Lamborghini THE COMPLETE STORY **DIABLO**

Other Titles in the Crowood AutoClassics series

Alfa Romeo 105 Series Spider
Alfa Romeo 916 GTV & Spider
Alfa Romeo 2000 and 2600
Alfa Romeo Alfasud
Alfa Romeo Spider
Aston Martin DB4, 5, 6
Aston Martin DB7
Aston Martin V8
Austin Healey
Austin Healey Sprite
BMW E30
BMW M3
BMW M5
BMW Classic Coupes 1965–1989
BMW Z3 and Z4
Citroën Traction Avant
Classic Jaguar XK – The Six-Cylinder Cars
Ferrari 308, 328 & 348
Frogeye Sprite
Ginetta: Road & Track Cars
Jaguar E-Type
Jaguar F-Type
Jaguar Mks 1 & 2, S-Type & 420
Jaguar XJ-S
Jaguar XK8
Jensen V8
Land Rover Defender 90 & 110
Land Rover Freelander
Lotus Elan
Lotus Elise & Exige 1995–2020
MGA
MGB
MGF and TF
Mazda MX-5
Mercedes-Benz Ponton and 190SL
Mercedes-Benz S-Class 1972–2013
Mercedes SL Series
Mercedes-Benz SL & SLC 107 Series
Mercedes-Benz Saloon Coupé
Mercedes-Benz Sport-Light Coupé
Mercedes-Benz W114 and W115
Mercedes-Benz W123
Mercedes-Benz W124
Mercedes-Benz W126 S-Class 1979–1991
Mercedes-Benz W201 (190)
Mercedes W113
Morgan 4/4: The First 75 Years
NSU Ro80
Peugeot 205
Porsche 924/928/944/968
Porsche Boxster and Cayman
Porsche Carrera – The Air-Cooled Era
Porsche Carrera - The Water-Cooled Era
Porsche Air-Cooled Turbos 1974–1996
Porsche Water-Cooled Turbos 1979–2019
Range Rover First Generation
Range Rover Second Generation
Range Rover Third Generation
Range Rover Sport 2005–2013
Reliant Three-Wheelers
Riley – The Legendary RMs
Rolls-Royce Silver Cloud
Rover 75 and MG ZT
Rover P5 & P5B
Rover P6: 2000, 2200, 3500
Rover SDI
Saab 92–96V4
Saab 99 and 900
Shelby and AC Cobra
Subaru Impreza WRX & WRX STI
Sunbeam Alpine and Tiger
Toyota MR2
Triumph Spitfire and GT6
Triumph TR6
Triumph TR7
Volkswagen Golf GTI
Volvo 1800
Volvo Amazon

Lamborghini DIABLO

THE COMPLETE STORY

Thillainathan Pathmanathan & Anne Christina Reck

THE CROWOOD PRESS

Dedication

To Nallini Pathmanathan, Supreme Court Judge,
Master of Middle Temple, sibling and surrogate parent.

First published in 2023 by
The Crowood Press Ltd
Ramsbury, Marlborough
Wiltshire SN8 2HR

enquiries@crowood.com

www.crowood.com

British Library Cataloguing-in-Publication Data
A catalogue record for this book is available from the British Library.

ISBN 978 0 7198 4244 3

Typeset by Simon and Sons
Cover design by Blue Sunflower Creative
Printed and bound in India by Parksons Graphics Pvt. Ltd.

CONTENTS

INTRODUCTION

The Lamborghini Diablo was the product of three immutable factors: the supercar heritage of Sant'Agata Bolognese, the unrelenting pressure from new technology adopted by rival supercar manufacturers, and the ever-fluid and inexorably forward-moving social, political, economic and environmental influences of the late twentieth century. The Diablo story can only truly be understood by studying each of these elements.

If Sant'Agata readily gained entry into the very highest echelons of the supercar world by way of the Lamborghini Miura, this Emilia-Romagna based manufacturer definitively established its name by designing and building another of the defining supercars of all time, the refulgent Lamborghini Countach. The Miura's supposedly novel mid-engine layout had been seen in earlier racing and road cars, but the Countach's revolutionary south-north engine-gearbox orientation, its extreme wedge shape and its startling scissor doors were all unique and had not been seen before in any production car. With these features the Countach started a dynasty that continues today, and the Lamborghini Diablo was the first evolution of this Countach bloodline.

But the Countach had faults and foibles aplenty. Rival supercar manufacturers stood eager and ready to topple this acknowledged King of the Supercars. The Countach was largely early 1970s technology, and teams in Stuttgart and Maranello, in 1985 and 1987 respectively, demonstrated just how far the 'Science of Supercars' had progressed when they launched the Porsche 959 and the Ferrari F40. By the late 1980s the Countach had been comprehensively outclassed in many different areas, but most notably in the field of aerodynamics. A completely new replacement car, which came to be the Lamborghini Diablo, was the only pragmatic solution. If the Countach begat the Diablo, then aerodynamics was its midwife.

Lamborghini could call upon expert designers, highly specialised engineers and skilled artisans from within its existing ranks to produce a worthy successor to the Countach. Money, or rather the lack of money, was also no longer a restraining factor. For much of its history Lamborghini had been shackled by financial woes, but not any more. While the Diablo was still on the drawing board, Lamborghini was bought by Chrysler. Given Detroit's immense financial firepower, money would no longer limit innovation and progress at Sant'Agata.

The greater challenge facing Lamborghini was how to respond to the fluid demands of customers, politicians and activists. The Diablo had to be faster, and faster accelerating, than the Countach: customers would accept nothing less, if only for bar-room bragging rights. The Diablo also had to be more spacious, more comfortable, more user-friendly and more reliable. Ralph Nader's seminal 1965 treatise *Unsafe at Any Speed: The Designed-In Dangers of the American Automobile* still reverberated into the late 1980s, and politicians were forced to legislate on ever more stringent pedestrian, passenger and driver safety mandates. The Diablo had to accommodate these new government decrees, just as it had to entertain the fallout from the 1973 OPEC oil crisis, which demanded huge improvements in fuel efficiency. Similarly, strident calls for air pollution controls from environmental activists, that had started with William Wordsworth's Romantic Movement in the nineteenth century, had morphed into the Earth Day protests of the 1970s, and there was no way a massive North America-based multinational like Chrysler could ignore, or swerve around, demands for less polluting cars.

Lamborghini certainly had its work cut out in designing, testing, developing and finally building the Diablo while still working within the limits of these multi-faceted constraints. Later in its production cycle the Diablo faced even more stringent legislation, as well as more advanced rivals like the Bugatti EB110 and the McLaren F1, both of which really pushed the technological envelope far forwards.

That the Lamborghini Diablo succeeded so spectacularly is a reflection of Sant'Agata's inherent strengths. Today, more than twenty years after its debut, the Diablo still retains the power to startle and stupefy any driver, passenger or casual bystander.

TIMELINE

1916 Ferruccio Lamborghini born in Renazzo di Cento, near Bologna

1963 Automobili Lamborghini SpA presents its first car, the 350GTV, in prototype form

1964 Launch of the 350GT, the first production Lamborghini car

1966 The Miura makes its debut at the Geneva Motor Show

1971 The prototype Countach, the LP500, is shown on the Bertone stand at the Geneva Motor Show

1974 The first production Countach is delivered

1990 The Lamborghini Diablo, Sant'Agata's replacement flagship for the Countach, makes its debut in January at the Sporting Club de Monte Carlo

1993 The four-wheel-drive Diablo VT is launched in March at the Geneva Motor Show. Limited edition Diablo SE30 launched in September

1995 The stripped-down Diablo SV makes its debut in March at the Geneva Motor Show. Lamborghini Diablo Roadster is launched in December at the Bologna Motor Show

1998 Now under the ownership of the VW-Audi conglomerate, in September Lamborghini presents a 1999 Model Year facelifted trio: the Diablo VT, Diablo SV and Diablo Roadster

1999 Diablo GT makes its debut in March at the Geneva Motor Show

2000 The Diablo 6.0 VT is launched in January at the Detroit Auto Show

2001 The Diablo's replacement, the Murciélago, is presented in September on the foothills of a still-smoking Mount Etna in Sicily

CHAPTER 1

FERRUCCIO LAMBORGHINI AND HIS EPONYMOUS SUPERCAR COMPANY

The Lamborghini Diablo, in its earliest guises and most common forms, was the product of Ferruccio Lamborghini's singular diktat that his supercar company should never make racing cars, or indulge in motor sport. It would be long after Ferruccio had relinquished his ownership of Lamborghini, more than three decades later in fact, that Sant'Agata finally broke with this policy and produced a track car. This first factory-sanctioned Lamborghini racing car was a Diablo derivative. The Diablo, however, like its illustrious predecessors the Countach and the Miura – and indeed its earliest ancestors, the 350GTV, 350GT, 400GT, Jarama and Espada – was conceived and designed purely as a road car. This remains a key defining feature of the Lamborghini Diablo.

Ferruccio's influence also permeated through the Diablo by virtue of his shrewd appointments at the very beginning of the company's history. Giotto Bizzarrini had designed Lamborghini's stalwart 60-degree V12 engine in 1963, but a modernised version of this powerplant was used in the Diablo throughout its production life. Ferruccio quickly identified the very young Giampaolo Dallara as the most promising automotive engineer of his generation, and appointed him as Lamborghini's first Technical Director in 1963. Dallara was responsible for the Miura's rear-wheel drive and transverse mid-engine layout, which set the scene for the Diablo's own layout. When Dallara left in 1967, Ferruccio immediately asked Paolo Stanzani to take over as Lamborghini's next Technical Director. Stanzani was a true genius who realised that a longitudinal mid-engine layout, as he adopted for the Countach, held many advantages and the Diablo religiously followed the Countach with a longitudinally oriented V12 engine. But Stanzani's real engineering brilliance was shown in the conception, design and delivery to production of the Countach's revolutionary south-north engine-gearbox orientation. Here again, the Diablo obediently followed the Countach's novel design. And why not? It was a supremely elegant engineering solution, which would also be adopted for the Murciélago and Aventador. It was also Ferruccio Lamborghini who brought in Nuccio Bertone and Marcello Gandini, who in time would almost become Lamborghini's

Ferruccio Lamborghini: hemp farmer, schoolboy artisan, wartime mechanic, tractor manufacturer, Italian industrialist and supercar visionary.

Lamborghini was born on 28 April 1916. His birth sign, Taurus, became the emblem of Automobili Lamborghini S.p.A.

in-house stylists. Gandini's extreme wedge-shaped cars, and his jaw-dropping guillotine doors, would go on to influence a generation and a half of supercar design, including the Diablo.

No comprehensive story about the Lamborghini Diablo would be complete without examining Ferruccio Lamborghini's own history, the life experiences that moulded him and guided his business decisions, simply because without him there would never have been a Lamborghini supercar manufacturer, let alone a Lamborghini Diablo supercar.

The period after Ferruccio Lamborghini was forced to sell his car company should also be examined as this was a particularly turbulent time for Sant'Agata, with multiple changes of ownership, lawsuits, receivership and creditors constantly at the door asking for cash. This was the world in which the Lamborghini Diablo was conceived, developed, manufactured and marketed, and the Diablo was the child of all this chaos and uncertainty.

FERRUCCIO LAMBORGHINI

Ferruccio Lamborghini's distaste for racing cars and motor sport only extended as far as the involvement of his own supercar company. As a young man he was a keen amateur racer, who designed and built racing car parts, and even extensively modified a whole car. While still in his early thirties, and at a time when he was not yet a rich man, he nevertheless indulged his craving for motor sport by taking part in the Mille Miglia. His reluctance to get Lamborghini SpA involved with racing stemmed from sheer pragmatism, and to understand the origins of this hard-headed, unsentimental rationality we will need to examine his childhood and early adult life.

Seen across what would have been the Lamborghini family's hemp fields and fruit orchards in 1916, the red house is where Ferruccio Lamborghini was born. His early mechanical exploits were carried out in an adjacent barn, which he burned down in the course of one of his technical experiments.

Ferruccio Elio Arturo Lamborghini was born on 28 April 1916 into a family of canepa (hemp) and fruit farmers. His forefathers had cultivated their land in Renazzo, a village in the commune of Cento, for generations. Renazzo lies about 24 kilometres north of Bologna, and his parents Antonio and Evelina earned a comfortable if not luxurious living from their labours off this ancestral land. From an early age Antonio and Evelina taught Ferruccio the vital importance of hard work, but he was also brought up within the unforgiving environment of farming, where luck in terms of the weather and plant disease was equally as important to success as hard work. Ferruccio quickly learned to make his own luck.

Antonio and Evelina quite reasonably expected Ferruccio to follow in their footsteps and become an agricultural farmer. But he was fascinated by machinery, and while still a child persuaded his parents to give him some space within one of their barns to set up a small machine shop. This was one of the earliest recorded instances of Ferruccio making his own luck by enthusiastically and aggressively pursuing what he wanted, rather than simply following the path that was expected of him. His fabled battle with Enzo Ferrari was a later example of this same dogged fighting spirit, wherein he decided to enter into direct competition with Ferrari rather than meekly tolerate the abuse that the patrician Enzo felt he could direct at a simple Emilian farm boy.

Through hard work and an instinctive feel for mechanical components and basic engineering principles, the young Ferruccio was soon modifying and improving his parents' farm machinery. Not every task went exactly to plan though, and on at least one occasion Ferruccio set his workshop alight! His parents recognised Ferruccio's love and aptitude for engineering, and, being modestly well-to-do, were able to support his ambition to become an engineer. They paid for his education at the Fratelli Taddia Technical Institute where he studied engineering and industrial design.

Ferruccio Lamborghini turned global disaster into personal luck with World War II. In many ways this was the making of his personal and professional life. Ferruccio enrolled in the Italian Infantry (and not, as his son Tonino Lamborghini patiently explained to the authors during one of several interviews, the Regia Aeronautica, as is so commonly misstated in many publications) and was sent to the island of Rhodes. There he started as a junior mechanic with the rank of Caporale in the 50th Autoreparto Misto di Manovra. Again his enthusiasm and aptitude soon gained his promotion to Head of the Workshop Division, but Ferruccio also made his own luck by getting to know and earning the trust of the base's commanding officer by expertly servicing and modifying the commander's beloved red Alfa Romeo 1750. But as with the burnt-out barn back home, not every modification went smoothly. Ferruccio conducted a 'modification and improvement' exercise on the Alfa Romeo's braking system that failed spectacularly while the commander was driving along one of Rhodes's coastal roads. The 1750 ended up in the Mediterranean, but the commander forgave the very likeable Ferruccio.

In 1944 the British overran Rhodes. Ferruccio was taken prisoner and put to work servicing and repairing British army vehicles. During this time, when he met his future wife Clelia Monti, he also gained experience and insight into the workings of British engines. This knowledge would turn out to be instrumental in his future success when building tractors.

On his return to Renazzo in 1946 Ferruccio found that mainland Italy's industrial base had been devastated by the war, and that Italian farmers throughout the country were desperate for tractors. His wife Clelia, sadly, had died shortly after giving birth to their first child, Antonio (Tonino) Lamborghini. Soon after, however, Ferruccio married his second wife, Annita Borgatti, and it was during their honeymoon in Romagna that Ferruccio happened upon a discovery that would change his life. He heard that the British military were selling off their surplus war equipment, and he bought a 4-cylinder Morris truck from the occupying force. He drove the truck back to Renazzo and converted its 1548cc petrol engine to run on Italian agricultural fuel, which was then both cheaper and more readily available. With further modifications, Ferruccio then made his first carioca, a lightweight tractor that would soon gain immense popularity in post-war Italy.

Ferruccio made more of his own luck by choosing to launch his new tractor in the town of Cento, the region's agricultural centre, on 3 February 1948, which happened to be the feast day of St Blaise (Biagio in Italian), Cento's patron saint. On this one day all the region's usually hard-working farmers would be partying late into the night in Cento's central piazza, and Ferruccio astutely parked one of his new cariocas nearby. By the end of Cento's San Biagio festivities, Ferruccio had secured eleven orders for his new carioche (as they became known in Emilia-Romagna).

Lamborghini made his first fortune from lightweight tractors known as carioche.

This was just the start of a very successful period for Ferruccio. By the end of 1948 he had garnered so many orders for carioche that he set up a purpose-built tractor factory in Pieve, not far from Renazzo. By 1952 he was manufacturing all new tractors of his own design, and by 1954 he was building air-cooled diesel tractors. By the early 1960s about 5,000 tractors were being produced every year under the Lamborghini Trattori banner.

In 1960 Ferruccio Lamborghini visited the United States as part of an Italian trade delegation. He was hugely impressed by what he saw happening across the Atlantic, and on his return to Italy decided to enlarge and diversify his already massive industrial empire. He founded Lamborghini Bruciatori to manufacture domestic and industrial air-conditioning and heating equipment.

Part of Lamborghini Bruciatori's almost immediate success was due to Ferruccio following the same sales, marketing and after-sales protocol that he had established for Lamborghini Trattori. Central to this strategy was his novel approach to customer care, establishing in-house quality control protocols that were strictly adhered to, and his companies were among the first in Italy to offer comprehensive after-sales service plans for their products. Ferruccio's supercar company would later follow this same customer-oriented doctrine. He said that he wanted to produce only the finest cars, and that he wanted his customers to be delighted with their vehicles. It didn't always turn out this way, but that was his stated intention. By the time he was in his mid-forties he was one of Italy's key industrialists and a very rich man.

Ferruccio had always had a passion for motor cars and motor racing. As a young man he modified an old Fiat 500 Topolino and entered it into the 1948 Mille Miglia. The Topolino's 569cc engine was bored out to 750cc, and Ferruccio cast his own cylinder head out of bronze to squeeze as much power and torque as possible out of this still minuscule engine. His Topolino would have to compete with purpose-built 6- and 12-cylinder giants from the likes

Lamborghini made his second fortune through heating and air-conditioning machinery.

of Alfa Romeo, Ferrari and Maserati on the Mille Miglia's tortuous 1,000-mile, figure-of-eight public road circuit between Brescia and Rome and back. For the first 700 miles (1,126km) Ferruccio did well, but he lost control of his car when passing through the commune of Fiano at speed and crashed into a roadside restaurant. Later he would often quip: 'I finished my Mille Miglia in an osteria, which I entered by driving through a wall.'

Ferruccio's passion for motor sport and racing cars cooled following his Mille Miglia accident, but not his infatuation with road cars. His considerable wealth allowed him almost unlimited licence to indulge in this craving, and his fleet included cars from Mercedes, Mustang, Buick and Maserati.

By the early 1960s Ferrari had established a reputation that transcended motor sport. Its road cars were commonly acknowledged as some of the fastest, most beautiful and most prestigious available. Naturally these very special cars would soon come to Ferruccio's attention: he bought a white two-seater Ferrari 250 GT short-wheelbase Berlinetta in 1958, and then another, and later a grey 2+2 Ferrari 250 GTE. Contrary to common belief, Tonino Lamborghini emphasised to the authors during an interview in 2019 that his father loved his Ferraris. Ferruccio was very impressed by the quality of their design and engineering, particularly their 'perfect balance, and the strong engine that went very well'. Tonino stressed that his father's only complaint about his Ferraris related to their clutches.

Again there is a popular belief that Ferruccio Lamborghini's battle with Enzo Ferrari over clutch wear was the sole factor that led him to establish his eponymous supercar company. This is almost certainly an over-simplification of the myriad of considerations that probably led to the establishment of Automobili Lamborghini SpA, but it was certainly a very important factor.

Ferruccio was a proud man: not at all arrogant, but proud, open and honest about his humble beginnings and how far he had come through hard work, and he hated the disdain with which Enzo Ferrari treated him.

The infamous Lamborghini-Ferrari fight was a long time coming. Ferruccio used all his cars hard, extracting the most from their acceleration, braking and cornering potential, driving them in this extreme manner more frequently than the average supercar customer might. Time and again he found that the clutches of his Ferraris would slip under hard acceleration, even immediately after a brand new clutch replacement. After a few visits to the Ferrari works at Maranello, none of which permanently resolved this clutch problem, Ferruccio decided to look into the matter himself. With the help of one of his tractor mechanics, he stripped down a Ferrari clutch mechanism and discovered that the clutch plate was too small in diameter to cope with the engine's torque output. The problem was cured by replacing the Ferrari's original clutch with a larger diameter clutch from one of his tractors.

Having found a solution to this previously apparently unsolvable problem, Ferruccio decided that it would be in everyone's interest to inform Enzo Ferrari about the primary cause of the clutch issue and how it could easily be resolved. Ferruccio was a very straightforward character, maybe blunt to a fault, but never one to bear malice. Tonino explained that Ferruccio approached Enzo politely and in good faith.

The Commendatore was, however, cut from quite different cloth. As a way of keeping people in their place, Enzo was known to intentionally make customers and guests wait for long periods in an ante-room before granting them an audience – and he kept Ferruccio waiting for hours after the appointed time before receiving him. When Ferruccio complained about this delay, Enzo's reply was 'One day I kept the King of Belgium waiting, so you Mr Lamborghini, builders of tractors and boilers, really have no cause for complaint.' From then their conversation took a progressively downward trajectory. When Ferruccio complained about the clutch and politely explained his new-found solution, the Commendatore became furious and said, 'Lamborghini, you may be able to drive a tractor, but you will never be able to drive a Ferrari properly.'

According to Ferruccio Lamborghini, it was this singularly venomous statement, said aloud at their meeting, that ignited his momentous decision to set up a rival supercar company. Ferruccio has been widely quoted as saying, 'This was the point when I finally decided to make a perfect car.'

AUTOMOBILI LAMBORGHINI SpA

It is highly unlikely, however, that the shrewd, worldly-wise and financially astute Ferruccio Lamborghini would have committed to such a major undertaking solely after an insult from someone he barely knew. Rather there were almost certainly other major factors at play. By the early 1960s Ferruccio had more money than he knew what to do with. What he wanted now was power and recognition. Establishing a bespoke supercar company catering to the world's most exclusive clientele, and directly entering battle with Ferrari at Maranello, was surely the fastest way of grabbing everyone's attention, particularly in car-mad Italy. Another reason for setting up Automobili Lamborghini SpA was to diversify his industrial empire. From his work on his tractor and heating and air-conditioning businesses, he already knew exactly how to work his way around Italian government legislation and how to exploit generous government subsidies, so this new venture promised lucrative gains for relatively little effort and risk. Thirdly, a Ferrari-rivalling supercar would garner wide and positive publicity for the Lamborghini name, and this reflected glory would bestow much welcome publicity upon his tractor, heating and air-conditioning businesses. And finally, of course, he was a genuine petrolhead who had been an engineer and mechanic at heart from childhood.

The lead author with Automobili Lamborghini's first car, the concept 350GTV, at the factory museum in Sant'Agata Bolognese.

Not one to procrastinate, Ferruccio bought 9 hectares of land on the outskirts of Sant'Agata Bolognese in 1962. This was an inspired choice of location because it was close to Modena, from which Ferruccio could recruit specialist workers skilled in engineering, manufacturing and tooling, and also because Sant'Agata had excellent transport links through which raw materials could be brought in efficiently, and gleaming supercars could be shipped out effortlessly. The two-flavoured icing on the cake was that the local council was offering concessions and grants to attract new businesses to the region, and additionally Sant'Agata was close to Cento, where the Lamborghini tractor, heating and air-conditioning factories were already established.

By the middle of 1963 Ferruccio had established Automobili Lamborghini SpA and had spent 500 million lire on the first phase of the factory build. At that time this was a vast amount of money for a small car factory, but Ferruccio was determined that his new plant should be outstanding in itself, and not just for the products that came out of it. It was a well thought-through and modern factory, with half a million square feet of factory floor space housed within two long buildings, and it featured a twin-track production line, a spare parts repository and a service department. The factory boasted a very futuristic feel with natural sunlight flooding onto the production line from large galleried windows, and there was of course the now famous terracotta tiled flooring. Clerical staff were based in offices on the first floor of the buildings, a service road encircled the whole factory perimeter, and the word Lamborghini stood out proudly in bright yellow lettering from the top of the factory roof. Despite the many substantial factory renovations that have taken place since 1963, some of these original features can still be seen today, and many were present in an unaltered form when the authors visited the factory at the end of the Diablo's production run in 2001.

When Ferruccio Lamborghini launched his first prototype, the Lamborghini 350 GTV, on 20 October 1963, the invited motoring journalists, potential customers and high-ranking government guests were as stunned by the cutting-edge factory as they were by his avant-garde prototype supercar. He had just won one of the prizes he most coveted – recognition. At first this recognition was limited to local dignitaries, petrolheads and the specialist motoring press, but with the launch of the Lamborghini Miura in 1966 the wider motoring world would come to recognise that they had a genuine Ferrari-beater in Lamborghini. The launch of the Lamborghini Countach prototype in 1971 brought instant worldwide fame and recognition from all those who swooned in automotive lust at Ferruccio's wedge-shaped, guillotine-doored, wonder car. The Lamborghini Diablo would continue in this tradition – sprinkling the fairy dust of expensive, elusive and much-wanted publicity on the Lamborghini name and all its associated brands and products. Ferruccio had succeeded in his second aim too.

The company banner flutters at the entrance to the Sant'Agata factory.

Making a success of Automobili Lamborghini SpA as a self-financing business, however, would prove to be greatest of the three challenges. Base raw materials flowed into one end of Lamborghini's Sant'Agata factory and, through some glorious alchemy, the most astounding and extraordinary cars came out of the other. The Lamborghini 350 GT, 400 GT, Jarama, Espada, Miura and Countach were usually in high demand by very well-heeled customers worldwide, but this was not always the case and keeping the balance sheet in the black during bleak recessions and lesser economic downturns would plague Automobili Lamborghini SpA throughout its early history. The Lamborghini Diablo's conception, birth and development would almost be defined by the company's financial fortunes and misfortunes.

The high point of Ferruccio Lamborghini's involvement with supercar manufacture probably came with the Miura. The company gained instant and widespread recognition through this revolutionary supercar, and it was also in rude financial health at this time. In 1966 Ferruccio's industrial empire employed about 4,500 people and he was one of Italy's most important industrialists. He was awarded the title of Commendatore Ordine al Meritodella Repubblica Italiana for his services to Italian manufacturing, and later in 1969 was awarded the further honour of Cavaliere del Lavaro.

But industrial unrest was just round the corner. Strike action began in earnest in 1970. The seeds of this unrest had actually begun with students staging protests about the cost of living and university fees in 1967, and trade unionists started agitating about pay and employment terms and conditions in 1968. When the students joined forces with the more militant trade unionists the touchpaper was lit for crippling economic chaos. By 1973 more than 6 million Italians were on strike, and all industrialists were seen as exploitative mega-capitalists who should be treated as social pariahs. Ferruccio had never forgotten his roots, had never knowingly abused any of his workers, and was in fact recognised as a very considerate boss who was ever ready to roll up his sleeves and crawl underneath a faulty tractor or a misbehaving supercar. He was very upset at being cast as an unscrupulous and uncaring plutocrat, and his misgivings about business began at this time, which also coincided with the Countach prototype's debut. The additional fame that the Countach brought Ferruccio was therefore something that he both desired but also eschewed. In happier times he would merely have bathed in all the exaltation. Any unhappiness was further fired up when his own workers, with whom he had previously had an excellent relationship, also became more bellicose and militant purely through osmosis.

LOSING CONTROL

The killer blow came in 1972 when the Bolivian government cancelled an order for tractors. This hit was intensified by the 1973 oil crisis and the subsequent 1973–4 stock market crash. The Bolivian government had previously placed an order for 5,000 tractors in good faith, and in equally good faith Lamborghini Trattori had sourced the necessary materials and built these tractors without taking a deposit or any other form of pre-payment. In 1972 political and economic turmoil in Bolivia sent shock waves far and wide, including to Emilia-Romagna in Italy. The Bolivian government's abrupt cancellation of their tractor order came with no financial compensation, and Ferruccio was left with a serious cashflow problem. He managed to get through this sudden downturn by selling off some of his tractor factory buildings to Giovanni Agnelli, the 'Godfather of Fiat', at well below market value. At Agnelli's insistence, an unwilling Ferruccio also had to transfer some of his best tractor factory staff onto Fiat's payroll. When this proved insufficient to keep his creditors at bay, he sold 51 per cent of Lamborghini Trattori to the giant Italian tractor company S.A.M.E., which had been pursuing Ferruccio for years in the hope of buying into Lamborghini Trattori and thereby gaining a seat on the board of the Emilian tractor company. The Bolivian debacle gave them just the opportunity they had been looking for.

The impact of the Yom Kippur war extended as far as Sant'Agata. In October 1973 the Organisation of Arab Petroleum Exporting Countries (OAPEC) imposed an oil embargo on all those countries they deemed supportive of Israel. This embargo lasted until March 1974 and during this time the price of oil quadrupled, resulting in petrol rationing in some countries, the introduction of stringently monitored and fiercely enforced speed limits, and societal rejection of gas guzzlers. None of this advanced Sant'Agata's cause, or indeed that of any other company producing 170mph, petrol-thirsty supercars. When both the New York and London Stock Exchanges dived in 1973 it was the start of a global recession that impacted exactly the sort of potential Lamborghini customers who otherwise would have had the financial wherewithal to indulge their supercar cravings. And meanwhile the union-led industrial problems were continuing apace.

The 1972 Bolivian tractor debacle soon forced Ferruccio to sell 51 per cent of Automobili Lamborghini SpA to the Swiss businessman Georges-Henri Rossetti. The completion of this quick and involuntary sale was necessary simply to keep the company afloat. A more considered sale of his remaining 49 per cent stake in Automobili Lamborghini SpA to René Leimer, one of Rossetti's many business associates, took place over the following eighteen months. This came about partly because Ferruccio was tired and traumatised by the never-ending ups and downs of his business empire, and partly because he was reluctant to give in to the combative, constantly demanding and never happy trade unionists in his supercar factory. A further factor was that he recognised that society's new environmental, safety and social concerns would make it ever more difficult to sell extravagant, very high-speed, highly polluting, bespoke supercars.

In 1974, having divested himself of any further involvement with Automobili Lamborghini SpA, Ferruccio Lamborghini retired to La Fiorita, a 32-hectare vineyard near Lake Trasimeno in Umbria. He lived out the rest of his days on this estate, actively participating in his new wine business surrounded by his beloved Sangiovese, Merlot, Gamay and Ciliegiolo vines. One of the most famous wines his vineyard produced was officially called 'Colli del Trasimeno', but unofficially this outstanding red wine was called 'Sangue di Miura' (Miura's blood). This final stage of Ferruccio's life was peaceful and happy. He passed away on 20 February 1993 after an unexpected heart attack, and his body was taken back to Renazzo where it was interred alongside those of his ancestors.

La Fiorita, the Umbrian vineyard where Ferruccio spent his last days.

Ferruccio Lamborghini's fingerprints are all over every Diablo ever produced, although he had officially left the supercar company a full decade and a half before the Diablo made its debut, and even though the Diablo was barely a fifth of its way through its production life cycle when Ferruccio drew his last breath. Sant'Agata's recognition of his contribution to the Diablo was most tellingly demonstrated when one of the earliest Diablo pre-production prototypes was sent across the Apennines from the factory to La Fiorita, just to get Ferruccio's blessing for Automobili Lamborghini's latest flagship car. The authors visited La Fiorita in 2018 and were lucky enough to meet and interview Ferruccio's long-standing secretary from this period, Giuseppina Maccioni. Signora Maccioni said that Ferruccio was delighted that Sant'Agata had remembered him, and recollected the Diablo's arrival at La Fiorita. In the peace of his vineyard Ferruccio had inspected the Diablo closely and at leisure. His considered verdict on the Lamborghini Diablo: 'A true Lamborghini'.

FERRUCCIO'S HEIRS

The stewardship of Automobili Lamborghini SpA by Georges-Henri Rossetti and René Leimer makes for a sorry story. They were very hands-off owners with little interest in their new acquisition, and even less understanding of the complexities of supercar manufacturing. They hardly ever visited Sant'Agata, abdicating almost all responsibility for the running of the business to the factory managers. The Countach almost single-handedly kept the company afloat during their tenure as sales of the Espada, Jarama and Urraco during this period were thoroughly underwhelming. Combative trade union policies and practices made running the factory efficiently very difficult, and this was compounded by the continuing fallout from the oil crisis and the stock market crash, both of which were adversely affecting the global economy. Chronic poor management might have been the primary factor that drove the company to the wall, but it was an acute cashflow problem that rang the death knell for Rossetti's and Leimer's ownership.

In August 1978, after essentially running out of money, the company went before the Italian courts. Judge Mirone, who was well disposed to the company and Italian industry, astutely placed Automobili Lamborghini SpA under the control of Alessandro Artese, a shrewd and insightful accountant. He in turn appointed Giulio Alfieri, the

Giampaolo Dallara, Lamborghini's first Technical Director, examines a copy of Crowood Press's *Lamborghini Countach: The Complete Story* and a photograph of 5000 QV F920OYR (*see* Chapter 14).

acclaimed ex-Maserati engineer, as Technical Director, and retained the experienced and industrious Ubaldo Sgarzi as Sales Director. This triumvirate provided new dynamism and direction for the company, and they almost succeeded in finding a new owner for Automobili Lamborghini SpA Sadly, at the very last moment, a conglomerate headed up by Hubert Hahne was unable to secure the money needed to buy the company. A huge amount of work and hope had gone into this potential sale and both parties were deeply disappointed when the deal fell through. Worse was to follow: on 28 February 1980 Automobili Lamborghini SpA was declared bankrupt and placed into receivership.

In July 1980 two French brothers, Patrick and Jean-Claude Mimran, took over management of the company and renamed it Nuova Automobili Ferruccio Lamborghini SpA. Heirs to a vast industrial empire stretching across most of the globe and encompassing a multitude of industries, the Mimrans were superbly well placed to run the company. Patrick Mimran in particular was a genuine car and Lamborghini enthusiast, and both brothers were young, energetic and enthusiastic. They revamped the company's management structure with Patrick Mimran becoming Chairman, Emile Novaro his immediate abettor, Alfieri promoted to Technical Director-cum-General Manager and Sgarzi retained as Sales and Marketing Director. In May 1981, happy with the growth and improvement they had been able to inject into the company, the Mimrans bought Nuova Automobili Ferruccio Lamborghini SpA outright. They paid 3,850 million lire for the company (about US$3 million). Patrick Mimran was quickly able to establish his new acquisition on a genuinely solid financial footing, and he was also instrumental in providing the direction and funding for the Countach's further development. The Countach LP 400 was still in production when Patrick Mimran took over the company, but over the course of his tenure at Nuova Automobili Ferruccio Lamborghini SpA the company developed and produced the Countach LP 400 S, the Countach LP 500 S, the Countach 5000 QV and laid the groundwork for the 88 1/2 Countach 5000 QV. Patrick Mimran saved Automobili Lamborghini from oblivion and successfully re-established the company as one of the world's foremost supercar manufacturers, an astounding achievement bearing in mind that he was barely twenty-four years old when he took over the management in 1980. The Mimran brothers sold Nuova Automobili Ferruccio Lamborghini SpA to the Chrysler Corporation in 1987. Chrysler paid US$25 million for their trophy Italian supercar company, thereby netting the Mimrans a very healthy profit.

Lamborghini's successor flagship to the Countach was first mooted in the Mimran era, but the Diablo only came to market in 1990 under Chrysler. Chrysler, and in particular its chairman Lee Iacocca, had been looking to buy into, or preferably buy outright, a high-profile, top-drawer supercar manufacturer with which to crown and hopefully lift up Chrysler's rather utilitarian image. Chrysler's market was largely based in North America and catered to a mainly down-to-earth clientele. What better way to sprinkle a pinch of fairy dust upon Chrysler, than to have a bespoke, ultra high-performance, European subsidiary within Chrysler's portfolio. As Lee Iacocca was of Italian ancestry, and very partial to his heritage and culture, an Italian supercar manufacturer was the ideal candidate. Iacocca started off by buying a 15 per cent share in Maserati, but no Maserati could compare with the contemporary Lamborghini Countach 5000 QV. In fact nothing in series production by any manufacturer on the planet could remotely compare with this latest Countach. By a happy coincidence the Mimrans were looking to sell just when Iacocca was looking to buy. Patrick Mimran had invested money, time and some of his soul into Nuova Automobili Ferruccio Lamborghini SpA and he was determined only to sell the company to someone, or to some entity, that would cherish, nurture and advance it. In Lee Iacocca he saw someone genuinely keen on Sant'Agata, and in Chrysler he saw a major player with the financial

LAMBORGHINI MIURA

The Miura was the car that first called the world's attention to Automobili Lamborghini. Its low, wide, curvaceous form, penned by a very young Marcello Gandini, defined automotive voluptuousness, and the Miura has repeatedly been voted the most beautiful car ever produced by motoring journalists, art connoisseurs and the general public alike. But more importantly, the Miura also represented the cutting edge of 1960s automotive technology. The Miura's naked chassis, which made its first appearance on 3 November 1965 at the Turin Motor Show, showcased a radical transversely oriented V12 engine within a rear mid-engine layout.

For the last six decades there has been constant disagreement in the car and design world as to whether Gandini or his then boss, Bertone's chief designer Giorgetto Giugiaro, should be credited with the Miura's sensual styling. The current consensus is that Gandini should take that honour, with the caveat that Giugiaro's guiding hand also deserves recognition. Gandini has said that in designing the Miura he was acutely aware that Automobili Lamborghini was a fledgling company, and that he could not risk the company's very survival with a car that did not meet the expectations and approval of its then current and future customers. The racing cars of the 1950s and 1960s were rounded and arciform, and Automobili Lamborghini's potential clientele were used to these shapes and expected their road cars to look like these racers. With the Countach, and later with the Diablo, Gandini felt at liberty to adopt a more brave and adventurous design language, as by that time Sant'Agata was financially secure and had already become a pillar of the supercar establishment. When Nuccio Bertone and Gandini presented the first renderings of the Miura styling concept to Ferruccio Lamborghini and Giampaolo Dallara, Ferruccio was immediately besotted, and without a moment's hesitation turned to Bertone and simply said, 'Make it'.

The Miura's retractable headlights operated by Ducellier electric motors gave Automobili Lamborghini's latest supercar a futuristic twenty-first-century appearance, but it was the car's audacious transverse mid-engine layout that made it really stand out. Once Bizzarrini's four-camshaft V12 engine was thrown into the equation there was simply no other road car quite like the Miura; the 1962 1108cc single-camshaft, 4-cylinder Bonnet/Matra Djet was the only other road car to boast a rear mid-engine layout, but it belonged to an altogether inferior class. The very limited production, V8-engined Ford GT40 of the mid- to late 1960s, designed by Ron Bradshaw, also employed a rear mid-engine layout, but this iconic car was designed principally as a racer to beat Ferrari at Le Mans, rather than to rule the public highway.

The Miura P400 (standing for Posteriore 4 litri) prototype was launched at the 1966 Geneva Motor Show where it overshadowed its fellow debutants, the Bizzarrini 5300 GT and the Ferrari 365 California Spyder. It was the talk of the show even before Automobili Lamborghini added spice to the sauce by claiming that the Miura P400 would be the fastest production road car ever: without providing any supporting evidence, Sant'Agata happily put about the rumour that the Miura had a top speed of 318km/h (198mph). The first customer P400 Miura was delivered in December 1966 with a 3929cc engine producing 350bhp at 7,000rpm, and 262lb ft torque at 5,000rpm. The P400 weighed in at 1,125kg and Lamborghini claimed a 0–100km/h time of 6.7 seconds and a top speed of 280km/h (174mph).

The first Miura variant suffered from high-speed front-end lift as well as very significant chassis flex, so in 1968 Sant'Agata launched the Miura P400S (the S standing for Spinto or 'tuned'), a modified Miura running a new rear suspension set-up, new Pirelli radial tyres and a substantially modified chassis constructed of heavier gauge steel. On the powertrain front larger carburettors, redesigned engine combustion chambers and inlet manifolds, and reprofiled camshafts increased the V12's output to 370bhp, albeit at the expense of the Miura P400S weighing in at 1,198kg.

The ultimate production Miura, the hallowed Miura P400SV (the SV standing for Super Veloce) was produced between 1971 and 1973. One of the key engineering innovations with the SV variant was the SV's split sump, which allowed the engines and gearboxes to have their own individual lubrication systems. The SV variant was easily distinguished from its earlier and lesser brethren by the loss of the P400 and P400S's signature 'eyelashes' surrounding the headlights, and by its much wider rear wheel arches. The SV variant had new carburettors and cam timing allowing Sant'Agata to claim that its flagship now developed 385bhp, and that Lamborghini produced the fastest production car in the world.

The Miura startled the world's motoring press and gave instant recognition to the Lamborghini name.

wherewithal and the business acumen to take the company forwards.

Chrysler invested heavily into Lamborghini, providing not only money but also technical resources. The 88 1/2 Countach 5000 Quattrovalvole was said to be built to a higher standard than any of its predecessors purely because the factory workers now had all the exact parts they needed: prior to Chrysler's takeover they often had to modify whatever parts they needed from whatever was then available in the parts bin. Chrysler also helped by insisting on more stringent build and quality control than Sant'Agata had ever previously judged necessary.

Tonino Lamborghini, Ferruccio Lamborghini's son, expands on the family's long association with farming, tractors and supercars.

If the Countach's replacement had originally been conceived under the Mimran administration, it was under Chrysler that the Diablo was gestated, developed, refined and finally launched in 1990, as will be described in detail in the following chapters. Suffice it to say here that the Diablo was received with great acclaim by potential customers, the motoring press and the general public alike. The order book filled up almost immediately, and a long waiting list full of customers hungry for Lamborghini's latest flagship soon developed. For once Lamborghini was destined for that rarest of treats – it was going to make a profit. The Sant'Agata engineers and designers, the Chrysler accountants and Lee Iacocca were all delighted, and the latter two parties felt totally vindicated in their decision to cross the Atlantic and buy a tiny, almost loss-making car manufacturer. But as so often in Lamborghini's history these halcyon days were short-lived. Rising inflation caused the world's major central banks to raise interest rates and enact restrictive monetary policies that, combined with the 1990 oil price shock, pushed the West into recession. Existing Diablo orders were cancelled and new orders simply never materialised. Soon Lamborghini was back to its hitherto normal state of making losses and Chrysler's love affair with Sant'Agata went cold. By 1992 Chrysler quietly made it known that it wanted to offload its now tarnished Italian jewel.

A rescue of sorts came from an unlikely source. MegaTech, an Indonesian conglomerate headed up by Setiawan Djody and Tommy Suharto, bought Lamborghini. Djody already part-owned Vector Motors, an American supercar manufacturer destined for obsolescence, and he felt that collaboration between Vector and Lamborghini would magically lead to profitability. Tommy Suharto, the quintessential playboy, was the youngest son of Indonesia's infamous second president, who in a previous incarnation as Indonesia's military Chief of Staff had led a murderous anti-communist purge. It was an unfortunate combination of hopeful but ultimately hopeless new owners, and was essentially a replay of the Georges-Henri Rossetti and René Leimer scenario. By 1995 Lamborghini had to be restructured, with Tommy Suharto retaining a majority share through an Indonesian company called V Power Corporation, and a Malaysian company, MyCom Bhd, acquiring the remaining 40 per cent of Lamborghini. Even this reorganisation was doomed to failure by yet another recession. In 1997 the economies of both Indonesia and Malaysia were badly hit by the Asian financial crisis. The Indonesian rupiah, together with many other South-East Asian currencies, was devalued in response, leading to widespread rioting in Indonesia and President Suharto was forced to step down. Tommy the playboy soon found himself in dire financial straits and Lamborghini was once again placed on the market.

Enter Ferdinand Piech, the grandson of Ferdinand Porsche who had designed the Volkswagen Beetle and later established his own eponymous sports car company. Piech was a formidable engineer and businessman. He was instrumental in the design and engineering of the iconic Porsche 906 and 917 racing cars, and as chairman of the Volkswagen Group had saved the company from near-certain bankruptcy before turning it around and acquiring a number of smaller premium-brand car companies including Bentley and Bugatti. Piech was also set on taking over Lamborghini and this came

Tonino Lamborghini's own Diablo at the Museo Ferruccio Lamborghini in Funo di Argelato, Bologna.

to pass in September 1998. For the princely sum of US$110 million Volkswagen AG purchased Lamborghini through its subsidiary, Audi AG.

It was Piech who appointed Luc Donckerwolke, an ex-Audi designer, as Chief Stylist at Lamborghini and it was Donckerwolke who redesigned and modernised the styling on the final Diablo variants. Piech insisted that Lamborghini meet the quality standards of all the other offerings from the Volkswagen Group, and as a direct result of this diktat the last of the Diablos are some of the best-constructed Diablos of all. The Diablo's successor, the Murciélago, took initial design, prototype testing, manufacturing and final quality control to a previously unknown and altogether higher level.

Lamborghini's turbulent history, marked by recurrent financial misfortune, took a sudden and very positive turn when Piech, through Volkswagen-Audi, took over ownership of the company. At the time of writing in 2022, Lamborghini under the Volkswagen-Audi umbrella has been transformed into one of the world's most successful and profitable car companies, producing truly delectable *objets d'art* that can travel at incredible speeds and wow all onlookers. Patrick Mimran and Ferdinand Piech, together with dedicated Sant'Agata engineers and managers like Paolo Stanzani, Giulio Alfieri, Ubaldo Sgarzi and Emile Novaro, were the certain saviours of Lamborghini, but there would never have been anything to save, and certainly no Diablo supercar, without the visionary and tenacious Ferruccio Lamborghini.

Ferruccio Lamborghini described the early pre-production Diablo that Chrysler sent to his Umbrian vineyard as a 'true Lamborghini'.

CHAPTER 2

THE COUNTACH INFORMS THE DIABLO

The Lamborghini Countach was a genuinely revolutionary car in terms of design and engineering, and the Lamborghini Diablo was a direct evolution of this radical supercar. But the Countach had its problems – all of which became more evident and more constraining with the passage of time. Lamborghini's rival supercar manufacturers were constantly improvising and improving, and with each passing year the Countach was having to do battle with increasingly challenging competitors. The Lamborghini Diablo was Sant'Agata's answer, and this new flagship tackled the Countach's glaring deficiencies, particularly in the field of aerodynamics and material sciences, and thereby moved the game forwards. But at its heart, the Diablo, particularly in its earliest iterations, was a modernised, revised and upgraded Countach, based on the same engineering and design building blocks as its iconic predecessor. And there is absolutely no shame in this – the Murciélago and Aventador would go on to do exactly the same.

The Countach's extreme wedge shape and guillotine doors defined it aesthetically.

The Lamborghini Miura's innovative mid-engine layout had introduced Lamborghini to the motoring world as an avant-garde supercar manufacturer that was not intimidated by its more established competitors, and one which was ready to embrace the latest and most advanced technological solutions. The Miura made its debut in 1966, but such was the rate of progress in supercar development at that time that a wholly new successor was needed just four years later.

STANZANI AND THE COUNTACH'S POWERTRAIN LAYOUT

By 1970 Paolo Stanzani had succeeded Giampaolo Dallara as Technical Director at Lamborghini. Stanzani was a true engineering genius and dreamt up the unorthodox, but ultimately very successful, concept of placing the Countach's gearbox in front of the engine and having the drive then directed back to the rear wheels through a sealed tube in the engine's sump. This was a thoroughly bizarre idea that should have been beset by a million real-world problems, but Stanzani was also a very meticulous engineer and he was able to get this revolutionary south-north engine-gearbox layout to work almost perfectly at his first attempt. Stanzani also recognised the importance of retaining the Miura's mid-engine layout, but realised that it could be improved by adopting a longitudinal rather than a transverse engine orientation. Finally Stanzani showed his brilliance again by adopting an ultra-lightweight frame for the Countach in the form of a spaceframe chassis. Each of these fundamental engineering principles was carried forward, albeit in an updated form, into the Diablo, and so need to be examined in any comprehensive assessment of the Countach's successor.

To clothe Stanzani's cutting-edge spaceframe chassis, Sant'Agata once again turned to another true automotive genius. Marcello Gandini had done Lamborghini proud through his designing of the Miura's sensuous body, which even today is often voted the most beautiful car ever built in polling within the specialist motoring press and the general public at large. For the Countach Gandini introduced the extreme wedge shape and the breathtaking idea of guillotine doors, both concepts of which were carried forward into the Lamborghini Diablo.

We also need to examine two further topics, the increasingly important role of material science in supercar design and the application of aerodynamic studies. The last of the Countachs embraced advances in material science by adopting composites, but its successor would have to do so much more comprehensively. Similarly the original LP 500 Countach prototype of 1971 did undergo rudimentary aerodynamic testing in a wind tunnel, but aerodynamic drag was to remain the Countach's ever present and unyielding enemy. The only way to sort out this aerodynamic problem was to design a totally new car, and so the Countach's unresolvable Achilles heel led directly to the Lamborghini Diablo.

Paolo Stanzani, the father of the Countach, pictured here at the 2001 Murciélago launch.

The Countach's rear mid-engine layout placed its major masses – the engine and gearbox – near the car's centre of gravity and rotational axis. This gave the Countach a low moment of inertia, which in turn gave the car great agility and manoeuvrability. By placing the major masses in the centre of the Countach, Stanzani and Gandini were also able to approach the ideal 50/50 front-to-rear weight distribution sought by high-performance car designers. A 50/50 weight distribution is desirable because it means that the car's weight is distributed equally between the car's four tyres, which in turn affords the car more neutral handling characteristics and greater balance. The Countach only had a 42/58 front-to-rear distribution, but this was better than many of its rival supercar competitors.

The Countach also retained the Miura's rear-wheel-drive configuration. This configuration works particularly well when combined with the rear mid-engine layout that Stanzani had already adopted for the Countach. This arrangement places significant mass over the driven tyres, which helps in transmitting the engine's torque to the tarmac efficiently. This translates into better traction and hence better acceleration, but the rewards of adopting this

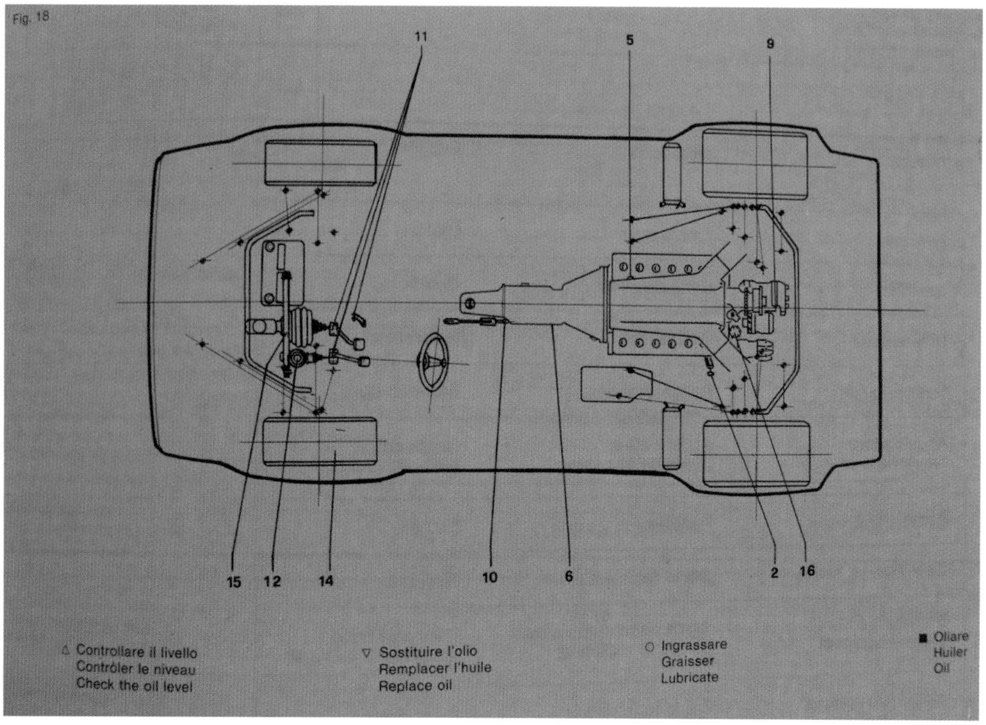

The Countach's rear mid-engine layout placed its major masses – the engine and gearbox – near the car's centre of gravity and rotational axis.

combined arrangement do not end here. With more weight over the rear tyres, the two rear tyres are better able to help the front tyres during hard-braking manoeuvres and in high-speed, high-G-force cornering.

Where the Countach differed radically from the Miura was in placing Bizzarrini's V12 engine in a longitudinal orientation rather than in the Miura's transverse orientation. Again Stanzani was following fundamental and sound physics in choosing to make this change. The Miura's high-speed, front-end lift and its snap oversteer were among its major weaknesses and most frightening foibles. With the Countach Stanzani sought to exorcise these demons by placing the massive V12 engine longitudinally. A longitudinal engine orientation meant that the weight of the Countach's single highest mass was more evenly distributed between the front and rear axles, leading to less front-end lift, more accurate and dependable steering, and better directional stability. This engine orientation also enabled more efficient engine cooling, so addressing another major issue that had plagued the Miura. The longitudinal engine orientation did bring with it the disadvantage of a higher moment of inertia than a transversely oriented engine, but Stanzani was prepared to trade off some reduction in the Countach's agility for greater stability, and for more dependable, and more easily exploitable roadholding and handling.

THE COUNTACH'S V12 ENGINE AND SPACEFRAME CHASSIS

Lamborghini's stalwart V12 engine was designed by Giotto Bizzarrini in 1963. It would go on to power all of Sant'Agata's flagship supercars for the next forty-seven years, including the Countach, the Diablo and the Murciélago. Only with the advent of the Aventador would Lamborghini finally abandon this magnificent powerplant. In 1963 Ferruccio needed a V12 engine, which was the bare minimum requirement for the upstart Automobili Lamborghini SpA to challenge the patrician and already well-established and hugely respected Italian supercar manufacturers like Ferrari and Maserati.

Each new Lamborghini flagship, and often each new variant of an already existing flagship, would feature some upgrade, modification or more comprehensive reworking of Bizzarrini's gem. But the basic architecture and design of this longstanding, complex but reliable and melodious

PAOLO STANZANI

Paolo Stanzani did not have any direct involvement in the conception or development of the Lamborghini Diablo, but his fingerprints are all over it. His principal contributions to the Diablo were, first, working out that a longitudinal engine orientation had major benefits when dealing with a massive V12 engine, and then coming up with the revolutionary idea of re-orienting the traditional engine gearbox placement. Lamborghini has retained these concepts in the flagship cars that have followed the Miura, adhering to Stanzani's brilliant plan of placing the gearbox in front the engine, and then passing the drive from the engine first forwards to the gearbox, and then down through a series of drop-gears, before finally sending the power and torque backwards to the rear differential through a sealed tube in the sump. This unique south-north engine-gearbox orientation, first seen in the Countach, was continued in the Diablo and is still employed in the Aventador and the smaller V10-engined Gallardo and Huracan. Sant'Agata's adoption of four-wheel drive for the Diablo VT in 1993 never posed a problem for Stanzani's novel drivetrain layout, because the forward placement of the gearbox was ideal for delivering additional drive to the front wheels by the simple expedient of adding two extra driveshafts, and the not-so-simple expedient of designing a viscous-traction system to deliver just the right amount of torque to each of the four wheels when needed. In this way Paolo Stanzani's legacy lives on in today's Lamborghinis.

Paolo Stanzani was born on 20 July 1936 in Bologna and gained a degree in mechanical engineering from Bologna University in 1961. He joined Lamborghini in 1963 as deputy to the even younger Giampaolo Dallara, Sant'Agata's first Technical Director. Together they were instrumental in the conception, design and development of the Lamborghini Miura, but Stanzani was also intimately involved with the 350GT, the 400GT and the Islero.

Ferruccio trusted Stanzani implicitly, not just because of his obvious engineering ability, but also because of his work ethic and his attention to detail. This became evident with Stanzani's first mock-up of his complex and novel south-north engine-gearbox prototype. In spite of this all-new system's intricacy it worked almost perfectly straight out of the box, a testimony to Stanzani's thoroughly meticulous planning and painstaking engineering. Stanzani is the acknowledged father of the Lamborghini Countach – or at the very least its co-parent together with Marcello Gandini, the Countach's stylist.

In 1975, with the Countach already fully in series production, Stanzani left Sant'Agata. There were many reasons for his unwelcome departure from Lamborghini, including Ferruccio's own retirement to an Umbrian vineyard and the sale of his eponymous supercar company to two disinterested businessmen, the latter's rejection of Stanzani's plan for a smaller, cheaper, sibling to the Countach based on the Bravo concept car, and the prevailing labour militancy that made running any business difficult and sometimes even dangerous.

After leaving Lamborghini Stanzani set up his own engineering consultancy in Bologna. In the late 1980s he was recruited by Romano Artioli for the twin posts of Chief Executive Officer and Chief Technical Officer at Bugatti Automobili SpA. Working together with Maurizio Reggiani, who is the current Chief Technical Officer at Lamborghini, and who as a younger man was intimately involved with the development of the later Diablo variants, Stanzani produced the carbon-fibre chassised, 60-valve, quad-turbo Bugatti EB110. This was launched in September 1991, but by then Stanzani had already left Bugatti, resigning in August 1990 after a dispute with Artioli over funding. He then briefly dabbled in the high-profile world of Formula One motor sport, working with Scuderia Italia and then Minardi, before setting up his own company specialising in renewable energy machinery. He was a master of many trades, and it was a sad day for engineering when the highly talented and generous Stanzani – the authors can personally vouch for his generosity – passed away on 18 January 2017.

powerplant would remain fundamentally unchanged, and Lamborghini's Bizzarrini engine would go on to become one of Sant'Agata's most appealing calling cards.

The other signature feature of the Countach that would be carried forward into the Diablo was its spaceframe chassis. The Countach used a truly bewildering lattice of round-section hollow pipes for its frame, while the Diablo used cheaper square-section hollow pipes that were easier and quicker to weld. A square-section spaceframe was less exotic, less bespoke and less glamorous, but Ferruccio Lamborghini and Paolo Stanzani had originally conceived the Countach as a very limited-volume, no-expense-spared

Bizzarrini's V12 masterpiece served Sant'Agata from 1963 to 2010.

supercar that was designed to annihilate all competitors to the extent that the term 'rival supercar' would be irrelevant when discussing the Countach.

By the time Automobili Lamborghini SpA had emerged from the financially turbulent 1970s and 1980s, and now with Chrysler's accountants in Detroit closely scrutinising every lira that Sant'Agata spent, it was inevitable that the Diablo would have to be an altogether more realistic proposition, cheaper and faster to produce in order to sell in higher volumes, and more competitively priced. All this was needed simply for Lamborghini to stay afloat. The move to a square-section spaceframe chassis for the Diablo was less than ideal, but it was a perfectly reasonable real-world compromise that did not adversely affect the Diablo's dynamics, even if it made for a less utopian specification sheet and a less romantic sales and marketing brochure.

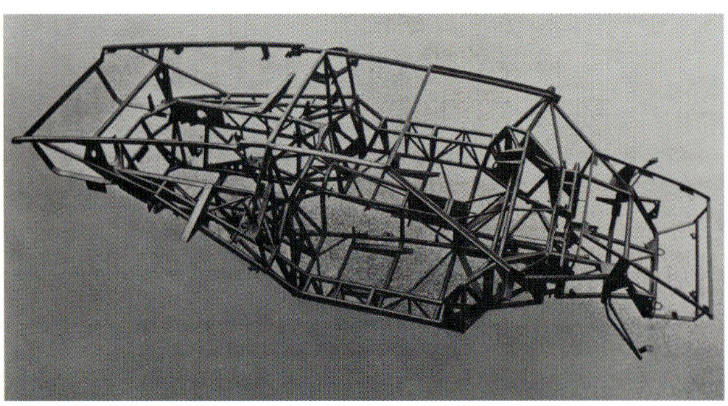

Marchesi built the Countach's intricate spaceframe chassis.

5167cc of stalwart Lamborghini powertrain sits within a Countach 5000 QV.

Umberto Marchesi autographing Crowood Press's book on the Countach.

MARCELLO GANDINI AND THE COUNTACH'S SPECTACULAR DESIGN

The other genius intimately involved with the Countach was Marcello Gandini. Widely accepted as the supercar designer of his generation, Gandini had clothed the Miura's chassis with a gloriously tight-fitting and sensuous body, and would later be instrumental in the design of the Diablo. For the Countach, Marcello Gandini departed radically from the Miura's script. Where the Miura was lithe, delicate and almost feminine, and followed the then prevailing racing car fashion of voluptuous curves, the Countach was angular, angry even at a standstill, and defiantly masculine. Gandini said that when he was designing the Miura, Automobili Lamborghini SpA was still a young company trying to find its feet and establish itself in the highly competitive supercar firmament. He therefore had to be attentive to market demands, and make sure that his Miura design would be accepted immediately by the motoring press and potential customers alike. With the Countach, Gandini felt that that he had much more licence, since Lamborghini was now firmly established on the back of the acclaim and success garnered by the Miura. In addition, Ferruccio Lamborghini himself had requested that the Countach's design should be diametrically opposed to that of its iconic predecessor. Automobili Lamborghini SpA had by now established a reputation for avant-garde design and bold and innovative engineering. Ferruccio recognised that this newly established reputation was hard won and that it distinguished his supercar company from its more established rivals. He was determined not to lose this advantage, so he readily accepted Marcello Gandini's extreme origami design for the Countach, just as he did Paolo Stanzani's revolutionary south-north engine-gearbox orientation for Lamborghini's latest flagship supercar.

Gandini's design for the Countach was sharp-cornered in the extreme. Jagged edges abounded in a manner that would give today's pedestrian safety legislators nightmares. The early 1970s, however, was a different era. The Countach's spectacular appearance gave it and Sant'Agata immediate worldwide recognition within days of its debut at the 1971 Geneva Motor Show. The Countach's nose was impossibly narrow and sharp, and from this forward tip the bodywork rose in an uninterrupted straight line across the front bonnet and the windscreen to the leading edge of the roof. The roof itself was almost completely flat, and from its posterior aspect the bodywork fell, again in an uninterrupted straight line, to the farthest extent of the car. Here the one-millimetre-thick aluminium alloy bodywork ended at a cliff-edge in the form of a vertically cut-off Kammback tail. In profile, the Countach was like an arrow, the epitome of the layperson's image of the most aerodynamic shape possible. This extreme shape was only possible because the Countach adopted electrically activated retractable headlights, which were carried forward to the early Diablo variants. The Countach's outrageous angularity was further accentuated by Marcello Gandini's signature design feature – the slashed and uprising rear wheel arch. This exaggerated styling element was also carried forward to the Diablo.

The Countach's guillotine doors were carried through to the Diablo and the Murciélago.

A high-pressure gas strut was an integral part of the guillotine door's complex operating mechanism.

If Gandini's Countach immediately called attention to itself through its origami-like angularity, its extreme wedge profile and its retractable headlights, it had an even more spectacular party piece guaranteed to make children, teenagers and adults alike swoon: guillotine doors. Although guillotine doors had featured in concept cars like the 1968 Alfa Romeo Carabo prototype, which was also designed by Marcello Gandini while he was at Bertone, the Countach was pretty much the first series production car to boast the extravagance of scissor doors.

Two of Gandini's design innovations that made their debut in the Countach – the extreme wedge profile and the guillotine doors – would go on to define the next generation of supercars, including the Diablo.

MATERIAL SCIENCES

The Lamborghini Countach was a pioneer in the use of exotic materials. The Lamborghini Diablo would build upon this foundation, in particular utilising the knowledge learnt from the carbon fibre-rich Countach Evoluzione prototype. Paolo Stanzani used some rudimentary composites in the LP500 Countach prototype, which made its debut at the 1971 Geneva Motor Show. Later production Countachs used glass-fibre in their bulkheads, front compartment floors, wheel arch liners, central transmission tunnel covers, fuel filler housings, and in numerous smaller body parts.

At this early stage, however, the truly cutting-edge materials that Sant'Agata employed in the Countach were not composites, but other-worldly sounding alloys like Elektron and Avional, which were very rare and hugely expensive, as well as more commonly known elements like aluminium and magnesium. The latter elements are highly abundant (aluminium is the most abundant material by mass in the Earth's crust, and magnesium is the second most abundant) but were almost never used in the construction of everyday cars in the 1960s and 1970s. Each of these four materials had the singular benefit of a high tensile strength-to-weight ratio, which, when employed in bespoke, very high-performance, outrageously expensive supercars, outweighed the fact that they were difficult to mould and manipulate. Avional, for example, was highly favoured by Stanzani for its low density and high resistance to compression, extension and shearing forces, but simply could not be produced in sufficient quantities even for the very limited number of Countachs that Automobili Lamborghini originally planned to build. This aluminium-manganese-magnesium alloy, with a 4 per cent copper content, therefore only featured in the LP500 prototype, and all the production cars had to make do with a more prosaic aluminium alloy for their body panels. Similarly the LP500 prototype debuted with Bertone-designed cast magnesium wheels, manufactured by Campagnolo, but these were too delicate for everyday use, and it would be a further forty-nine years before Sant'Agata revisited magnesium wheels with their Lamborghini Essenza SCV12 hypercar.

Glaverbel glass – very lightweight and super-thin safety glass manufactured in Belgium – was another no-expense-spared material that Stanzani originally specified for Sant'Agata's revolutionary and ultra-exclusive flagship. The Lamborghini Diablo took a similar path, although somewhat

GIOTTO BIZZARRINI'S STALWART V12 ENGINE

The engine powering the Lamborghini Diablo has a rich and longstanding heritage. Few other engines, the Porsche 911's flat six air-cooled engine included, endured for as long. The Diablo's powerplant was a variant of the V12 engine that Giotto Bizzarrini had designed in 1963 at Ferruccio Lamborghini's behest. Versions of this engine powered Lamborghini's flagship cars from the original 1963 Lamborghini 350 GTV concept car right through to the final iteration of the Murciélago in 2010. By comparison, Porsche's commonly mischaracterised air-cooled 'boxer' engine only lasted from 1963 to 1998, just thirty-five years versus the Bizzarrini's forty-seven.

Right from the beginning the story of Bizzarrini's Lamborghini V12 engine was studded with mystery and drama. Popular lore suggests that Lamborghini's supercar company was established in a pique of anger at Enzo Ferrari's rude and arrogant attitude towards him, so it is ironic that the engine that established Automobili Lamborghini SpA as a credible rival to Ferrari SpA had specifically been rejected by Enzo.

Giotto Bizzarrini, a brilliant student, was born into a rich Livornese family in 1926. He graduated from the University of Pisa with a degree in mechanical engineering, having come out top in each of his examination papers. With such an academic pedigree he was immediately recruited by Alfa Romeo and started his engineering career in Milan. He was very unhappy, however, when he was sent to Alfa's chassis department rather than its engine department. Soon after, together with his new friend and fellow Alfa Romeo colleague, the legendary Carlo Chiti, he moved to Ferrari at Maranello, where they were responsible for, amongst other tasty morsels, the iconic Ferrari Testa Rossa and the Ferrari 250 GTO. Both Bizzarrini and Chiti were dismissed by Enzo Ferrari as part of his 1961 'Palace Revolution'. Bizzarrini subsequently set up various engineering consultancies including Automobili Turismo e Sport (ATS) and Società Autostar.

Ferruccio Lamborghini recognised that at the very least he needed a V12 engine to power his cars if he were to compete within the highest tier of supercar manufacturers and have a realistic chance of achieving his stated ambition of producing the 'perfect grand touring road car'. In the course of the considerable time he spent scouting around for talented engine designers and builders, Società Autostar was recommended by the highly reputable coachbuilders Neri & Bonacini as a reliable and technologically advanced engine design company.

Giotto Bizzarrini was interviewed by Ferruccio in 1962 and Società Autostar received a commission later that year for the design and development of a V12 engine producing a minimum power output of 350bhp. Società Autostar would receive a fee of 4,500,000 lire for this work – half upfront and the other half upon completion. If the engine produced more than 350bhp Bizzarrini would receive a bonus payment for his brilliance, but the contract also stipulated that money would be deducted from the second instalment if the engine produced less than the agreed 350bhp.

Bizzarrini had previously designed a very promising state-of-the-art, 1.5-litre, four camshaft, V12 competition engine for Formula One, but Enzo Ferrari had dismissed this engine for use in any of his race cars. Both Bizzarrini and Lamborghini saw huge potential in a scaled-up, road-focused version of this cutting-edge powerplant, and the former set about his task with his typical diligence and intelligence.

On 15 May 1963 Bizzarrini put his 60-degree, 3465cc, dry-sump V12 engine on the dynamometer and it produced 358bhp at 9,800rpm and 240lb ft torque at 6,000rpm. This engine had a bore of 77mm and a stroke of 62mm, and ran 38mm down-draught Weber racing carburettors. One might have thought that would be job done, with a bonus as well, but life was never so straightforward in the emotive world of 1960s Italian automotive engineering. Lamborghini was furious because the engine presented to him was essentially a racing engine that was totally unsuited to a grand touring car. This engine's power and torque outputs only reached adequate levels at unacceptably high engine speeds for a GT car, which by definition was designed to be easy on its driver, and serene and cossetting for its passenger. Ferruccio's anger manifested itself in a completely uncharacteristic refusal to pay Bizzarrini and Società Autostar the full 4,500,000 lire, let alone the bonus payment for the additional 8bhp that Giotto had magicked out of the engine's 3465cc. Bizzarrini was forced to take Lamborghini to court, where Ferruccio lost and finally paid up.

It was left to Giampaolo Dallara and Paolo Stanzani to tame this promising but wild powerplant. They did so by jettisoning the dry-sump lubrication system in favour of a cheaper and less complex wet-sump system, by using side-draught carburettors instead of down-draught carburettors, and by modifying the engine's valve stems, valve timing, tappets and distributors. All their work culminated in an engine that produced much less power and torque than Ferruccio had initially wanted – only 270bhp at 6,500rpm and 240lb ft torque at 4,000rpm – but Ferruccio was finally happy. This engine was now civilised enough for his 'perfect grand touring car'.

In the years that followed Giotto Bizzarrini worked on the Iso Rivolta and the Iso Grifo, manufactured the spectacular Bizzarrini 5300 GT Strada road car, and entered the P538 racing car for the Le Mans 24 Hours. His V12 Lamborghini engine was equally successful and it became one of the defining features of Automobili Lamborghini's early history.

The Countach made extensive use of aluminium and composite materials.

tempered by the economic realities dictated by Chrysler's Detroit accountants.

The Countach Evoluzione was a turning point in Lamborghini's involvement with the material sciences, and in particular the more advanced composites. The Evoluzione was a prototype car produced and developed in the early to mid-1980s under the stewardship of Giulio Alfieri, Horacio Pagani and Rosario Vizzini. All three were outstanding engineers and designers in their own right, but when brought together they formed a formidable team that would direct Lamborghini's course for decades to come. The Countach Evoluzione was a one-off mobile laboratory for testing the viability of promising new materials under consideration to replace the more traditional metals that had been the mainstay of the automotive industry since the birth of the motor car. Foremost amongst the materials that Vizzini, an aeronautical engineer by training, investigated were Kevlar and carbon fibre. Kevlar, famous through its use in bullet-proof vests and military helmets, readily gained acceptance within Sant'Agata and was used as early as 1985 in the series production Countach 5000 Quattrovalvole model. This para-aramid synthetic fibre had already been used in racing tyres and in Formula One monocoques. In the Countach it was used as the base material for the front compartment and engine compartment lids. In the Lamborghini Diablo Kevlar was used in some of the seat frames and after-market clutches; in the Diablo 6.0 VT cockpit it was also a component of a special Lamborghini carbon-fibre twill, which imparted a very attractive blue thread-like pattern to the weave.

The Countach Evoluzione's major contribution to the Diablo and its successors, however, came through its investigation and development of automotive carbon fibre. Carbon fibre, which was first produced in 1860 by Joseph Swan, is composed almost exclusively of carbon atoms bonded together into microscopic crystals that are then aligned into fibres. These fibres are then joined into filaments, which are twisted to form a yarn and then woven into a fabric. When impregnated with a plastic polymer resin and baked at high temperature and under high pressure in an autoclave, a carbon-fibre reinforced polymer is produced with an exceptionally high strength-to-weight ratio and phenomenal rigidity.

McLaren were the first Formula One team to use a complete carbon fibre monocoque in their 1981 MP4/1 racing car, and the Lamborghini Diablo was one of the first products from a mainstream car manufacturer to employ carbon fibre extensively. The amount of carbon fibre employed increased significantly with each successive Diablo variant, and by the end of the Diablo's production run carbon fibre was used for the car's front and engine compartment lids, its bumpers, sills, front and rear spoilers, and for an assortment of cockpit parts. Some of these carbon fibre components were for structural strength, while others were essentially chosen for their visual appeal, since by then carbon fibre had become a must-have accessory for the fashionistas. The Diablo's successor, the Murciélago, would have a body made almost exclusively of carbon fibre, and with the Murciélago's successor, the Aventador, this had extended to the chassis as well as the body. The Countach had a far-reaching and long-lasting influence that extended well beyond the Diablo.

AERODYNAMICS

The arrow-like profile of the Countach might have screamed aerodynamic efficiency, but in fact it was one of the most aerodynamically inefficient of cars, even at this stage of the automotive timeline. A full-scale Countach was never put through formal wind tunnel testing, although a Bertone scale model underwent testing in the Politecnico di Torino's wind tunnel. The sleek scale model used looked like the original smooth and uncluttered LP500 prototype, and was quite different in overall shape and detail to the rather messy series production cars, which were strewn with aerodynamic drag-inducing vents, conduits and engine-cooling protuberances,

The Countach looked aerodynamic, but its Cd of 0.42 said otherwise.

such as the elephant ear RAM ducts that stood directly in the way of the oncoming airstream. Even so this scale model had an appalling coefficient of aerodynamic drag (Cd) of 0.42, which just goes to show how misleading appearances can be in aerodynamics.

The true Cd of the less sleek production Countachs would almost certainly have been much worse. In contrast, contemporary cars and immediate rivals boasted much better Cd figures than the Countach, including the 1969 Saab Sonnet (0.32), the 1969 Alfa Romeo Giulia (0.34), the 1970 Citroën SM (0.33), the 1974 Ferrari 365 GT/4 Berlinetta Boxer (0.35) and the 1984 Ferrari Testarossa (0.36). When the CdA (coefficient of aerodynamic drag multiplied by the car's frontal area), the true real-world measure of aerodynamic efficiency, was considered, the outlook for the Countach darkened further. The Countach not only had a larger than average bodywork frontal area, but this was further aggravated by its employment of very wide tyres, particularly the massive rear tyres found in later variants. Aerodynamic inefficiency was the Countach's greatest weakness, and each subsequent model variant attempted to sidestep this glaring fault by increasing the engine's power and torque output. By 1985 it had become clear to Sant'Agata's engineers that such compensatory powertrain measures could not adequately deal with the Countach's fundamental aerodynamic failings, and they started thinking about a brand new replacement flagship with class-leading aerodynamics, which would later become the Diablo.

As aerodynamics played such an important role in the Lamborghini Diablo's conception, and as aerodynamics has such an influential role on the way any car accelerates, brakes, steers and corners, a very brief overview of automotive aerodynamics is called for here.

The word aerodynamics is derived from two Ancient Greek words, *aër*, which itself comes from *aemi*, meaning 'to breathe unconsciously', and *dunamis*, meaning 'strength or power'. Aerodynamics is a branch of gas dynamics, and so itself part of fluid dynamics. Aerodynamics studies how moving air passes around and through a solid body, and how this moving air interacts with said solid body. The most important and fundamental parameters in aerodynamics include weight (a function of mass and gravitational force), lift, thrust and drag.

The basic scientific principles underlying automotive aerodynamics were first identified by five acclaimed mathematicians and physicists. The concept of aerodynamic drag was postulated by Sir Isaac Newton (1642–1726) in his 1687 treatise *Philosophiae Naturalis Principia Mathematica*. The behaviour of fluids in motion was described by Daniel Bernoulli (1700–1782) in his *Hydrodynamica* of 1738, in which more specifically he put forward what became known as Bernoulli's Principle, which links together pressure, density and flow velocity. Sir George Cayley (1773–1857) identified the four vectors of flight (weight, lift, drag and thrust), which are just as important to the way a Countach or Diablo drives as they are to the way an aeroplane flies. Lord Rayleigh (1842–1919) further developed Newton's aerodynamic drag theory and formulated the circulation theory of aerodynamic lift – all of which was immediately relevant for the Countach and Diablo to realise their potential top speeds, and to prevent them from becoming airborne. Henri Coanda (1886–1972) described the Coanda Effect, which details how and why a fluid stream in contact with a curved surface follows that surface's curvature, rather than simply continuing on in a straight line. The Coanda Effect was brought to life at the rear of the Countach's and Diablo's bodywork, where their overall aerodynamic drag was substantially reduced by the abrupt cliff-like cut-off of their Kammback tails.

In addition to Bernoulli's Principle and the Coanda Effect there are three further important laws of physics that are of immediate relevance to automotive aerodynamics: the Law of Conservation of Mass, the Law of Conservation of Momentum, and the Law of Conservation of Energy. The Countach and Diablo were pierced by a multitude of vents, ducts and conduits, and these five physical principles and laws dictated how air would flow through and around these cars, and thereby influence how they behaved on the road. Flow speed, fluid viscosity and fluid compressibility are other immediately relevant topics that the reader might want to pursue further in their search for a more thorough understanding of the Countach and the Diablo.

Aerodynamics also tied in neatly with another issue that had plagued Sant'Agata right from the company's inception. Bizzarrini's V12 engine was massive and its many reciprocating parts generated frictional forces, which in turn translated into wasteful heat energy that had to be quickly and reliably dissipated. With each new iteration of the Countach and Diablo, the Bizzarrini engine grew in size, power and torque output, and generated more and more unwanted heat energy. The sleek and smooth LP500 Countach prototype had to be progressively desecrated into an ever more cluttered caricature, with a never-ending

Note the Countach's cliff-like Kammback tail.

variety of RAM ducts, NACA ducts and other bodily piercings tacked on to each new Countach variant, simply to get the hot engine-bay air out as quickly as possible from what would otherwise be a furnace-like engine compartment. Sant'Agata's engineers learnt from their distressing Miura and Countach experiences, and engine bay heat management was an important consideration right from the earliest moment of the Diablo's conception. Gandini designed the Diablo's bodywork to allow heat energy to escape easily, and by doing this he avoided having to tack on protuberances that stuck out into the oncoming airstream. This in turn meant that the Diablo was aerodynamically efficient, so it was able to cleave through the air cleanly and easily. The Diablo therefore needed less power, less torque and less fuel to accelerate to, and maintain, any given speed, while also generating less unwanted heat energy. Intelligently applied aerodynamic principles resulted in good aerodynamics, which allowed for better engine heat management, which in turn allowed for an aerodynamically efficient body shape: the paragon of a thoroughly virtuous circle. The Lamborghini Diablo had a genuine, real-world aerodynamic drag coefficient of 0.31, which was much, much better than the Countach's impossibly optimistic 0.42 – a figure derived from a smooth, uncluttered and wholly unrepresentative scale model.

A BRIEF HISTORY OF THE COUNTACH

The Lamborghini Countach LP500 prototype was unveiled on 11 March 1971 in the Palexpo Halls at the Geneva Motor Show. It made its debut on the Bertone stand rather than the Lamborghini stand as it remained a concept car at this stage, although Ferruccio Lamborghini and the Countach's two key designers, Paolo Stanzani and Marcello Gandini, had every expectation that it would enter series production in the very near future. In fact it took a further three years to iron out the numerous teething problems thrown up by this revolutionary supercar before the first Countach could be delivered to a paying customer, but once in production the Countach remained at the very pinnacle of the supercar tree for an almost unimaginable sixteen years. During this time it went through six major iterations, the last two of which, the 88 ½ and the Anniversary, have particular resonance here as they were produced under Chrysler and featured design details that would influence the Lamborghini Diablo.

Drivetrain cooling problems were the single most troublesome issue that Sant'Agata's engineers faced in getting the Countach LP500 prototype road ready. The only way they could resolve this cooling issue was by desecrating the

The Countach's cockpit was simple and elegant, even if it could double up as a leather fetishist's boudoir.

LP500's impossibly sleek and smooth bodywork with additional ducts and vents – carbuncles that would markedly increase the car's drag coefficient and indirectly lead to the Diablo's conception and birth. Other problems that beset the LP500 were issues with engine reliability, dynamic stability, cockpit instrumentation and comfort.

The first production Countach, the LP400 model variant, was delivered to a Milanese customer in April 1974, and 157 such cars were produced between 1974 and 1978. They featured a 3929cc engine producing a very optimistically claimed 375bhp at 8,000rpm and 266lb ft torque at 5,500rpm. Lamborghini's fashion conscious and never satisfied customers demanded another fix fairly soon thereafter, and Sant'Agata obliged by delivering a radically redesigned car in the Countach LP400S. Produced between 1978 and 1982, the LP400S retained the 3,929cc displacement of its predecessor, but Lamborghini were now more honest and realistic in claiming just 353bhp at 7,500rpm for their latest flagship. The profound bodywork changes found in the LP400S were forced upon Lamborghini by its decision to use the newly available Pirelli P7 tyres. These massive low-profile tyres, measuring a previously unheard-of 345/35VR15 at the rears, demanded vast flared wheel-arch extensions. To fit in with these new arches aesthetically, Lamborghini also redesigned the front of the car with a deep chin spoiler, and balanced this out with an optional arrow-shaped rear wing spoiler.

With wide tyres and no power steering, manoeuvring a Countach at low speeds can be hard work.

In 1982 Sant'Agata launched the Countach LP500S to counter the competition from Ferrari's Boxer, and also to compensate for the additional aerodynamic drag produced by the previous variant's new bodywork and tyres. Power was now back to a genuine 375bhp at 7,000rpm and torque was elevated to 303lb ft at 4,500rpm, courtesy of an enlarged engine displacing 4574cc. But Maranello was still taking aim at Lamborghini's supercar crown, and in 1984 Ferrari launched both its very aerodynamically efficient Testarossa, and its powerful twin-turbo limited edition 288 GTO.

Sant'Agata riposted in 1985 by launching the Countach 5000 Quattrovalvole, which featured a fundamentally redesigned engine. Under the direction of Giulio Alfieri, one of Italy's most renowned post-war automotive engineers, whose curriculum vitae included the iconic Maserati 250F and the Maserati Tipo 61 Birdcage race cars, Sant'Agata's engineers increased the engine's stroke to 75mm while keeping its bore size unchanged for a total swept capacity of 5167cc. In addition Alfieri developed a completely new cylinder head featuring four valves per cylinder, introduced downdraught Weber 44 DCNF carburettors, and increased the engine's compression ratio to 9.5:1. This combination allowed the Countach 5000 Quattrovalvole to boast substantially increased power and torque outputs – 455bhp at 7,000rpm and 369lb ft at 5,200rpm – enough to see off the Testarossa's 390bhp and the admittedly much lighter 288 GTO's 395bhp.

The word Countach translates from Piedmontese into 'Wow!' Enough said.

The 88 ½ Countach 5000 Quattrovalvole was a pivotal version. It was the first Countach produced wholly under Chrysler, who quite rightly demanded much stricter, mass market-led, quality control procedures than Sant'Agata had previously been accustomed to. Lamborghini would carry these vetting and cross-checking logistics forward into the future, long after Chrysler had sold its Italian trophy purchase, and the Diablo would be a direct beneficiary of these additional procedures and checks. The 88 ½ was the first Countach to exploit the knowledge distilled from the experimental Countach Evoluzione, and it also featured bodywork alterations that would go on to inform both the Diablo and the Murciélago. The 88 ½ had improved aerodynamics, and also used cutting edge materials, such as Kevlar for its engine compartment lid. Finally the 88 ½ could reasonably be seen as the ultimate production Countach as it improved upon its predecessors by having an improved suspension set-up and the most advanced Countach production engine, while also retaining the full glory of Marcello Gandini's unadulterated design masterpiece, the Countach's spectacular bodywork. (Most would agree that the Countach variant that followed on from the 88 ½, the 25th Anniversary, had highly debatable aesthetics that were very much an acquired taste.)

The 88 ½ was easily distinguished from its earlier brethren because it sacrificed the Countach's signature dolphin lower body voluptuousness for the Evoluzione's new linear, extended, straked and perforated side sills. This radical departure from the established norm was done to increase the Countach's total under-surface area, which in accordance with Bernoulli's Principle reduced lift at the rear of the car. The strakes also acted as air conduits to cool the rear brake discs and pads, the rear tyres and the lower parts of the engine compartment. These new side sills were designed by none other than Horacio Pagani of Zonda and Huayra fame. The Lamborghini Diablo and Murciélago took a leaf from the 88 ½, and their side sills too adopted the extended, linear, perforated lower bodywork of the 88 ½. The 88 ½ was only produced for a very short period,

Approaching a Countach is always daunting, made worse by its narrow door aperture and wide sill. The Diablo improved on both these aspects.

from the tail end of 1987 to the middle of 1988, and this is one of the rarest of the series production Countachs: only fourteen right-hand-drive 88 ½ Countachs were ever manufactured.

The final production Countach had lashings of Chrysler input. It was called the 25th Anniversary because it commemorated Lamborghini's 25th milestone year. Chrysler had originally hoped that the Diablo could be launched in that celebratory year, but when it became clear that this was an over-ambitious target, a farewell Countach version was launched instead. The Anniversary had a complete cosmetic makeover, although whether it benefited from this is entirely in the eyes of the beholder. On a more positive note, its suspension geometry was comprehensively reworked by the multiple world rally champion Sandro Munari, and the 25th Anniversary is rightly considered the most dynamically stable of all the Countach variants. The 88 ½ and the 25th Anniversary employed essentially the same powerplant and drivetrain as the 1985 5000 Quattrovalvole variant.

One of the authors tests the structural integrity of a 25th Anniversary Countach. Note the historical timeline with the Countach being sandwiched by a Miura and a Diablo.

At moderate to high engine speeds the Countach enters an ethereal plane. The steering lightens to perfection, the gear lever slots in cleanly, and the car accelerates forward savagely – all accompanied by Bizzarrini's glorious V12 symphony playing at its best. Bellissima.

Only 1,997 Lamborghini Countachs were ever produced. From 1971, when the LP500 prototype made its debut, until the last Anniversary rolled off the production line in 1990, the Countach defined the word supercar. No single supercar has dominated its segment for such a long period – only the Porsche 911, the Volkswagen Beetle and the Mazda MX5 are as long-lived and as globally recognised – but they each belong to an entirely different class of car. Even today, over a half century after its initial debut, and more than thirty years after the final car rolled off the Sant'Agata production line, the Countach and the Miura remain the two models that best symbolise and define Lamborghini.

CHAPTER 3

PROGETTO 132: A STAR IS CONCEIVED

The Place: Sant'Agata.
The Date: June 1985.
The Subject: Progetto 132.
The Parents: Patrick Mimran, Emile Novaro and Ubaldo Sgarzi.
The Midwives: Luigi Marmiroli, Marcello Gandini and Valentino Balboni.
The Inspiration: the Countach.
The Motivation: technological progress, intermanufacturer rivalry, aerodynamic efficiency, sociopolitical, safety and environmental factors.
The Result: the Lamborghini Diablo.

The Lamborghini Diablo had a particularly difficult gestation because it was conceived under the *ancien régime* of Patrick and Jean-Claude Mimran, but developed and refined for series production under the revolutionary American administration of Chrysler.

The Mimrans' management team was packed with traditional Italian executives and engineers like Emile Novaro, Ubaldo Sgarzi, Giulio Alfieri, Valentino Balboni and later Luigi Marmiroli, who had all spent a lifetime in Pianeta Modena ('Planet Modena', that small, discrete and densely packed supercar valley containing Ferrari, Maserati and Lamborghini, manufacturers of bespoke, low-volume, hugely expensive, specialist cars) and were steeped in Italian supercar knowledge, as well as confident in what they thought the Diablo should be.

In contrast, Chrysler's management team was led by the likes of Lee Iacocca, Gerry Grenwald and Bob Lutz, who had been nurtured in the very different world of America's 'Big Three' (General Motors, Ford and Chrysler), which were all geared to making mass-market, high-volume, low-cost, utilitarian cars. Pianeta Modena and the Big Three had very dissimilar histories, traditions, market expectations and ideas on design, production, marketing and sales. A fight was almost inevitable.

The Diablo's body design would become the key battleground between the Italian connoisseurs and their American paymasters. The disharmony created through this conflict would delay the Diablo's debut, and would also sully relations between Lamborghini and Chrysler for years to come.

PROTOTYPE DEVELOPMENT

June 1985 was a pivotal moment for the Diablo. Sant'Agata had for some years now identified key problem areas that would soon render the Countach unable to meet forthcoming governmental legislation or match forthcoming supercar rivals. But a powerful group within Lamborghini was loath to abandon this historic car, which had kept the company afloat during its most turbulent period. Sant'Agata therefore invested in a development team to work on modernising and revamping the Countach to make it fit for purpose for the next decade, and even for the next millennium.

By early 1985 even the Countach's most ardent supporters had to concede that a wholly new Lamborghini flagship was the only avenue open for Sant'Agata if it wanted to remain a key player in the supercar world. Even a comprehensive overhaul of the Countach's drivetrain and bodywork would not allow it to meet the homologation challenges that lay immediately ahead, let alone into the next century.

The P132 was the concept car for the Countach's successor.

In June 1985 Patrick Mimran, Lamborghini's owner, and Emile Novaro, Lamborghini's president, formally initiated a study to design and develop a brand new successor flagship to take over from the Countach. This study was called Progetto 132. Together with Ubaldo Sgarzi, Lamborghini's long-standing and long-suffering Commercial Director, Mimran and Novaro set down very clear guidelines for Progetto 132.

The rear mid-engine layout of the Miura and Countach was by now a Lamborghini trademark and had to be retained, as did a classic naturally aspirated, quad camshaft 60-degree V12 engine and a weight-saving spaceframe chassis. The Countach's longitudinally aligned engine had proven itself to be a technological and dynamic advance on the Miura's transversely aligned engine, so this too had to be preserved. Above all, Paolo Stanzani's revolutionary south-north engine-gearbox orientation had come to define both the Countach and Automobili Lamborghini, and had brought with it huge benefits in terms of roadholding, handling and space-efficiency, so this too had to be carried through into Progetto 132. An additional benefit of this unique engine-gearbox orientation was that it allowed Progetto 132 to be easily, quickly and relatively cheaply converted from a two-wheel-drive car into a four-wheel-drive car, a future development that Sant'Agata already had on its radar.

From an aesthetic standpoint, the extreme wedge shape of the Countach had immediately become emblematic of what a supercar's profile should be to most car aficionados and non-enthusiasts alike, and this too had to be retained. The same went for the Countach's spectacular guillotine doors, which were now synonymous with Lamborghini.

By Darwinian standards, however, the Countach in the late 1980s deserved to be extinct. It was no longer the fittest, and so had no entitlement to continued survival. Porsche's 959 was a technological tour de force that made the Countach look like something from the Dark Ages. A prototype 959 was shown at the 1983 Frankfurt Motor Show, and by the time the production 959 made its debut at the same event in 1985 this advanced engineering platform had already proven itself by winning the gruelling 1984 Paris–Dakar Rally. The 959 was also reliable despite its complex drivetrain, comfortable, spacious, easy to get into and out of, and afforded excellent outward visibility. While Stuttgart had been busy, Maranello had not been sitting on its 288GTO laurels either.

The P132 was designed to address the Countach's many shortcomings. WIKIMEDIA/ARNAUD 25

In 1984 Nicola Materazzi put forward the basic technical plans for the Ferrari F40 to Enzo Ferrari. The F40, although not as technologically advanced as the 959, made extensive use of cutting-edge Kevlar and carbon fibre, as well as state-of-the-art intercooler-enhanced turbo technology. With a claimed top speed of 323km/h (201mph), and a 0–62mph time of 4.1 seconds, the F40 blew the Countach's primary *raison d'être* – top speed and acceleration – right out of the water. Lamborghini, that most avant garde of supercar manufacturers, no longer produced the most advanced, the fastest or the fastest accelerating supercar. Sant'Agata had no choice but to respond.

Progetto 132 was set up to address these formidable performance shortcomings. Automobili Lamborghini had evolved from Ferruccio's original vision of a manufacturer producing the ultimate and consummate Gran Turismo cars. Now its calling card was as a manufacturer of outrageous, attention-seeking cars, which backed up extravagant aesthetics with exorbitant performance. Lamborghini willingly surrendering its claim to the 'Top Speed Crown' would be tantamount to declaring that it no longer had any reason to exist.

Patrick Mimran, Emile Novaro and Ubaldo Sgarzi were not in the market for any such ready renunciation or capitulation. The primary design specification that this trio laid down for Sant'Agata's engineers and designers was that Progetto 132 had to be the fastest series production car in the world, which in concrete terms translated into a car capable of reaching a minimum top speed of 315km/h (195.7km/h). Ubaldo Sgarzi, whose responsibility as Commercial Director was to sell the Progetto 132 to a sometimes uninformed and fickle clientele, knew that his mission would be that much easier if he could market this new Lamborghini flagship car as the fastest supercar available to the public.

To meet this principal design target Progetto 132 had to be much more aerodynamic than its predecessor. Despite its extreme wedge profile, the Countach had truly awful aerodynamics with origami-sharp edges, exposed protuberances such as its elephant-ear RAM ducts and the optional rear wing, and a multitude of drag-inducing vents. A totally new bodyshell was therefore urgently needed. This was a blessing in disguise, as it also allowed for essential and long-overdue improvements in cockpit space and cabin comfort.

Lamborghini now knew what Mercedes Benz had already researched and proven: humans in the 1980s were physically larger than their 1960s counterparts. Lamborghini also knew that the customers for its new flagship were likely to be more demanding of luxury features like fully functioning air-conditioning than the die-hard Countach enthusiasts of the 1970s. Early Lamborghini customers were happy to suffer a good bit of inconvenience and bother simply to experience the Miura's and Countach's exhilarating performance and crowd-pleasing oddity. Redesigned guillotine doors that allowed for easier ingress and exit, broader and more comfortable seats, a proper climate-control system, better headroom and legroom, wing mirrors that gave something more than a view of the car's own flanks, decent forward and side visibility, and, most important of all, better passive safety features (and indirectly, active safety features too) to improve crashworthiness; these were all improvements that a wholly new bodyshell could provide Progetto 132.

Progetto 132's new bodyshell would also have to be beautiful and dramatic. Many Lamborghini customers are extroverts, and their cars need to cater for their exhibitionist tendencies – and anyway, a supercar surely needs to be startling, thrilling and sensational even at rest. But the truth was that Progetto 132's designers would have their work cut out to even begin to match the sensuous beauty of the Miura or the sheer theatrical drama of the Countach. The grandfather and father are aesthetic icons that remain unsurpassed today.

Progetto 132 would also need outstanding levels of grip and road handling to keep up with the new breed of supercars now making an appearance. Noise, vibration and harshness levels would have to be on a different plane to that experienced in the Countach. The new car would need to be more forgiving at the extremes of its performance envelope, and have a less demanding clutch and gearchange – all of which were serious Countach foibles.

Progetto 132 would also have to be more fuel efficient and less polluting. Homologation regulations in Lamborghini's then key markets of the United States, Northern Europe and Japan had already instituted such legislation, and other markets like the Middle East and Australasia were also considering similar restrictive statutes.

On 1 January 1985 Patrick Mimran and Emile Novaro appointed Luigi Marmiroli as Lamborghini's Technical Director in place of Giulio Alfieri. Marmiroli was an accomplished engineer who had worked with Mauro Forghieri at Ferrari and with Carlo Chiti at Alfa Romeo, and had been instrumental in the design and development of Minardi's Formula Two race cars. Marmiroli was initially asked to carry out feasibility studies on how the Countach's drivetrain

A treasured magazine from the authors' library, the 22 June 1988 issue of *Autocar*.

Four-wheel drive and 480bhp plus are the keys to the car designed to top the Testarossa. By Michael Harvey

DIABLO: LAMBO NEW COUNTACH

32 AUTOCAR 22 June 1988

22 June 1988 AUTOCAR 33

***Autocar*'s 22 June 1988 issue quotes Luigi Marmiroli, Lamborghini's Technical Director, as saying that the P132 was designed 'to take the performance levels of the Countach one step further'.**

could be modified for substantially more power, torque and refinement. With the launch of Progetto 132 in June 1985, Marmiroli was also appointed to carry out the extensive engineering work needed to make Lamborghini's stalwart south-north engine-gearbox drivetrain, now almost fifteen years old, fit for purpose in the new flagship car.

Although much painstaking experimental work and many detailed technical modifications had to be carried out to enable Progetto 132 to meet its performance targets, the heart of this drivetrain, which itself was the very anima of the car, remained Bizzarrini's V12 engine, by then almost a quarter of a century old. Anima is also an Italian word, and interestingly Sant'Agata calls its latest selectable driving mode system, as found in the Lamborghini Urus, ANIMA. Progetto 132's soul was an evolution of the beating heart that powered the Countach, the Miura and the 350GTV, its classic Bizzarrini engine.

If Progetto 132's engineering was evolutionary and non-controversial, its bodyshell design was new and hugely contentious, and would be the cause of deep and longstanding animosity between Lamborghini's design team and Chrysler's management. The new flagship had to retain Lamborghini's now signature wedge shape, but it was also imperative that the car was very aerodynamically efficient: dire aerodynamics had been the Countach's Achilles heel.

The Miura and Countach had been styled by Bertone. This design house, based in Grugliasco, was also responsible for the Espada, Urraco, Jarama and Silhouette, so at first sight Bertone would have appeared to be the ideal and natural stylist for Progetto 132. But Carrozzeria Bertone's chief stylist was now Marc Deschamps, and Lamborghini had been less than impressed with the Frenchman's styling of its V8-engined Jalpa, which had debuted at the 1981 Geneva Motor Show. Sant'Agata needed Progetto 132 to be more dramatic, more coherent and more aerodynamic than what Deschamps had been able to produce with the Jalpa. Other styling houses did not measure up for various reasons: Pininfarina was too closely aligned with Ferrari for comfort, and Zagato, Ghia and Touring were unable to deliver suitable proposals. Giorgetto Giugiaro of Italdesign had produced a four-seater, two gull-winged door concept car called the Lamborghini Marco Polo for Sant'Agata in 1982, and Lamborghini was very impressed with the remarkable aerodynamic efficiency of this show car, which boasted an aerodynamic drag coefficient of only 0.24. When Giugiaro submitted a proposal for Progetto 132 in the form of a 1:8

Sant'Agata's in-house proposal for the Countach's successor.

painted wooden scale model, however, it was a scant remodelling of his 1984 Lotus Etna concept car, and Lamborghini felt compelled to reject it almost immediately.

But everything was far from lost. Marcello Gandini had always been the front-runner for styling Lamborghini's new flagship. After all it was Gandini who had styled the Miura and the Countach during his time as Chief Designer at Carrozzeria Bertone. Gandini's name was therefore already inextricably linked with Lamborghini's and had in fact become a byword for Sant'Agata's most outrageous and iconic supercars. Gandini knew the movers and shakers within Lamborghini, and they in turn knew him, trusted him, and were comfortable with his style and renowned work ethic. Gandini could be relied upon to deliver the goods.

After leaving Bertone, the reclusive Gandini had taken refuge in his beautiful and secluded seventeenth-century Villa Gran Vigna in Almese, a small commune 27 kilometres west of Turin. There he set up his own design studio and took on freelance projects. Gandini readily accepted Lamborghini's offer of the design brief. Sant'Agata stressed that his proposal had to be highly aerodynamic so that they could reclaim what they considered their birthright: the 'Fastest Production Car' crown. They also impressed upon him that Progetto 132's design brief required the car to be spacious, comfortable, user-friendly, safe, fuel efficient and environmentally friendly. Gandini was not deterred by any of these challenging but mandatory design parameters.

Working in his characteristically urgent manner, Gandini produced a first rendering of Progetto 132's body design

This proposal was rejected in fairly short order.

within a mere few weeks. He continued to refine his proposal over the subsequent months, and in January 1986 Gandini and Luigi Marmiroli presented the Lamborghini Management Board with detailed drawings and established engineering hard-points for the new car. Patrick Mimran and Emile Novaro liked Gandini's and Marmiroli's proposals and they sanctioned the further development of Progetto 132 in early spring. Work on the first prototype car began in June 1986.

By early March 1987 the first prototype car had been assembled. This hand-built vehicle was Chassis 12000, and was painted in a neutral, many would say ugly, grey. Marmiroli chose this colour on purpose, having taken onboard Battista Pininfarina's longstanding edict that prototype cars should always be in a neutral colour so that the car's shape and styling details would not be overshadowed by its hue. This car was fitted with a Type 521 engine, with a 5.2-litre displacement, in late March 1987. The car was then sent for aerodynamic testing to a wind tunnel facility just outside Paris as secrecy and confidentiality were paramount to Lamborghini. Sant'Agata simply did not trust any nearby Italian aerodynamic test centre not to leak highly sought-after photographic scoops to the clamouring motoring press who were hungry for any information on the forthcoming Lamborghini supercar. Wind tunnel tests were carried out between 29 and 31 March 1987, and the data that spewed out was hugely heartening to both Gandini and Lamborghini. This first prototype, which featured a large and curvaceous engine cover made of glass, was very streamlined and cleaved through the air with great aerodynamic efficiency.

The proposal put forward by Marcello Gandini for the Countach's successor. Emile Novaro, amongst others, favoured this styling exercise as the basis for the P132 project.

MARCELLO GANDINI

Marcello Gandini is commonly acknowledged as the pre-eminent supercar stylist of the twentieth century, and his name is almost synonymous with the most important and dramatic cars that Lamborghini has ever produced. While it is true that designers like Giorgio Prevedi, Franco Scaglione, Luc Donckerwolke and Mitja Borkert have also contributed, Gandini was so intimately entwined with Lamborghini, and for so long, that his association with, and influence on, Sant'Agata remains without parallel. Giorgetto Giugiaro and even Giuseppe 'Nuccio' Bertone have suggested that they contributed to the Lamborghini Miura's design, but if so their contribution must have been minuscule compared to Gandini's. It has never been disputed that the Lamborghini Countach was Gandini's work, pure and simple. And Gandini's extreme wedge-shaped, origami-based styling set the design template for the vast majority of the twentieth- and twenty-first-century supercars that have followed since the Countach.

While Gandini's first styling exercise for the Lamborghini Diablo was rejected by Chrysler, and his second proposal was diluted and mutilated by Detroit's own stylists, enough of his original design made it through to series production for Sant'Agata to stick a small plaque carrying the words 'disegno Marcello Gandini' on the lower flanks of every Diablo produced. Lamborghini, with Chrysler's blessing, thereby acknowledged Gandini's immense contribution to bringing the Diablo to life.

Gandini was born in Turin on 26 August 1938. His father was an orchestral conductor, so Marcello's later artistic brilliance may reasonably be attributed to both nature and nurture. On the latter front his early interest in mechanics was sparked by a Meccano set given to him by his parents at the age of five. This genuine interest in how things worked, and how individual components interacted to form a whole functioning object, distinguished Gandini from his contemporary fellow designers for whom the outward form of a car eclipsed its inner workings, and for whom appearance was often the sole consideration. Gandini wanted to know about, and could understand, the mechanics of the cars he was clothing. Giampaolo Dallara, Lamborghini's first Technical Director, said that Gandini was unusual amongst automotive stylists in being able to understand complex technical issues, and almost unique in then being able to proffer pragmatic mechanical solutions to resolve these problems.

Gandini's first job was with Abarth, but he stayed there for only a short time. In 1963 Gandini approached Nuccio Bertone for a job at his eponymous design studio. His appointment as a stylist at Bertone was fiercely opposed by Giorgetto Giugiaro, who was then Head of Design. There must have been a flicker of smug satisfaction and sweet revenge when Nuccio immediately appointed Gandini as Head of Design in 1965, a direct and unhesitating riposte to Giugiaro's abrupt and unexpected departure from the Bertone styling house to its almost equally prestigious rival Ghia. Gandini stayed at Bertone for fourteen years, during which time he rewarded Nuccio's trust in him by designing some truly spectacular cars.

Gandini's designs at Bertone included both sensational supercars and mass-market daily drivers, including the Miura (1966), the Espada (1968), the BMW 2500 (1969), the Iso Lele (1969), the Uracco (1971), the BMW 520 (1972), the Fiat X1/9 (1973), the Lancia Stratos (1974), the Volkswagen Polo (1975) and the Alfa Romeo Alfetta 2000 (1977). He was also responsible for two seminal concept cars that would guide supercar styling for decades to come: the Alfa Romeo Carabo of 1968 and the Lancia Stratos HF Zero of 1970.

Gandini was always explicit that his involvement in styling the Lamborghini Diablo was uncomfortable to the point of being tortuous, but he was content with the end result, despite relatively unknown Detroit stylists attempting to steal the limelight from all his hard work and true genius. His early drawings for the Diablo that had been rejected by Chrysler did not go to waste, as many of these ideas and concepts were recycled into the 1991 Cizeta Moroder V16-T supercar. In the late 1980s Marcello Gandini rejoined his old friend and former Countach colleague Paolo Stanzani in designing and developing the Bugatti EB110, which boasted a carbon fibre chassis made by Aérospatiale. This quad-turbo supercar, the immediate predecessor to the Bugatti Veyron, made its debut in 1991.

Marcello Gandini is famously reclusive and has a reputation for not standing fools willingly. He continues to work alone in a design studio cloistered within his grand seventeenth-century villa, situated outside the village of Almese, in the quiet solitude of the Susa Valley.

Emile Novaro, President of Automobili Lamborghini during the Diablo's early years.

It was also around this time that Emile Novaro started searching around for a name for Sant'Agata's new flagship car. The name had to have some link with Ferruccio Lamborghini's Taurus birth sign or with bullfighting, and the name Lamborghini Diablo was finally chosen. This topic is covered in detail in Chapter Four.

CHRYSLER TAKES CONTROL

A momentous turning point that would change the Diablo's further development, and indeed Lamborghini's future direction, took place on 23 April 1987 when, after months of secret negotiations, Lee A. Iacocca, the President of the Chrysler Corporation, purchased Lamborghini for a rumoured price, never officially disclosed, of about US$25 million. Patrick Mimran had bought the moribund company in 1981 and had successfully resurrected it and turned it around within six short years. Mimran, however, was aware that putting the Diablo into production would require the expertise and massive investment that could be best provided by an experienced and established car manufacturer with plenty of fiscal firepower readily available. He deserves recognition not only for rescuing and turning around Lamborghini, but also for passing the company on to a responsible and well-financed successor at just the right time.

By the time Chrysler acquired Lamborghini, a Diablo prototype with a fully functioning drivetrain had already undergone extensive wind tunnel testing. In addition, both

Lee Iacocca, Chairman of Chrysler. He had a major influence on the P132 prototype's later development and on the external appearance of the production Diablo.

Marmiroli and Mimran had actually driven the prototype within the factory grounds before the official signing ceremony on 23 April 1987. Chrysler was buying a company in rude health and its next product had even been gift-wrapped ready for its new owner to put straight into series production. To have thought along these lines, however, would have been to forget the ability of Lamborghini's new American paymaster to ignore polite convention, and to meddle carelessly with a highly specialised, bespoke and very expensive product, exactly the sort of merchandise with which Chrysler had little or no prior experience.

Chrysler had promised Lamborghini that it would allow the Italian company its independence, and would provide Lamborghini with financial, technological and logistical support to enable Lamborghini to continue designing and manufacturing class-beating supercars in the Italian mould. Marcello Gandini was indeed *the* supercar designer of the moment, Italian or otherwise, and there was no other contemporary car designer whose name was so intimately intertwined with sensuous, revolutionary, covetable supercars. Yet, in one of its first acts as Lamborghini's new owner, Chrysler spurned Gandini's Progetto 132 offering, the functioning prototype that had already undergone wind tunnel testing in France.

Starting in late April 1987, and continuing throughout May, the prototype Diablo was tested on public roads immediately around the factory. As confidence in the mechanical capabilities of this prototype rose with each outing, factory test drivers drove the car further and further away from Sant'Agata, investigating the car's performance, handling and roadholding on lightly trafficked, high-speed dual and triple carriage motorways. The Imola-Ravenna toll road was fairly close to the factory and was a favourite testing ground for the Diablo prototype. The car was always heavily disguised to make it look like a revised Countach so that rival manufacturers and prying motoring journalists were kept in the dark. For the same reason, much of this initial testing on public roads was conducted at dead of night. But by mid-May the still camouflaged prototype was being tested during daylight hours, and speeds in excess of 210km/h (130mph) were being reached.

Valentino Balboni, Lamborghini's legendary test driver, has previously said that he spent more than two years testing and developing the Diablo, and that the Countach was always his and Lamborghini's reference point. The aim was for the Diablo to be at least 40 per cent more drivable than its predecessor, and Valentino felt that this goal was achieved fairly early in the test programme.

The morning of 1 June 1987 was critically important for the Diablo project, but it turned out to be a false dawn. That Monday Lee Iacocca made his first visit to Sant'Agata as its new owner to check on the Lamborghini factory. As well as inspecting the site and reviewing Emile Novaro's plans for the company, Iacocca was also here to scrutinise the Diablo, and probe just how well it stood up against both its predecessor and its main rival from Maranello. Iacocca asked that the Progetto 132 prototype be available for inspection together with a Countach 5000 Quattrovalvole and a Ferrari Testarossa. All were to be placed side-by-side so that each could be easily compared and contrasted against the other. Having scrutinised all three carefully, the commandant-controller's verdict on the Diablo prototype was that it was 'Terrific'.

If Novaro, Gandini, Marmiroli and Sgarzi were pleased with Iacocca's lavish compliment, their relief was to be short-lived. By mid-June Chrysler's middle management started sending messages to Sant'Agata that they felt that Lamborghini's forthcoming flagship was somewhat less than terrific and that it needed minor modifications. With each passing week, Chrysler's stylists, led by Tom Gale, suggested further alterations and more extensive modifications to this already running and already wind tunnel-tested prototype. Gandini and Marmiroli began to suspect that Chrysler wanted a substantial reworking of the Diablo prototype simply so that their Detroit-based Chrysler Design Centre styling team could take credit for the final production car, and so claim the prestige and kudos that would inevitably come with what was surely going to become one of the pre-eminent supercars of its time. This degree of interference with Progetto 132's design by Chrysler's middle management stylists could only have been executed after being sanctioned from the very highest level of Chrysler's management team. Iacocca's 'Terrific' was beginning to sound very hollow, even duplicitous.

Gandini and Marmiroli were hugely upset by Chrysler's constant interference and deliberate obstruction as they both felt that Progetto 132's design was perfect, and that the car was ready to go into series production as the Lamborghini Diablo. They relied on Emile Novaro as president of Lamborghini to fight their corner, and Novaro did this valiantly until he was involved in a near fatal car accident while driving to Monte Carlo in the summer of 1987.

Novaro suffered multiple fractures as well as internal organ damage, and his enforced hospital stay gave free rein to Lamborghini's American paymasters, who used this calamity to further impose their will on the forthcoming Diablo.

Tom Gale and his fellow young designers at Chrysler's Design Centre had taken exception to Gandini's avant-garde styling of Progetto 132, and they instead put forward a radically different proposal, which was essentially a modernised and reworked Countach.

Gandini in particular was hugely offended. He has always maintained that any design masterpiece must look forward and not be a copy – poor or otherwise – of a past icon, so it is not surprising that in 2021 he reiterated this strongly held conviction in a shower of scathing comments about the unfortunate hybrid-electric Countach LPI 800-4 announced in that year. In his opinion this retro-supercar was a caricature copy of the original 1971 Lamborghini Countach and he decried that Sant'Agata had the temerity to call this a 'new for 2021 Countach'. Gandini wasted no time in expressing his true opinions in a formal press statement distancing himself from the Countach LPI 800-4, and stating that this new car did not reflect his 'spirit and vision', which was aimed at 'breaking the mould' and creating genuinely new and fresh styles and designs. His Twitter release read:

> *I have built my identity as a designer, especially when working on supercars for Lamborghini, on a unique concept: each new model I would work on would be an innovation, a breaker, something so completely different from the previous one. Courage, the ability to create a break without sticking to the success of the previous car, the confidence to not wanting to give in to habit were the very essence of my work. To repeat a model of the past represents in my opinion the negation of the founding principles of my DNA.*

Those were Gandini's words in 2021. You can just imagine the anger of a younger, much more driven and impassioned Gandini in 1987 when some chancers at Chrysler tried to hitch a ride to success on his genius and have the temerity to plunge the knife in deeply, and twist it around more violently, by criticising and then openly condemning his Progetto 132 design.

Still, Gandini was now a freelance designer, paid work is paid work, and the chance to design a flagship Lamborghini comes but once a decade. So Gandini rejected the proposals from the young guns at Detroit, but agreed to go back to the drawing board. By this time the Diablo prototype had undergone high-speed testing at Nardo, where Valentino Balboni had recorded a top speed of 310km/h (192.6mph), and he had felt so confident in the car's inherent stability that he was able to release the steering wheel at 240km/h, only to find that the car continued to track straight and true. The only significant problem that the Nardo crew identified during this test session was that the engine oil temperature rose above 150°C after sustained high-speed runs, accompanied by a concurrent drop in engine oil pressure.

To appease Chrysler, Gandini now started work on redesigning the Diablo's bodywork. In October 1987 he put forward a second design proposal. He presented this as an asymmetrical two-sided mock-up, with the left-hand side of the mock-up being essentially the same as his original Progetto 132 design, while the right-hand side displayed his newly modified Diablo styling.

For this new offering, Gandini had smoothed off Progetto 132's sharp edges, and in doing so had made it less aggressive, less Lamborghini. Some of Progetto 132's origami bends were now tempered, while others were abandoned altogether, so the car's new styling was more 'soap bar' than the original proposal, but it was not all bad news. The car now looked very modern and, crucially, its aerodynamics were not compromised through this restyling exercise. The new design had a much larger glass area, a more rounded nose, a less pronounced rear spoiler, and redesigned headlights. Just as with the 1971 LP500 Countach prototype, engine compartment heat dissipation had been identified as an important problem during high-speed testing, and this demanded urgent attention. Marmiroli and Gandini immediately collaborated closely on this pressing issue, and a redesigned engine lid cover sorted out this problem. The new engine lid was flat and featured multiple louvred hot-air exit vents.

Lee Iacocca and his Chrysler management team, however, were still not happy with Gandini's second and latest proposal. In particular they condemned the rear of this second car, with Iacocca levelling the specific criticism that the bodywork in this area was 'too busy'. He elaborated on this by claiming that the styling of the tail end was too convoluted and complex, and expressed strong reservations about such tangled and tortuous design features, stating that they were out of keeping with modern, cohesive supercar styling.

Marcello Gandini's signature slashed and uprising rear wheel arch featured once again on the P132.

Pop-up headlights were de rigueur for 1980s and early 1990s supercars, and they featured on the P132 concept car.

The American mass production car executive was now dictating styling terms to the universally acknowledged maestro of Italian supercar design. The madness did not end here, as in the final months of 1987 Tom Gale and his Chrysler Design Centre styling team made a final push to take control of the production Diablo's body styling. These youthful and inexperienced stylists, with the tacit approval of Chrysler's most senior management, now started sending whole clay models of their proposals to Sant'Agata – none of which impressed Novaro, Marmiroli, Gandini or Sgarzi. The Americans and Italians had reached a Mexican standoff.

DIABLO COMPROMISE

Happily Marmiroli had by now largely recovered from his injuries and he entered the fray with characteristic vigour. Bashing heads together, he restarted the styling debate, seeking compromise between the two parties so as to arrive at a design that could be put into series production. The delays, adjournments and procrastination had gone on for far too long, and speed was now of the essence. The Countach was already well past its sell-by date, and was clearly not up to meeting the challenge of its imminent rivals. Furthermore, Countach homologation permits were due to expire by the end of the decade in several countries. Sant'Agata desperately needed its new model on the market very quickly if it were not to completely disappear off the map as a serious car manufacturer in these countries.

In June 1988 Gandini put forward his third Diablo styling proposal. While the front end of the car was largely carried over unchanged from his second proposal, the rear end was now simpler, smoother and less cluttered so as to meet Lee Iacocca's demands. The Diablo was getting progressively less striking and less startling with each revision of Gandini's original proposal and this troubled the Maestro greatly. But Marcello had no choice but to bend his knee before the power of the mighty American dollar. Gandini was very proud of his initial styling suggestions for Progetto 132, which Chrysler had rejected off-hand, so when Claudio Zampolli, Giorgio Moroder and Paolo Stanzani approached him to design the bodywork for their new 16-cylinder supercar, he simply dusted off and mildly reworked his early Progetto 132 drawings before handing them over to Modena-based Automobili Cizeta-Moroder. The Cizeta-Moroder V16T made its debut at a private gathering in Los Angeles hosted by Jay Leno in December 1988 before being presented to the public at the 1989 Geneva and Los Angeles Motor Shows. So the V16T was launched a year before the Diablo made its debut. Blame that delay wholly on Lee Iacocca, his senior management team and the Chrysler designers. Look today at the Cizeta-Moroder V16T and you will see what the Lamborghini Diablo might have looked like if Detroit had never interfered with Gandini's and Sant'Agata's original design proposal.

Novaro, Marmiroli and Sgarzi were perfectly happy with Gandini's third proposal and approved it. But the designers at the Detroit Styling Centre led by Tom Gale were still not content and kept asking for further alterations to this latest design. Considering that Chrysler had about 350 people working in their Detroit design studio, while Gandini was working all alone, it was an unequal battle, but he was not easily quelled and defended his third proposal vigorously. The continued interference of Gale and his team was by now delaying the Diablo's proposed production schedule, and thereby putting at risk Lamborghini's and Chrysler's profit margins and financial security. Marmiroli arranged a meeting with Iacocca during which the Lamborghini chairman very bluntly told his overlord that the Chrysler designers had to be reined in or he would resign. Iacocca agreed to do this, with the caveat that the Diablo's finer styling points be tackled jointly at a later date. This compromise allowed Marmiroli and his team to definitively fix the engineering hard points of the Diablo, thus enabling the technical and mechanical work on the car to move forward unimpeded.

The Diablo's cockpit and interior was designed almost exclusively by Chrysler designers led by William A. Dayton. Marcello Gandini was never particularly keen on interior car design and his focus was always biased towards a car's bodyshell design and its outside aesthetics. Speaking to Michael Harvey for *Autocar* in June 1988, Gandini mounted a fierce defence of his design ideas for Progetto 132 and the second and third proposals that followed, but did not comment on the interior design of the forthcoming Diablo:

> *The Countach is not an easy car to replace. It has now the same fresh feel as the day I first constructed those planes on the drawing board. I wanted the Diablo to have the same feel as the Countach, only more so. The Diablo is much simpler than the Countach. The Countach arrests you because of the intensity of the detailing. The Diablo will make you stop because*

The downward-swooping sideglass windows on the P132 concept made it onto the production cars and became among the Diablo's aesthetic highlights. WIKIMEDIA/ARNAUD 25

> *of its silhouette. Its proportions are deliberately out of shape. The rear of the car is much longer than the front. It looks longer than the Countach.*

Dayton and his team of young stylists at Detroit had almost full licence to design the Diablo's interior as they saw fit, free from interference from Gandini and Lamborghini. Their only restrictions were from the already established engineering hardpoints that flowed naturally from Gandini's proposed bodyshell and from existing and forthcoming homologation rules and safety legislation. The results of Detroit's endeavours are detailed in the next chapter.

If Progetto 132's engineering was previously labelled as evolutionary and non-controversial, this must not belie the fact that much engineering blood, sweat and tears, and Chrysler dollars, were spent on making the new Diablo chassis and drivetrain production ready. Sant'Agata under the stewardship of the Mimran brothers had already determined that the Diablo would continue with the Countach's spaceframe chassis, its south-north engine-gearbox configuration and a development of its venerable Bizzarrini naturally aspirated V12 engine. Marmiroli and Chrysler took these basic ingredients and ran with them, but always kept in mind their own desired objectives: the fastest series production car in the world with a top speed in excess of 315km/h (195.7mph) and with commensurately spectacular handling and roadholding.

Progetto 132's spaceframe chassis was developed and refined using computer-assisted analysis by Antonella Bertuzzi. The resulting spaceframe used fewer box sections

A treasured model from the authors' collection.

than the Countach's spaceframe, but more tubular sections. In a significant deviation from the Countach, the production Diablo used square-section tubes instead of the round-section tubes of its predecessor. Square-section tubes require less expertise to weld into a spaceframe lattice, which meant that Sant'Agata and Vaccari & Bosi could employ slightly less talented welders. This was an important consideration. Lamborghini needed to produce many more Diablos than it had Countachs, and Marchesi's ability to deliver Countach spaceframes had already been a significant choke point that had limited Countach production. Eliminating this bottleneck was therefore crucial for Sant'Agata's balance sheet. Welding square-section tubes was also faster than welding circular tubes, meaning lower production costs. A further benefit was cheaper and easier subsequent repair work should the chassis be damaged in an accident. Crucially the Diablo's spaceframe retained all the rigidity and more of the Countach's spaceframe, while weighing only 80kg (176lb). This made it 30kg lighter than the Countach's less rigid spaceframe. Again this was vitally important, as every gram of mass saved translated directly into better acceleration: class-leading 0–60mph and 0–100mph times were crucial parameters for gaining future sales in favour of the Diablo instead of one of its rival supercar competitors.

UPGRADING THE BIZZARRINI V12

The classic 60-degree naturally aspirated Bizzarrini V12 engine needed to be substantially upgraded to produce the necessary power and torque needed for the Diablo to seize the crown of the fastest production car. This extensively reworked 5.2-litre, four valve per cylinder powerplant engine, known by its internal Sant'Agata designation as 'Type 521', was ready to be installed into the first prototype Progetto 132 by March 1987.

This engine actually had a twin, the other one being put to work on a static test bench where its power and torque curves were measured and plotted, and its all-important output emissions determined. This test engine was repeatedly modified to produce the optimum performance and emissions parameters. Strict homologation rules, especially in the critical United States market, simply had to be met, and many alternative set-ups were examined to get the Type 521 engine to satisfy these unalterable and immutable legislative demands. In this regard, Marmiroli and his team were greatly helped by the Type 521 engine employing the latest generation Weber-Marelli fuel injection system. Detailed and precise fuelling, air, spark and emission calibration work was carried out by Massimo Ceccarani under Marmiroli's supervision. It is of note that Ceccarani, who had qualified from Bologna University with a degree in mechanical engineering, and who had worked at Ducati before joining Lamborghini in 1983, eventually succeeded Marmiroli as Technical Director at Automobili Lamborghini when the latter retired in August 1997. The bench-test Type 521 engine survived more than 200 hard test hours, during which it proved reliable and flexible while producing more than 470bhp and meeting the necessary homologation requirements. Concurrent real-life road testing using the other Type 521 engine installed in the Progetto 132 prototype car was equally promising.

As a result it was a surprise to find that Luigi Marmiroli was not satisfied with the Type 521 engine's performance. There were several reasons for this. First, rival supercar manufacturers were developing new models and the 521 engine's power and torque outputs, while adequate for the immediate present, would soon be eclipsed by the powertrains of these coming adversaries. Second, although the Type 521 engine had propelled Progetto 132's unfinished bodyshell to more than 300km/h in preliminary tests, when Marmiroli extrapolated forward he felt that this engine lacked adequate power and torque, and would struggle to propel the Diablo much faster than this. This would mean that one of the Diablo's key design briefs – the need to breach the 315km/h barrier and thus claim the title of the world's fastest production car – would not be realised. Finally all the tests to date had been carried out using a bodyshell based on Gandini's first proposal for Progetto 132. Marmiroli knew that this original bodyshell was more aerodynamic than the second and third bodyshell that Gandini had been forced to offer up at Chrysler's insistence, so again casting doubt on whether the final series production Diablo could meet its principal performance mandate.

Progetto 132's Type 521 engine was therefore removed from the prototype car and subjected to intense scrutiny to determine why it was not performing as well as expected. One crucial finding was that the engine was overheating, which in turn led to a drop in its power and torque outputs. Engine bay cooling, which had plagued the prototype LP500 Countach in 1971, was again proving to be a major problem with its successor in 1987. Marmiroli and Gandini tried to overcome this overheating problem by redesigning the Progetto 132's engine bay cover. The original version featured a large, very smooth, transparent bonnet, which in the search for aerodynamic efficiency eschewed all ducts, vents and scoops. A new engine bonnet incorporating numerous hot-air exit vents significantly reduced the engine bay temperature, but not by enough to alleviate Marmiroli's reservations about the Type 521's performance potential.

Marmiroli was by now convinced that only a significantly redesigned engine could produce the power and torque needed to meet the Diablo's performance brief. Happily he also knew that Lamborghini's existing Bizzarrini engine could be further developed to deliver the necessary power and torque. After convincing President Emile Novaro that the Diablo deserved, indeed needed, better, Marmiroli rejected the Type 521 engine and commissioned a new engine. Marmiroli was confident because earlier tests had already shown that with modifications the classic V12 powerplant could reliably produce 650bhp at 8,000rpm. Marmiroli was especially taken with the modified engine's roar at its redline, describing it as 'fantastic'. The ensuing Type 522 engine would go on to power the Lamborghini's new flagship car, and is covered in detail in the next chapter.

While development work on the Type 522 engine was being carried out, a second prototype Progetto 132 car was built. This was Chassis 12001 and its coachwork was based on Gandini's third proposal for Progetto 132's bodyshell, which he had put forward in June 1988. This second prototype was painted a dark grey. As it featured the production Diablo's eventual bodyshell, and as the first Type 522 engine would eventually be installed in it, Chassis 12001 can be considered the first Lamborghini Diablo car.

A total of five Progetto 132 prototype cars were built. Notable among these was Chassis 12004. This light blue car carried stickers on its guillotine doors reading 'F144' and 'MIRA', and its five-spoke gold wheels carried tyres whose side walls had been painted red. Thus adorned, and once laden with electronic sensors, Chassis 12004 was barrier

Note the P132's deep chin spoiler and front wing NACA ducts. The P132 was designed to be much more aerodynamic than the Countach.

crash-tested at the Motor Industry Research Association's test facility in the United Kingdom. The car's passenger cell survived this gruesome but essential test pretty much unscathed, and the Lamborghini Diablo model thereby gained its European Type Approval certification and E-mark.

Although the Lamborghini Diablo was always meant to be an evolution of the Countach rather than a radical new design, one can appreciate that it suffered a troubled gestation through both bodyshell and drivetrain problems, and never-ending disputes between Sant'Agata and Detroit. These difficulties inevitably led to delays, and as a direct consequence the Diablo's debut and production schedule suffered. Progetto 132 reputedly cost Chrysler a not inconsequential 6 billion lire. But in January 1990 Sant'Agata launched its long-awaited new flagship. Progetto 132 had finally delivered the production Lamborghini Diablo.

Valentino Balboni, Lamborghini's legendary test driver, was responsible for developing and honing the P132.

CHAPTER 4

THE ORIGINAL DIABLO: PURITY EXEMPLIFIED

It is fitting that the Lamborghini Diablo was unveiled – on 21 January 1990 at the Sporting Club de Monte Carlo – to the sounds of Puccini's 'Nessun dorma'. The Diablo's launch had been plagued by endless delays, mainly brought about by never ending disputes between Sant'Agata and Detroit about the car's external styling. As a result, Lamborghini's designers and engineers had repeatedly been forced to burn the midnight oil, spending countless days and even years reworking Gandini's and Marmiroli's original plans for the new flagship. In the same vein, at the start of Act 3 of *Turandot*, Calaf sings 'Nessun dorma' ('None shall sleep') as dawn approaches after the cruel Princess Turandot decrees that none of her subjects shall sleep until the riddle of the mysterious stranger's name has been revealed, and if they fail to uncover his identity they will all be killed. In this analogy, Chrysler is Princess Turandot, Calaf is the Diablo, and Marmiroli and Gandini are Turandot's subjects. If the reader is in any doubt as to the validity of this analogy, then a cursory examination of Gandini's revelations about his trials and tribulations when dealing with Detroit over the Diablo's design will surely settle the matter. Although the Diablo carries a plaque bearing Marcello Gandini's signature low down on its flanks, Chrysler had always been prepared to abandon Gandini's blueprints if his proposals did not conform with their perception of an avant-garde supercar.

THE DIABLO LAUNCH

In the autumn of 1989 Emile Novaro, the President of Automobili Lamborghini SpA, sent out invitations to selected motoring journalists and Lamborghini owners. The invitation is worth examining in some detail as hidden within it was a précis of the Diablo's whole development history and the tense chemistry between Sant'Agata and Chrysler.

The invitations arrived in the form of a twelve-page booklet sandwiched between stiff black covers splattered with gold writing and 'Raging Bull' logos. The front cover was emblazoned with the title 'Lamborghini Day 2 1990'. Inside, printed in four languages – Italian, English, French and German – was an invitation to attend the unveiling of Lamborghini's new flagship, and a request to existing owners to bring and parade their cars, the Diablo's forebears, in Monte Carlo.

An exclusive invitation to a rare event, the unveiling of a Lamborghini flagship.

The date set for this momentous event was the weekend of 20–21 January 1990. The fact that this was 1990 and not 1988 speaks volumes of the heartache, pain and misery that Marmiroli, Gandini and Novaro had been through to get the Diablo ready for series production. When Chrysler first bought Lamborghini from the Mimran brothers in April 1987, the Diablo prototype, Progetto 132, was already fairly advanced. The Mimran brothers had authorised initial funding for its basic design as far back as June 1985, and for its further development in anticipation of manufacture in early 1986. Chrysler had examined the blueprints for the Diablo prior to their purchase of Lamborghini, and their original plan had been to launch the Diablo on the twenty-fifth anniversary of Ferruccio Lamborghini's supercar company. To meet this deadline the Diablo should have been launched in May 1988, but it soon became clear that a worthy successor to the Countach could not be designed, developed and introduced within the timeframe afforded by this anniversary date. Lee Iacocca decided that a lavish party should be thrown to mark the occasion and highlight Chrysler's recent takeover of Lamborghini. This celebratory silver jubilee was called 'Lamborghini Day' and a cosmetically enhanced – some would say mutilated – end-of-line Countach was launched at that gathering instead. Held at the Autodromo Nazionale Monza on 10–11 September 1988, the weekend of the 1988 Formula One Grand Prix, the highlight of this party was the unveiling of the latest and final Countach model variant. With new and questionable body styling by Horacio Pagani, the 25th Anniversary Countach stood in for the still unfinished Diablo.

It was within this context that Emile Novaro sent out his gold on black invitations titled 'Lamborghini Day 2'. The weekend's festivities were organised by Sandro Munari, winner of multiple Monte Carlo rallies and world Rally Championships, and now a test driver-cum-public relations executive for Lamborghini. Novaro's booklet set out the programme for the weekend in some detail. Lamborghini also itemised the precise cost of attending – Fr3,700 for a single room for the weekend, and Fr6,000 for a double – and was not apologetic in stating exactly where and how to wire this remittance. Automobili Lamborghini SpA was after all first and foremost a business, and certainly not a high-end charity.

The highlight of the weekend was a Gala Soirée held on the evening of Saturday 20 January 1990 at the Sporting Club de Monte Carlo. The climax would be the unveiling of the

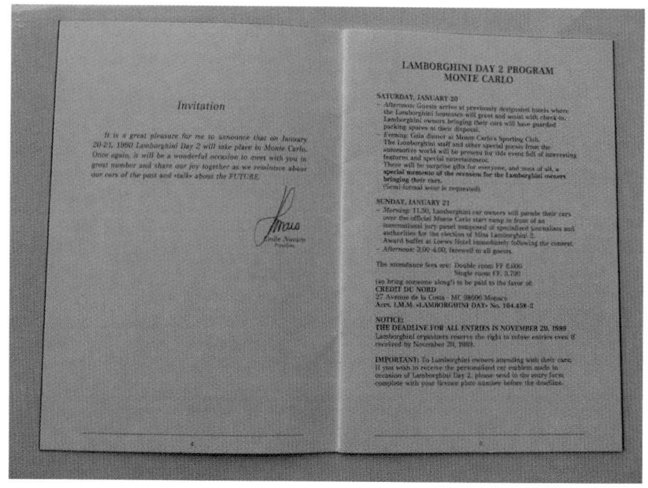

The weekend's festivities were tempting, but note the attendance fees.

Lamborghini Diablo. But for their fee the guests would also get another very special treat, an appearance by the tenor José Carreras, who had just undergone chemotherapy but apparently delivered a superb performance.

The Lamborghini Diablo was unveiled to the strains of 'Nessun dorma' sung by José Carreras. It was an inspired choice, made relevant because it mirrored the Diablo's tortuous gestation. 'Nessun dorma' requires a two-octave range and is particularly challenging because the soloist has to sustain its high tessitura and rise to a crowd-pleasing fortissimo high B natural. Few could meet these conflicting demands as well as the acclaimed Spanish operatic tenor. The Diablo's troubled start had brought its designers and engineers countless sleepless nights, but the comparisons did not end there. The Diablo was a technically advanced supercar based on cutting-edge aerodynamics and mechanical engineering. It, too, successfully straddled an extremely broad design brief, marrying world-class performance with the superlative comfort and luxury that pampered 1990s customers now demanded. It is appropriate that the aria closes with the words 'All'alba vincerò!' ('At dawn I will win!') After much *sangue, sudore, lacrime e denaro* (blood, sweat, tears and money) Marmiroli and Gandini had won the challenge of producing the world's fastest series production car, and recaptured the top speed crown for Lamborghini.

Sunday 21 January 1990 was a glorious day in Monte Carlo with bright sunshine and no rain. Novaro had asked all the guests to bring their Lamborghini cars to the festivities, if possible, and many had obliged. Sandro Munari had made sure that all the hotels into which Lamborghini guests were booked had specially designated parking spaces available for their supercars, and that plenty of dedicated guards would be in attendance throughout to watch over these mobile treasures. Thus reassured, about eighty guests had brought their Lamborghinis to Monte Carlo. One of the highlights of 'Lamborghini Day 2' was the Sunday morning parade of Sant'Agata's finest around Monaco starting from Casino Square. Among the many Countachs, Miuras, Jalpas and Silhouettes were one-off concept cars like the Carrozzeria Touring Lamborghini 4000GT Flying Star, and the unique Bertone-designed Lamborghini Miura P400 Roadster.

Most eyes, however, would have been on the four Lamborghini Diablos parked on Casino Square directly in front of the Hôtel de Paris Monte-Carlo. The glorious, classically styled dining room of the hotel's Le Louis XV restaurant opens directly onto an elevated balcony, and the view of the Diablos from this vantage point must have been matchless. Unfortunately the refreshment covered by the entertainment package only ran to an Automobili Lamborghini SpA buffet lunch at what was then the Loews Hôtel nearby. Two beautiful red Diablos were neatly parked next to each other, front to back, so that spectators could fully appreciate all aspects and facets of Sant'Agata's new flagship. The former Formula One driver Mario Andretti, who owned a Countach and had just ordered a Diablo, was given the privilege of entertaining the onlookers by firing up and revving one of these static display Diablos.

The Diablo was the last Lamborghini supercar that was conceived and launched while Ferruccio Lamborghini was still alive. Like its immediate predecessors, the Countach and the Miura, it made its debut with the indisputable advantage of being the fastest production car of its time. Sant'Agata and Chrysler had anticipated that the Diablo

Classic Lamborghini: a wedge-shaped missile with guillotine doors.

NAMING THE DIABLO

The Diablo followed the proud Lamborghini tradition of being named after a fearsome fighting bull. Ferruccio Lamborghini, who was born on 28 April 1916, was a firm believer in astrology and regarded his birth sign, Taurus, with almost religious reverence. This prompted the logo, a golden raging bull set against a black background, that adorns the front bonnet of all modern Lamborghini vehicles.

Much of the ancient Greeks' astronomical knowledge was inherited from the early civilizations of Mesopotamia, who had a particular interest in observing the constellation of Taurus, because at the height of their civilization, the sun rose through the Taurus constellation on the vernal equinox. The Mesopotamians therefore considered Taurus, which they called the 'Bull of Heaven', the first sign of their zodiac, and Lamborghini was delighted that he had been born under such an auspicious birth sign.

While his earliest cars were given simple alphanumeric names, this changed with the Miura. In 1962, the year before Ferruccio Lamborghini established his company, he visited Finca Zahariche, the fighting bull ranch founded by Don Eduardo Miura Fernández in 1842. Situated nearly 100 kilometres (60 miles) east of Seville in Andalusia, this hacienda was acclaimed for its massive, difficult, fierce and, most notably, cunning Miura bulls. There's a good reason why matadors say 'Never turn your back on a Miura'. Ernest Hemingway singled out the Miura bull in his 1932 book *Death in the Afternoon*:

Diablo manuals and books. Note the keyring with a gold bull on a blue background, which Automobili Lamborghini were dishing out even in the Countach era.

> *There are certain strains of bull which have a marked ability to learn from what goes on in the arena ... faster than the actual fight progresses, which makes it difficult from one minute to the next to control them ... these bulls are raised by Don Eduardo Miura's sons from old fighting stock.*

Ferruccio thereafter took to calling his supercars after famous fighting bulls and bull-fighting equipment. The Countach was an exception to this rule, but it may be that its extraordinary and stunningly dramatic aesthetics gave it a particular and wholly justified exemption. (The Piedmontese word Countach very fittingly translates into English as 'Wow'.) In contrast, the Islero, Espada, Jarama, Urraco, Jalpa, Murciélago, Gallardo, Reventon, Aventador, Huracan, Veneno and, of course, the Diablo did not get any such special dispensation, all having some association with the bullring.

The Lamborghini Diablo was named after a vicious bull that had a notable fight against the matador José Lara Jiménez, known as 'El Chicorro'. This particular bull was raised by Cristobal Colón y de la Cerda, 14th Duke of Veragua (the 1st Duke of Veragua was the grandson and heir of Christopher Columbus). Lara Jiménez was born in Algeciras on 19 March 1839, but was brought up in Jerez in a house almost adjacent to an abattoir. He was therefore intimate from a very early age with butchers, cattle dealers, livestock and bullfighters. He gravitated almost naturally into becoming a matador and toured South America making appearances in Peru and Cuba before returning to Spain, where he became known for his prowess with banderillas and poles. On 11 July 1869 Diablo and El Chicorro came head to head in a Madrid bullring. It was an extraordinarily long contest in which both antagonists exhibited exceptional bravery and consummate skill, with El Chicorro attacking and avoiding injury, while Diablo continued attacking and advancing despite being wounded. Honour fell to both sides on this occasion.

The word 'Diablo' ('Devil') suited Sant'Agata perfectly as it summoned up just the right note of power, unrestrained lust and controlled malice that Sant'Agata wanted to project for its flagship car and its corporate image. For most of the world an association with Beelzebub was of no material concern, but the strongly religious Mexican market could not overlook such a close partnership with Mephistopheles, and so for Mexico alone the Lamborghini Diablo was renamed as the Lamborghini Costanga, purely to soothe any cultural sensitivities.

would be in great demand, but had deliberately put on this lavish 'Lamborghini Day 2' to garner as much publicity and as many sales as possible. Emile Novaro was delighted with the marketing success that accompanied his Monte Carlo party, since by Sunday evening enough new commissions had been harvested to fill the order book for the year. In order to weed out speculators from genuine Lamborghini enthusiasts, Sant'Agata gave preferential early delivery slots to existing Lamborghini owners, and also demanded a 50 million lire deposit when placing an order. To further deter speculators, the delivery contract carried a clause stipulating that the car had to be registered in the name of the person who had placed the original order, otherwise the car would not be delivered and the deposit would be forfeited. Lee Iacocca, Emile Novaro, Luigi Marmiroli, Marcello Gandini and maybe most of all Ubaldo Sgarzi, who as Marketing Manager would have sell the car, were delighted with how the Lamborghini Diablo was received at its debut.

EXTERIOR DESIGN

No small part of the huge commercial success of the Diablo's launch was due to its spectacular styling. The Diablo's external styling was evolutionary, rather than the revolutionary and startling design exercise that had made the Countach an instant global hit. The Diablo continued with the extreme wedge-shape profile pioneered by the Countach, but the Countach's origami straight lines and acute angles were now substituted for a much more modern look with smoothed edges and aerodynamically efficient curves, which made it appear more twenty-first century than its predecessor. It had a more 'cab-forward' look, with a relatively short nose in front of the cabin compared to the long rear. The single most striking thing about the Diablo was its signature drooping side windows, which appeared to begin right in the very middle of the car, before flowing dramatically forwards and downwards almost to its nose. This was actually a visual illusion: Gandini had expertly positioned the fixed side glass

Note the deep chin spoiler and the front wing NACA ducts, which were first seen on the P132 concept car.

The massive rear wing adds to the Diablo's inherent drama.

so that it appeared to merge seamlessly into the movable side window as one single piece.

Underneath the Diablo's haute couture exterior was a classic Italian spaceframe chassis, built by Vaccari & Bosi. This spaceframe was constructed of square-section steel tubes welded together. Square-section tubing is easier and quicker to weld, so a square-section spaceframe is cheaper to produce than a round-section spaceframe. Theoretically round-section tubes give better torsional rigidity weight-for-weight, but Marmiroli claimed that by carefully calculating the tension and compression forces that would act on the Diablo's spaceframe, his team had been able to design a chassis that more than compensated for this hypothetical imperfection. Indeed, later structural analysis demonstrated that the Diablo's square-tube spaceframe was 30 per cent stiffer than the Countach's round-section spaceframe. Sant'Agata's artisans had previously found the process of attaching the Countach's aluminium body panels to its round-section steel spaceframe tubes to be a particularly difficult, time-consuming and hence expensive exercise, which was another reason why Lamborghini chose to move to square-section tubes for its new flagship car. In yet another move to contain costs and maximise production output, Marmiroli eschewed copying the manufacturing process used to make the Countach's outrageously expensive and infinitely time-consuming hand-beaten aluminium body panels, and instead organised for the Diablo's alloy body panels to be machine stamped.

While the Countach's outer skin was made up almost exclusively of aluminium, the Diablo's skin employed a variety of materials. The guillotine doors and front and rear wings were made of an extra-strong but very lightweight aluminium alloy, while steel was only used for the roof and the door shuts. The front and rear bumpers, side panels, sills, the entire lower part of the body, the front boot bonnet and the engine bay bonnet were all constructed from a composite material called Autoclave. Autoclave contains both Kevlar and fibreglass, and for a given degree of torsional rigidity Autoclave is 40 per cent lighter than aluminium, and 80 per cent lighter than steel. It is also easy to paint and highly resistant to chipping.

Marmiroli was particularly proud of finding the optimal mixture of high-strength alloy, high-strength steel and standard-strength steel for the Diablo's passenger safety cell and its front and rear crumple zones. All mid-engined cars pose distinct and peculiar challenges when designing their passenger survival cell. In mid-engined cars the whole drivetrain mass moves forward towards the cabin in a frontal impact, and the car's survival cell has to be able to absorb and dissipate this considerable energy without the huge mass of the engine smashing into the cockpit and injuring the driver and passenger. High-strength steel, although stronger, weighs considerably more than standard-strength steel, so there is no advantage in using it unless it is strictly necessary, particularly in a supercar where weight is a key consideration.

Move over if you see this in your rear-view mirror.

By carefully evaluating the likely impact forces, Marmiroli and his team were able to design the passenger safety cell and the crumple zones using the lightest possible materials, while still ensuring occupant well-being, and meeting all current and anticipated North American and European safety legislation.

Cognisant of the critical importance of superlative aerodynamics, Gandini had taken immense care to bury any necessary ducts and vents deep into the Diablo's bodywork. The Countach had featured two massive flank-mounted elephant-ear RAM ducts and two door-mounted NACA ducts. The Diablo eschewed both these in favour of three gently inward-curving vents, two high up behind the cockpit and one very low down just ahead of the rear wheels. The Diablo's side view was otherwise dominated by somewhat over-embellished 17-inch silver light alloy wheels, large

All the elements of Marcello Gandini's design come together perfectly in the original two-wheel-drive Diablo.

external wing mirrors and an integrated rear diffuser-cum-rear bumper. This bumper protruded proudly backwards and upwards, and was of necessity both massive and lofty to satisfy rear impact and bumper height regulations respectively. Gandini's signature 'slashed and ascending' rear wheel arch again featured on the Diablo, albeit this time in a rather muted form. The Countach's wheel arches were too tight to allow for 17-inch wheels and Gandini took care to address this constraining factor when designing the Diablo.

Low down on the right flank of the car, just ahead of the rear wheel, was a small silver plaque with 'Disegno Marcello Gandini' in black. This was a tacit admission that the Diablo's stunning aesthetics were principally the work of the maestro and no one else. Gandini himself has suggested that the Lamborghini Diablo's styling was 'perhaps 80 per cent' his own work, thus implying that Chrysler's William Dayton, Tom Gale and their teams were responsible for the remaining 20 per cent of the Diablo's aesthetics.

The frontal aspect of the car featured a very low, acutely angled snout, which carried retractable headlights. Below these motorised pods, the Diablo's parking lights and the turn indicator lights were mounted on the car's integrated front air dam-cum-front bumper, and below which again were the fog and flasher lights. The car's front bonnet was trapezoidal in shape, a styling feature first seen in the Countach, and carried the triangular gold-on-black Raging Bull emblem.

The rear of the Diablo was dominated by its massive engine bay bonnet, which carried six large air vents, three on each side. Inadequate ventilation in the prototype Progetto 132's rear bodyshell had caused overheating problems and secondary performance issues with the original Type 521 engine, and this new bonnet was designed to overcome the problem of hot air getting trapped within the engine compartment. There were four overwhelming aspects to the straight-on rear view of the Diablo: the rear brake and turn indicator lights housed within almost square pods; the Raging Bull logo and the Diablo name writ large in bright red; the massive air vents immediately below the rear light pods; and the quartet of upward-angled exhaust pipes. For the particularly extrovert owner, a rear wing could be fitted as an optional extra.

Marcello Gandini made an interesting aside at the Diablo's Monte Carlo launch when asked about this large and rather ungainly rear aerofoil: 'What aerofoil? I designed no aerofoil!' The Diablo does not need a rear wing for aerodynamic

The massive rear tyres, the quad bazooka tailpipes, the octet of engine vents and the rear wing are all astounding.

An early Diablo in southern Spain.

A Diablo at Brooklands. Note the quadrilateral air intake in front of the rear wheels and the two air intakes along the upper flanks.

At speed on a hill climb at Brooklands.

stability. Like its predecessor, the Diablo can be specified with a rear wing for aesthetic reasons, but this comes at a price: increased aerodynamic drag, with an accompanying decrease in top speed (it is estimated that the rear wing robs about 8km/h (5mph) from the Diablo's maximum velocity), high-speed acceleration and fuel economy. Here is a case of form triumphing over function, yet despite this the 1982 Formula One World Champion Keke Rosberg optioned his yellow Diablo with just this appendage. In doing so, Rosberg chose to disregard one of the key principles associated with nineteenth- and twentieth-century industrial design, and more recently with supercar construction and computer software composition.

In his masterful 1896 essay 'The Tall Office Building Artistically Considered', the architect Louis H. Sullivan argued that in any successful product 'form ever follows function'. Sullivan himself modestly claimed that he was merely adhering to the Roman architectural theorist Vitruvius' principles that products and structures should exhibit three key qualities: *firmitas*, *utilitas* and *venustas* (solidity, usefulness and beauty). One of the first brochures for the Diablo brochures mentions Vitruvius and his three virtues, alongside a full-page colour photo of a sleek red Diablo unfettered by an aesthetically questionable and aerodynamically injurious rear wing. An unadorned Diablo had a laudable aerodynamic drag coefficient of only 0.31, and Gandini's sleek and wind-cheating bodyshell design can take most of the credit for Lamborghini's new flagship meeting its performance targets, and thus becoming the world's fastest series production car.

The Diablo was 2,040mm wide, 4,460mm long and just 1,105mm high. Its wheelbase was 2,650mm, with a front track of 1,540mm and a rear track of 1,640mm. Its free front

The Diablo is just as dramatic under the Australian sun.

A Diablo looks good even when suspended in mid-air.

angle of ascent, so important for such a low car to navigate urban speed bumps and multi-storey car parks, was a creditable 8 degrees, while its free rear angle was a truly massive 19 degrees. Its ground clearance was 140mm, and it had a front overhang of 930mm and a rear overhang of 880mm. The Diablo had a front boot capacity of 141 litres, a fuel tank with a capacity for 100 litres of 95 RON unleaded petrol, and a kerb weight of 1,686kg.

The overall stance of the car – low, wide and long, with an almost theatrical side profile dominated by vents and scoops and the long side windows, and a large forward-placed glass canopy – was that of a General Dynamics F-16 fighter jet. Just what every child, teenager and Lamborghini customer expected and wanted from Sant'Agata.

INTERIOR STYLING

Chrysler was fully aware that if Lamborghini was to pay its way going into the future, the Diablo would have to appeal and sell to a much wider audience than its predecessor. The Countach was rightly criticised for its cramped, poorly laid

Even the petrol filler flap looks like it is travelling at speed in this stationary Diablo.

Low, wide and menacing.

The rear lights look like afterburners.

A single homogeneous unit – Marcello Gandini did well.

out cockpit. The hugely important North American market of the 1990s was in part made up of middle-aged men who were more comfort-loving and corpulent than their Countach-buying counterparts, and the Diablo's interior design had to not only accommodate them physically, but also had to accommodate their loathing of any discomfiture or discomposure. Ferruccio Lamborghini's original plan for the Countach was for an extreme car, made in extremely limited numbers, for those select customers who would be delighted to put up with multiple points of vexation simply to experience a unique car affording a singular driving experience.

More than a quarter of a century later, Chrysler, as a mass-market manufacturer, had a quite different agenda for its forthcoming supercar flagship: more user-friendly, more readily available to purchase, and aimed at a less exclusive target audience. At any rate, the Diablo's cockpit needed to be more comfortable than the Countach's, which was rooted in the very early 1970s. The rest of the world had moved on considerably since then, particularly in the field of ergonomics. Driver and passenger safety legislation had also been updated and tightened to the point that a complete cockpit redesign was the only practical way forward – and here Detroit did well.

William A. Dayton and his crew from Chrysler's Detroit Styling Centre were almost exclusively responsible for the Diablo's cabin styling. They had a major advantage over their Italian predecessors who had designed the Countach's interior, since they enjoyed the secondary benefits of the Diablo having larger external dimensions than the Countach. The Diablo's wider track and longer wheelbase brought with it increased internal space, and the increased height of the car brought improved headroom. Many potential Countach customers simply could not fit into its cabin, and Sant'Agata therefore lost many sales to Ferrari's more spacious and comfort-orientated Boxer and Testarossa. Dayton was tasked with addressing these shortcomings.

First on Dayton's list was to improve driver and passenger access into and out of the Diablo's cockpit. Here the Diablo benefited as its doors were longer, their opening angles were greater and its doorsills were lower, all of which made for a significantly bigger access aperture. Getting in and out of the Diablo was still a struggle, however, and Dayton explained the reasoning why this was necessary. The Diablo's cab-forward design was fittingly dramatic for a supercar, but automatically brought with it limited cockpit headroom. To

The Diablo's door aperture is more generous than that of the Countach.

Thinly padded bucket seats and a golf club-shaped gear knob. Note the fire extinguisher.

compensate for this and to gain the maximum possible cabin headroom, the Diablo's roof was dome-shaped. To utilise the additional height found close to the apex of the dome, the seats had to be placed as close to the car's centreline as possible. The seats were therefore very close to the transmission tunnel and thus quite far away from the car's outer sill, meaning that the occupants had to straddle a wide and awkward gap across the sills before reaching the seats. The compensation for this inconvenience was an additional 38mm (1½in) gained in cabin headroom.

The gas strut-assisted guillotine doors themselves were opened using a key and a button inset into the top of the door when the driver was outside the car, and opened by pulling up on a sill-mounted lever when the driver was already confined inside. Cars for the US market featured an additional warning buzzer, which bleeped when the ignition key was slotted into its barrel but the doors remained open or improperly closed.

Once seated the Diablo driver had more room than his Countach predecessor, primarily because the Diablo was 25mm wider. It was also 50mm wider than the Ferrari F40 and the Testarossa, and indeed wider than any other contemporary car then on sale in Europe. The new cockpit also felt lighter and more airy because the dramatic downward swooping side windows had a much larger glass area. It is of note that these windows drop down completely, unlike in the Countach. Although the Diablo had significantly more footwell space available, the three foot pedals were still packed fairly close to each other. Importantly the pedals were much less angled away from the straight-ahead driving position, and much less offset, than before. The steering wheel, gear lever and secondary controls were also much better positioned for the driver, and all this contributed to a more welcoming, albeit still very intimidating, introduction to this daunting supercar. Ergonomics had finally arrived at Sant'Agata.

Detroit's Diablo cockpit design was a leather fetishist's delight. Soft, hand-stitched hide that was pleasing to the eye and touch covered almost every surface save for the windscreen and the central console. The door cards featured diagonally slashed leather strips, which may have been fashionable but were a trifle fussy for some tastes. The quilted leather seats followed in the fashion of the door cards. They were manually adjustable for leg length and rake, and were thinly padded but more generous in size than the Countach's.

The Diablo's inertia-reel seat belts now resided in the centre of the car and had to be pulled downwards and outwards to meet up with the seat belt stalks, which were positioned just by the outer sill of the car. To allow for maximum comfort and some body movement under normal driving conditions, these seat belts were of a three-point cross thoracic and abdominal design, which included an emergency locking retractor mechanism. For the US market only, a somewhat different passive restraint system was offered as standard. This system used two separate belts: a lap belt with an integrated retractor mechanism and an automatic thoracic belt. US market cars also had two safety belt warning lights housed in the left-hand bank of the dashboard's lowest tier, which lit up when the seat belts were not correctly fastened into their stalks.

The satisfyingly thick-rimmed leather steering wheel was adjustable for both reach and rake, and the foot pedals were more spaced out than in the Countach. Each Diablo was delivered with two identical keys that operated the doors and the ignition system. The ignition barrel was located on the right-hand side of the steering column and a steering lock mechanism and steering wheel adjustment lever were both integrated within this column. Sprouting out of the steering column were two stalks: that on the left controlled the turn indicators, the horn and the high beam and daytime flasher lights, while that on the right controlled the windscreen wiper and washer mechanisms. At the base of the steering column was a small button, which, when pushed upwards, allowed the whole dashboard to be tilted upwards or downwards so that the dashboard angle could be altered to best suit the driver, and more especially to reduce distracting reflections in the dashboard glass cover.

The Diablo's side window glass was raised and lowered by operating two pushbuttons located on the central console immediately ahead of the gear lever. The outside rear view mirrors were also electrically adjustable, with a sill-mounted control unit allowing the mirrors to be moved up, down, inwards and outwards. In the event of an electrical failure the outside rear view mirrors could be adjusted manually by pressing directly on the mirror glass. The inside rear view mirror was mounted at the very top of the windscreen, sandwiched between the sun visors, and could be manually adjusted to reduce glare from a following vehicle's headlights.

The handbrake was unusual in being located just by the outer sill, and so would have obstructed a driver getting in or out when in an elevated position. Sant'Agata, however, designed a mechanism that allowed the handbrake lever to lie reclined whether or not the handbrake was operational.

If the car was not going to be used for an extended period of time, its battery could to some extent be protected against drainage by disconnecting it from the majority of the car's electrical systems by way of a screw-type switch located behind the driver's seat. Even when the screw device was turned off, however, the car's hazard lights, central locking system, clock, radio and injection control units remained connected and functional. The battery was housed within the rear wheel arch just ahead of the twin rear coil-over shock absorbers.

The front bonnet release lever was hidden underneath the dashboard at the base of the steering column, with an emergency pull release also hidden nearby in case the primary release lever failed. The front boot housed two roll-up bags, which were secured to the boot's side walls. One bag contained the emergency tool kit with a selection of spanners, ratchet heads and spare light bulbs, while the second bag contained the emergency tyre inflator kit. The Diablo did not carry a spare wheel or spare tyre. Lamborghini explicitly stated that the Diablo's Pirelli P Zero tyres should never be repaired, since any repairs to ZR rated tyres could not be considered safe, due to the high speeds and high temperatures that these tyres might be called upon to endure. A damaged Diablo tyre should simply be replaced at the earliest possible opportunity. The rear engine bonnet release lever was located in the door jamb, as on the Countach and Murciélago. Again two emergency pull releases were hidden within the rear wheel arches in case the primary lever failed. Within the cockpit were no fewer than three glove compartments: one behind each seat back and one centred between the two seats.

Handbrakes on Countachs and Diablos are notoriously poor. Always leave the car in first gear or reverse gear when parked up.

The Diablo's cockpit ergonomics were a revelation after the Countach. The ascending central console was beautifully laid out with the heating and ventilation controls, an analogue clock (an expensive Breguet timepiece was an option), and the in-car entertainment system located at the top, with a dual row of control buttons and the ashtray underneath. The car's climate control system could be set to a predetermined temperature using the digital monitor, which could be configured to either a Celsius or Fahrenheit readout. Hot or cold air could be sent to a choice of five different sets of air vents – upper, lower, front, side and

The early Diablo's multi-storey dashboard was not Renato Meduri's finest hour.

An economy class Diablo lacking an expensive optional extra: the removable Breguet mechanical clock.

windscreen – and at varying air speeds depending on the fan speed chosen. The dual row control buttons operated the parking, side, interior, fog and emergency lights, the central locking and window locking mechanisms, and the fuel filler flap release.

Lamborghini had already established a long-standing association with the Japanese high-fidelity stereo manufacturer Alpine, based in Iwaki, Fukushima Prefecture, as could be seen in the Alpine-Countach advertisements that adorned the inside pages of every high-performance car magazine of the 1970s and 1980s. It was therefore almost inevitable that Alpine would be Sant'Agata's preferred partner for the Diablo's in-car entertainment system. Alpine allocated one of their leading sound engineers, Marc Brazeau, to work on the Diablo, and he suggested the Alpine 7390 master unit controlling either a cassette deck with an integrated AM/FM radio or a six-disc CD player with an integrated AM/FM radio.

At the very base of the ascending central console column lay the switches for the driver and passenger side windows, and behind these, on the flat part of the console, the five forward speed gear lever stood proudly to attention within a semicircular well. This lever was topped by a golf club-shaped handle, which was very similar to that seen in the last Countachs and just as unattractive. I have never warmed to trying to grip a gear lever as though it were a Walther PPK: a pistol does not have to be manoeuvred and slotted through six differently oriented and narrow gear channels. A simpler and less contrived solution would surely be a perfectly spherical gear lever. A decade later a ball-topped gear lever like that was adopted for the Murciélago. On a more positive note, the Diablo's cockpit featured a dashboard-mounted passenger grab handle, which was bulky because it concealed a substantial amount of safety wadding as required by US homologation rules. The Lamborghini Miura had also featured a passenger grab handle mounted on the central console, but this necessary safety and comfort feature was inexplicably omitted in the Countach. Its reappearance in the Diablo was highly welcome.

The angle of the original Diablo's dash binnacle was adjustable and at the time this was touted as being highly ergonomic, based on optical principles espoused by an eye surgeon. In my opinion the Diablo's original double-decked dash binnacle is novel in design and aesthetically very attractive, but speaking as a driver who has actually piloted a Diablo and also has some knowledge of visual physiology, I find that it is one of the weakest parts of the original Diablo and is hugely compromised from a safety and ergonomic viewpoint.

This innovative dashboard was actually two and a half storeys tall, with the upper storey housing the speedometer on the extreme left, followed by the oil pressure gauge, then the coolant temperature gauge and finally the tachometer on the extreme right. The middle half storey housed a sequence of warning lights, starting on the left with a cautionary illuminated sign that lit up if the pressure in any of the tyres fell below 1.75bar (25psi), followed by a row of warning lights relating to the lighting system, and on the right the hazard indicator warning light. The lower storey housed a bank of warning lights at each extremity. The bank on the left held eight lights relating to the car's braking system and the driver and passenger seatbelts, while that on the right featured nine lights relating to the car's catalytic convertors, lambda sensor readings, engine oil pressure, fuel level warning light (which lit up when less than 25 litres of fuel remained in the tank), windscreen washer fluid level, alternator charging level and, for the Saudi Arabian market only, a speed limit warning light, which illuminated when the car exceeded 120km/h (75mph). Sandwiched between these two banks were the oil temperature gauge, the fuel level gauge and the battery amperage gauge.

The dash design was certainly dazzling in appearance and in keeping with the Diablo's spacecraft-like external appearance. The problem with having such a high multi-storey dashboard immediately in front of the driver is that it severely limits the driver's forward visibility. Vertically challenged drivers find that their sightline is directly level with the top of the binnacle, while even tall drivers find that their forward view is unnecessarily restricted to little more than a letter box slit, simply because the high binnacle obstructs most of the lower windscreen.

The second major fault with the original Diablo's novel tri-level dashboard was the location of the speedometer and tachometer dials. The tachometer is a vital gauge for spirited driving. It allows the driver to enjoy the thrill of using all the engine's maximum permitted revs without damaging its health by exceeding this mechanically important limit. The speedometer is an equally important gauge for the health of the Diablo pilot's driving licence and for the pilot's desire to avoid an extended diet of prison food. Both the tachometer and the speedometer therefore need to be immediately visible to the Diablo driver. Sadly, Sant'Agata employed Renato Meduri, a professor of ophthalmology at Bologna University, to advise them on the layout of the dashboard. He recommended that the tachometer and the speedometer be located at the extreme ends of the dashboard's top tier. His rationale for this extraordinary layout was that this arrangement allows the driver to see the tachometer and the speedometer using their peripheral vision, while keeping their central vision focused on the road straight ahead. Just how a visual physiologist could arrive at this bizarre conclusion is quite incomprehensible. Meduri's professional life was colourful, including visits to court for sending threats to a fellow ophthalmologist in the form of bullets, and his strange recommendations regarding the Diablo's dash layout should be seen in this context.

The steering wheel obscures many of the tri-level dash gauges, but more importantly the high binnacle cuts off much of the driver's forward view. Lamborghini never revisited this binnacle design.

In order to see the thin needles that reside within the speedometer and the tachometer gauges, the driver needs to use his central vision, since peripheral vision is simply not acute enough to even begin to pick up the necessary level of detail. Foveal vision (the most acute form of central vision) is limited to just 1 degree away from fixation, while parafoveal vision is limited to only about 6 degrees away from fixation. In contrast, the Diablo's speedometer and tachometer lie about 25 to 30 degrees from fixation, so are well outside the range of foveal and parafoveal vision. To add insult to injury, the location of these two gauges at the extremities of the top tier requires two separate and discrete eye movements: the driver first has to drop his gaze downwards from the road ahead, and then move his sightline to the right or left to read the gauge on that side. A more conventional dashboard layout with the speedometer and tachometer placed centrally would only require one downward movement of the eyes to read these dials. Any time spent looking away from the road ahead when driving, at high speed or otherwise, becomes an avoidable period of danger, and so is deeply undesirable. The suggestion that the driver can read either of these gauges using his peripheral vision while concentrating on the road ahead is simply not borne out either by the basic principles of visual optics or by real-life driver experience, and is compounded by the need for additional, unnecessary eye movements. It is telling that Sant'Agata revised the Diablo's dashboard later on in its production cycle, and never returned to this bizarre dashboard arrangement for the Murciélago, the Aventador or any of its subsequent models.

It is equally telling that when Paolo Stanzani, Marcello Gandini and Ferruccio Lamborghini planned and designed the revolutionary Countach, their very first prototype, the legendary LP500, had an extremely spartan – if space-age – dashboard design. They only allowed for a digital speedometer and tachometer, both of which were placed directly in front of the driver in a low dashboard, with all auxiliary systems monitored by banks of either red (urgent attention demanded) or orange (less immediate attention called for) warning lights. They formulated this novel dash design so that the driver could give the road ahead his full attention. It is also worth noting that the McLaren 720S available in 2022 has a similar trick dashboard system, by which the driver can select the 'Folding Driver Display' option. In this setting the normal full upright dash display folds down to a fraction of its usual height and only displays the most critical of parameters, so that the driver has an unimpeded view through the windscreen and is not distracted by any unnecessary gauges or information. But this one fault should not distract from the fact that the Diablo's cabin comfort and its cockpit ergonomics were a triumph over its predecessor's, and brought it right up to date and up to scratch with its rivals from other manufacturers.

Among the few optional extras that could be ordered were a custom-moulded driver's seat, a remote CD changer and subwoofer, and a factory-fitted luggage set. Not forgetting of course that removable Breguet mechanical clock for the central console, which was priced at a trifling additional US$10,500.

The Diablo's luggage compartment is at the front of the car and is fairly generous.

Factory-approved fitted luggage.

DRIVETRAIN

Pursuant to its goal of producing the fastest series production car in the world, Sant'Agata used the Type 522 engine variant of its classic 60-degree Bizzarrini V12 engine in the Lamborghini Diablo. Marmiroli had rejected the Type 521 engine due to its inadequate power and torque outputs, but was entirely satisfied by the performance parameters offered up by the Type 522 engine. This improved upon the Type 521 by having a larger cubic capacity, a new and stiffer engine block, more freely breathing cylinder heads, trapezoidal combustion chambers, new concave pistons, centrally located spark plugs, and Nikasil-lined cylinder bores to reduce blow-by and for increased longevity. The Type 522 engine also had fewer component parts for greater reliability and weighed less than the Type 521 powerplant.

The original Diablo adopted the classic mid-engine drivetrain layout of the Countach. The Bizzarrini V12 engine was placed longitudinally, and Paolo Stanzani's revolutionary south-north engine-gearbox orientation was retained.

The 5707cc naturally aspirated Bizzarrini engine in the original Diablo produced a maximum power of 492bhp @ 7,000rpm.

This all-alloy, 5707cc, quad camshaft, naturally aspirated, four valves per cylinder, wet sump engine had a bore of 87mm and a stroke of 80mm. Operating at a compression ratio of 10:1, this powerplant produced a maximum power output of 492bhp at 6,800rpm and a maximum torque output of 580Nm at 5,200rpm. Engine cooling was achieved through a pressurised circuit containing 15 litres of coolant, and two mid-mounted aluminium radiators with electric fans. The Type 522 engine used the latest technology timing chains with dampers and an automatic timing tensioner system, and ran on the following firing sequence:

1-7-4-10-2-8-6-12-3-9-5-11

Sant'Agata recommended Champion A59G or A59GC spark plugs with a gap of between 0.5 and 0.6mm. The battery was housed in the rear wheel arch in a cavity just ahead of the rear twin coaxial spring-shock absorber units.

Fuel, spark and emissions were controlled by a bespoke Marelli-Weber integrated injection-ignition arrangement that Sant'Agata called the LIE (Lamborghini Iniezione Elettronica) system. It managed each cylinder bank independently, depending on real time data sent by sensors monitoring the throttle position, the engine's rpm, piston position, and air intake and coolant temperatures. Sequential multipoint injection combined with lambda sensors and three-way catalytic convertors then ensured that the optimal air-fuel mixture was introduced into each cylinder at just the right moment. The LIE system thereby provided maximum engine responsiveness and flexibility throughout the Type 522 engine's rev range, so allowing for the most exhilarating driving pleasure whether at low, medium or high engine and road speeds. This electronically regulated system also enabled Sant'Agata to meet all existing and forthcoming global emissions regulations, while simultaneously optimising the Diablo's fuel consumption.

This Type 522 engine was mated to an all-new five-speed gearbox. Marmiroli explained that a six-speed gearbox was simply unnecessary because the Type 522 engine produced so much torque that for everyday onroad driving just three gears would have been more than sufficient. This gearbox was placed in the revolutionary south-north engine-gearbox orientation conceived by Paolo Stanzani, and first used in production form in the Lamborghini Countach, instantly

Note the V12's firing order embossed in red.

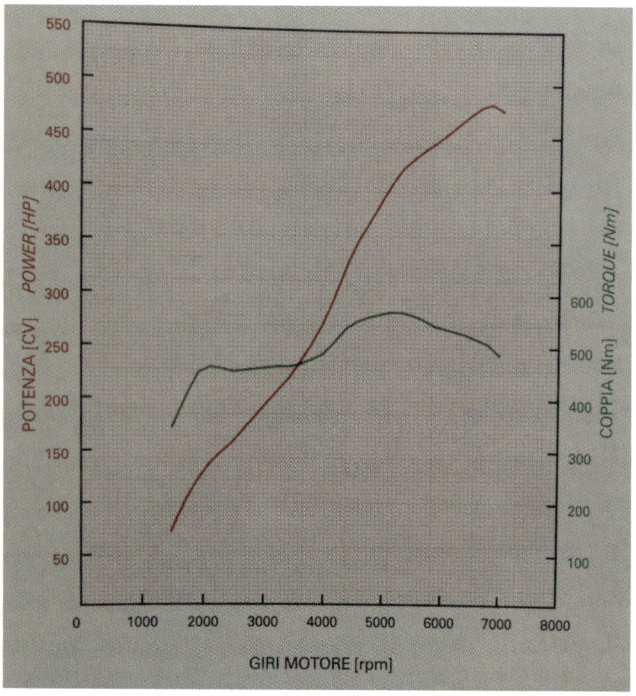

The original Diablo's power and torque curves.

With a compression ratio of 10.0, this Diablo engine produced 580Nm of torque @ 5,200rpm.

The Diablo's engine bay is much neater and tidier than that of the Countach 5000 QV seen in Chapter 2.

becoming one of its defining features. The Diablo used a dry single-plate clutch with a disc diameter of 254mm and a self-adjusting hydraulic clutch release. It had the following gear ratios:

	Ratio	***Maximum speed***
1st	1: 2.312	97km/h (60mph)
2nd	1:1.524	148km/h (92mph)
3rd	1:1.125	200km/h (124mph)
4th	1:0.888	255km/h (158mph)
5th	1:0.676	325 km/hg (202mph)
Reverse	1:2.125	106km/h (66mph)

From the beginning Sant'Agata had determined that the Lamborghini Diablo would at some stage feature a four-wheel-drive system. Marmiroli and his team felt that the Diablo's prodigious power and torque outputs could best be deployed onto tarmac without wasteful spinning of the wheels by using all the tractive forces at the Diablo's disposal. This meant sending power and torque to the front wheels as well as to the rear wheels, and Sant'Agata had a blueprint for this arrangement in its files. Budgetary, and more pressingly time, constraints, however, meant that this four-wheel-drive system was not ready at the Diablo's debut in 1990. The Diablo's launch had already been much delayed and Lamborghini could not suffer further postponement, so the original Diablo was presented with a two-wheel-drive system. The four-wheel-drive system would have to wait for the next variant in three years' time. In the meantime the original Diablo debuted with a limited slip differential made by Zahnradfabrik Friedrichshafen AG, more commonly known as ZF, and featuring a final ratio of 1:2.41.

The first production Lamborghini Diablos had non-assisted manual steering with three and a half steering wheel turns from lock to lock. A rack and pinion steering box attached to a collapsible steering column afforded a minimum turning circle of 13.2 metres (43ft). As with the Countach, the steering was heavy at parking speeds. Although the steering effort lightened considerably once above about 8km/h (5mph), low-speed manoeuvres were still limited by the steering weight. From the outset Lamborghini had anticipated this potential shortcoming, and had originally planned for the Diablo to have power-assisted steering right from its debut. This driver aid too was not ready for series production at the Diablo's launch in 1990, and power-assisted steering would have to wait for the next Diablo variant before making its first appearance.

Sant'Agata's new flagship needed a braking system commensurate with its high top speed and Marmiroli's team therefore employed a twin independent hydraulic braking system with brake booster assistance and ventilated discs at each of the car's four corners. The front and rear discs measured 330mm and 284mm in diameter respectively, and the mechanical handbrake worked on the rear discs. The brake fluid reservoir and the clutch fluid reservoir were both located behind a panel in the front luggage compartment. At the time the Diablo was lauded for its braking ability.

The Diablo featured independent double wishbone suspension at all four corners with single coaxial spring-shock absorber units on the front axle, and twin coaxial spring-shock absorber units on the rear axle. The suspension also featured non-adjustable anti-roll bars and incorporated anti-dive and anti-squat technology.

For the Diablo Lamborghini specified asymmetrical, tubeless, Pirelli P Zero radial ply tyres measuring 245/40 ZR 17 for the front, and 335/35 ZR 17 for the rear. Solely for the Swiss market, Sant'Agata specified Bridgestone tyres to comply with local noise regulations. These tyres were mounted on multi-piece lightweight aluminium alloy wheels measuring 8.5 x 17 inches for the front and 13 x 17 inches for the rear. These wheels were made by OZ Group, a specialist alloy wheel manufacturer founded in 1971 and based in San Martino di Lupari, near Venice. The factory stipulated different tyre pressures depending on the speed that the car was going to be driven at. For speeds below 260km/h (161mph), the recommended tyre pressures were 2.8bar for the front and 2.7bar for the rear, but if the car was going to be driven at speeds in excess of 260km/h then all four tyres needed to be further inflated to 3.2bar.

With its rear mid-mounted V12 engine, a south-north engine-gearbox orientation, and its Vaccari & Bosi square-tube spaceframe chassis weighing only 80kg, the Diablo tipped the scales with a dry weight of 1,576kg, and boasted an admirable weight distribution of 60 per cent rear and 40 per cent front.

Sandro Munari used all of his legendary car control skills, experience and knowledge to develop and refine the Diablo's suspension set-up so that the car handled in a safe and consistent manner. At its debut the car had servo-assisted steering, but none of the other cutting-edge driver aids then available from rival supercar manufacturers. Power steering, anti-brake-lock technology, four-wheel drive, four-wheel steering and active suspension would all have to wait for another day. Similarly, traction control and stability control were not available on the original Diablo, but Sant'Agata was confident that a calm and considered right foot from a sympathetic and circumspect driver would stand in admirably for these electronic safety nets. The Diablo's new electronic multipoint fuel injection system did help here by increasing engine flexibility, optimising torque output, and delivering this torque more smoothly and more consistently compared to its carburettor-bearing predecessor. As a result the Diablo had an exquisitely sensitive throttle pedal, with each additional millimetre of accelerator pedal movement prodding the fuel injection pump into ever greater action, which in turn translated into more power and thence into higher speed. All of this made accessing the Diablo's formidable performance potential that much easier and safer.

The Diablo was clocked circling around the Nardo test track in southern Italy at 325.2km/h (202mph), and in doing so it eclipsed the previous production car record held by the Ferrari F40. The new Lamborghini flagship's most important design brief had been met. Its acceleration figures were equally impressive. The 0–100km/h dash took only 4.09 seconds, while the claimed standing start to the 1km post sprint took only a claimed 20.7 seconds. The Diablo's petrol consumption figures were equally daunting: 20.21ltr/100km (14mpg) for the standard EPA highway cycle, dropping down to 31.44ltr/100km (9mpg) for the standard EPA city cycle. Expressed according to speed, this translated to 13.3ltr/100km at 90km/h and 15.2ltr/100km at 120km/h. Whichever standard one chose to express the Diablo's fuel consumption, it was clear that owning one's personal oilfield was almost a compulsory prerequisite for running a Diablo.

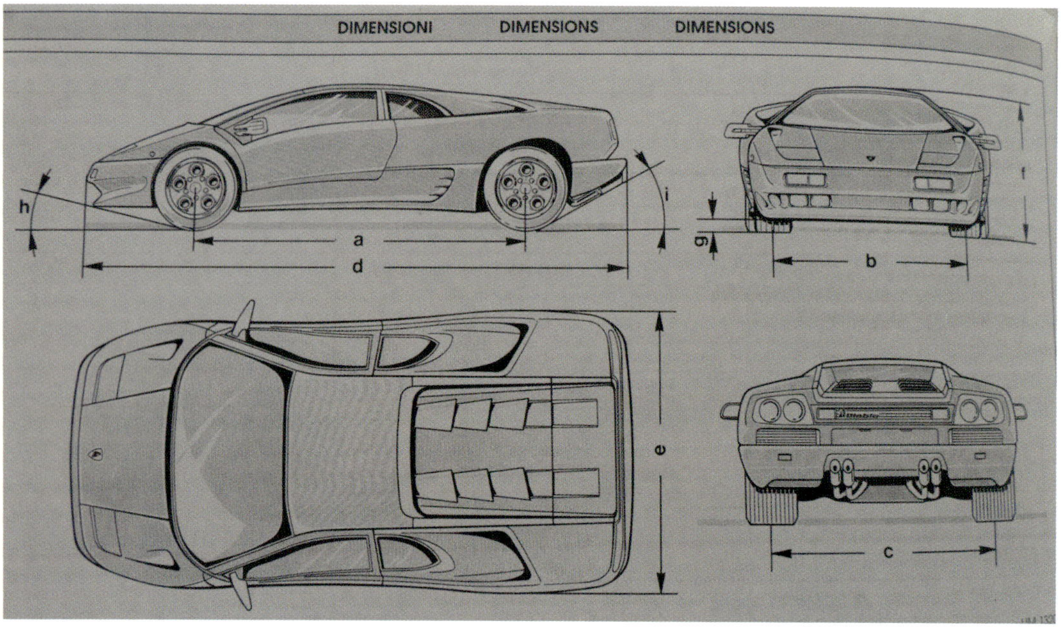

Schematic diagram of the Diablo's exterior from the Owner's Manual.

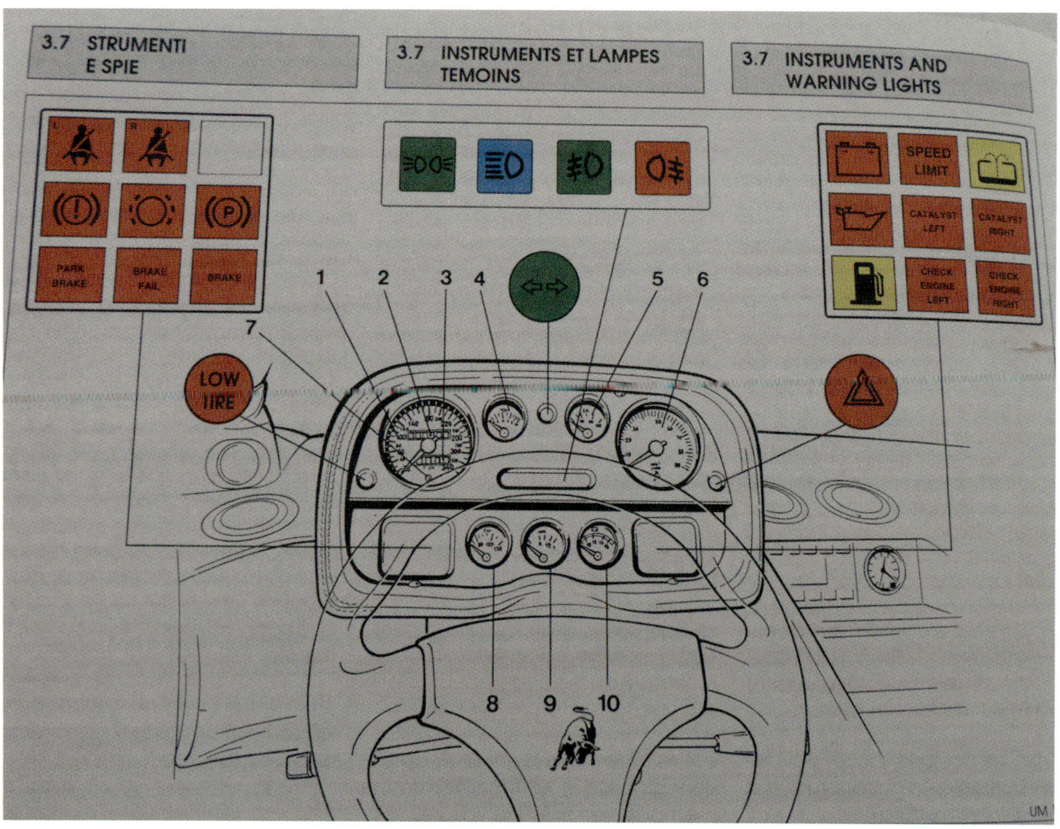

Schematic diagram of the Diablo's dashboard gauges and warning lights.

CHAPTER 5

BUILDING THE DIABLO

Despite their multinational and hugely diverse industrial empire, Patrick and Jean-Claude Mimran were acutely aware that they would not be able to finance the production phase of the Lamborghini Diablo. Ferruccio Lamborghini had been forced to sell his beloved supercar company because of a lack of money, and Georges-Henri Rossetti and René Leimer were hands-off owners who had left the company in a truly parlous state financially. The Mimrans were too astute to fall into the same trap.

The Countach had been designed in 1970 and had entered production in the early years of that decade when automation, robotics, electronics, quality control and 'just in time' production practices were barely known about. By 1990 the Countach was a dinosaur, and the building techniques and practices used to construct it were, relatively speaking, from the automotive Dark Ages.

Marmiroli, Novaro and the Mimrans knew that the first production Diablos would have to be rapidly followed by more advanced variants simply because Lamborghini's main rivals were constantly creating ever faster and more radical competitor supercars. They knew that developing these later versions would cost serious money. Electronic driver aids in the form of new braking, suspension and steering technologies were becoming the norm, none of which the Countach had, and each would demand significant financial investment. Lamborghini customers were also now demanding creature comforts that early Countach customers would never have dreamt about, like climate control and electrically operated wing mirrors. Twenty years on, clients were also much less tolerant of automotive faults: they expected their cars to start when the ignition key was turned, and then get them to their desired destination without having to call for breakdown assistance, or without throwing up unwelcome dashboard warning lights. All these things demanded money.

The Sant'Agata factory's Piazza Centrale a few years before Diablo production began.

The Mimran brothers were lucky that Chrysler was looking to burnish their image with an upmarket European acquisition at the exact moment that the Diablo's early development phase was coming to an end. The Mimrans were beautifully positioned to entice the Detroit giant with a promising plan and prototype, but without having to commit the investment needed to build actual Diablo cars.

Lee Iacocca's purchase of Automobili Lamborghini SpA at a rumoured cost of US$25 million was just the beginning of Chrysler's financial outlay. True glamour never comes cheap. When the Mimrans acquired Lamborghini in 1981 the company boasted a total factory floorspace of just 1,626m^2 (17,500ft^2). Nine years later, with Diablo production just about to commence, Chrysler had bankrolled a further 700m^2 (7,500ft^2), representing an almost 43 per cent increase in production space. New autoclaves for manufacturing composites, engine dynamometers, emissions testing stations and quality control stations were all needed to put the Diablo into series production, and these advanced facilities were eye-wateringly expensive. Most of these, however, were one-off costs. The most expensive item on Lamborghini's fiscal spreadsheet was its recurring salary bill. Chrysler had approved the hiring of new artisans, mechanics and engineers, all in anticipation of Sant'Agata's much increased output once the Diablo and its smaller Type 140 sibling went into production.

In October 1989 Emile Novaro launched an in-house magazine called *Automobili Lamborghini News*. Its stated aim was to establish 'better communications within the company and with collaborators and friends'. By friends, Novaro almost certainly meant potential customers for the Diablo and the Type 140, and it is no coincidence that the first issue of this publication concentrated on the theme of quality control. Over the decades Lamborghini's supercars had established a somewhat distant and uneasy relationship with quality and reliability, depending upon customers' unrequited love of their supercars to readily and willingly ignore sometimes glaring faults and omissions. This would no longer work with the new customers that Chrysler was now chasing after, who would demand a degree of fit and finish, reliability and after-sales care that had previously been associated more with Porsche at Stuttgart than Sant'Agata.

The first edition of *Automobili Lamborghini News* was a pre-emptive strike from Emile Novaro, acknowledging that Sant'Agata would have to do much better in quality control and laying out his plans to ensure that every Diablo that left the production line would not disappoint its eagerly awaiting first owner. Novaro pledged that Lamborghini's quality control would extend from the design phase through to component manufacturing and parts assembly. He also promised that the franchises would be more closely monitored and that dealer-customer interactions would be improved at every stage, from the moment of first contact, to the stage when the customer was deciding on the car's colour and optional extras, to when the vehicle was handed over, and then during the after-sales, servicing and repair stages.

Novaro claimed that the first steps in this quality assurance programme had been implemented at the beginning of 1989, and that he could already see the fruits of this scheme at the time of writing the first issue in October 1989. Novaro elaborated on Lamborghini's new Quality Assurance Project, saying that it 'will increase the company's worldwide success by strengthening its image' and 'the concept of Quality takes priority over every other theory known up to now'. He also indicated that a major advance in Sant'Agata's capabilities would be forthcoming shortly: 'Until recently we have had to use contract facilities for pollution and homologation tests – but by the end of the year Lamborghini will have a fully functioning laboratory which will make it possible for the company to programme most of this strategically important work in-house.'

Gianfranco Venturelli, the General Manager at Automobili Lamborghini, expanded further on this topic in early 1989, saying that Sant'Agata had chosen Philip Crosby Associates, a pioneering leader in the field of Quality Control, to advise

The Sant'Agata factory just as the last Diablo was rolling off the production line.

The production line's terracotta flooring. The Diablo was still in production when these photos were taken.

and guide Lamborghini through this chapter in its history. A key piece of advice that Philip Crosby had given Lamborghini, and one that Venturelli committed to taking onboard immediately, was that all future Lamborghini employees should be very carefully chosen and vetted, and that they should then receive comprehensive training followed by regular updates to ensure that every car that Lamborghini manufactured was of the topmost quality. To this end Lamborghini entrusted Dott. Galli and Ing. Guarneri, under the guidance of Philip Crosby Associates, to develop a Quality Education and Improvement Process through which all Lamborghini employees would have to be accredited before series production of the Diablo started.

Series production started in June 1990, although there was a brief overlap during which both Countachs and Diablos were being manufactured. The last Countach, a silver 25th Anniversary that now resides in the factory museum, rolled off the production line on 4 July 1990. Novaro, Venturelli and Marmiroli had by this time streamlined the inflow of components for the Diablo, and refined the manufacturing process in the search for increased efficiency.

The original Countach manufacturing plant was reconfigured for the Diablo, and it was here that the first parts of the Lamborghini flagship were put together. In this building the Vaccari & Bosi square-section spaceframe was clothed with the car's body panels, and the main mechanical components and cockpit parts were incorporated into the body. A sizeable portion of this building was reserved for machining all the rough metal castings used in the car's drivetrain, while a smaller section was reserved for quality control. Chrysler had financed a completely new building located behind the original factory building and the finishing touches, and the subsequent static and road-testing of the Diablos, were carried out in this new facility. The Customer Care Department, the Spare Parts Division and the new Emissions Testing Centre were all housed in a separate building within the factory compound.

By the start of Diablo series production in June 1990, Sant'Agata had increased its workforce to about 460 personnel, of which 330 worked in various roles on the production line and about 120 worked in homologation, emissions testing, type approval legislation, sales, marketing and customer liaison roles. At the top of the pyramid there were about ten senior managers and executives. The start of Diablo production was further complicated by delicate and complex negotiations that senior management had to undertake with the factory floor trade unions to renew various existing contracts that were about to expire.

SOURCING THE COMPONENTS

The Diablo was a bespoke hand-built supercar, although less so than its illustrious predecessor. In contrast to most 1990s car plants, the Lamborghini factory manufactured a very high proportion of the Diablo's components in-house rather than simply buying these parts in ready-made form from outside suppliers. There are three reasons why Sant'Agata chose this approach. First, many of the components were required in very small quantities and many potential suppliers were not prepared to make parts in such small volumes. Second, many of the Diablo's components were highly intricate parts beyond the ability of many outside manufacturers. Finally, and most importantly, by making components in-house Lamborghini could ensure that these parts were constructed under the strictest possible conditions and to the tightest tolerances, thereby maximising quality and reliability. Unlike Ferrari, Lamborghini did not own its own foundry. As a result Lamborghini bought in rough castings for the Diablo and then machined the parts in-house, whereas other manufacturers would have chosen the simpler and cheaper route of outsourcing. Classic examples of in-house machining were the Diablo's aluminium engine block, the engine's baseplate, oil pan, cylinder heads, differential casing, gearbox housing, oil pump, water pump and connecting rods. The Diablo's massive crankshaft and its intricate camshafts were particularly difficult to machine to the necessary tolerances, but Sant'Agata put its most talented artisans to work at machining these parts. At an early stage Lamborghini did try buying in completed engine components, composite parts and upholstery, but found that the quality of many of these items never matched their expectations. Having to reject a high proportion of bought-in components turned out to be more expensive in the long run than setting up an in-house manufacturing department and making the relevant parts within the factory.

Some Diablo components were bought in, including pistons and their iron liners from Mahle, fuel injectors from Magnetti Marelli, starter motors and alternators from Bosch, and the gearsets from a specialist transmission company. A local firm assembled the Diablo's engine management

Electronic Control Units, but Lamborghini wrote the software and did the programming in-house.

Assembling the Diablo was a complex and labour-intensive process with much traditional hand finishing. In 1990 all Lamborghini had was alphanumeric automated machines. They did not possess any electronically controlled robots. Carbon fibre panels were hand moulded, and any blisters or other defects in the Diablo's bodyshells were sanded out by hand. As the Diablo evolved through its many model variants, the components used and the techniques employed to construct the car changed, but these were relatively minor modifications based on the same basic themes and principles. For example, the later variants used many more carbon composite parts than the early models, but the same artisans used almost the same basic fixing techniques to attach these cutting-edge body parts to the car as previously. The last variants were no less bespoke or hand-manufactured than the earliest cars.

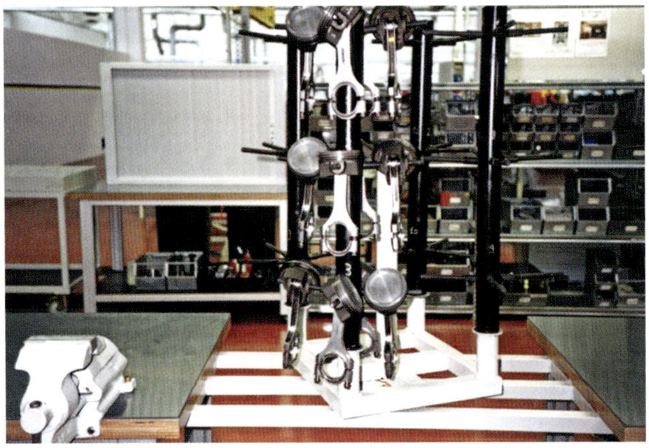

These were just about the last Diablo pistons and conrods to be used on the Sant'Agata production line.

ASSEMBLY

Building the Diablo started with the body-in-white arriving at Sant'Agata from an outside supplier called Golden Car, based in Caramagna Piemonte. Golden Car was established in 1949 by Alessandro Festa and soon established a reputation for producing extremely high-quality aluminium-alloy body panels. By 1970 Golden Car supplied Maserati, de Tomaso and Lamborghini, and more recently Ferrari has also been among its customers. Golden Car is particularly known for its *battilastri* (panel beaters), who perform three-dimensional alchemy by transforming plain flat alloy or aluminium sheets into the most curvaceous, sensuous and seductive bodyshells. In the 1990s Lamborghini was one of Golden Car's biggest clients, and the Diablo was one of its biggest projects. Vaccari & Bosi would send the intricate square-section Diablo spaceframe chassis to Golden Car, where the *battilastri* would perform their magic and attach the car's front and rear wings, its roof, sills, floorpan, inner wheel arches and bulkheads. These *battilastri* were very versatile, being quite comfortable working with materials other than aluminium: the Diablo GT's front fenders, for example,

The red door on the left of the photograph illustrates the signature downward swoop of the Diablo's side window aperture.

The last days of Diablo production. The galleried windows date back to the factory's inception. Note the surgical theatre cleanliness of the production floor.

were made of carbon fibre. The Diablo's rear wings were enormous and were welded up from between five and seven separate sections of aluminium alloy panelling. Before the body-in-white left Golden Car's factory the bodyshell was seam-sealed.

Clothing the Diablo's Vaccari & Bosi-built square-section spaceframe chassis on a jig, which the Italians call a 'cala'.

Smoothing off the Diablo's bodywork to perfection.

When the body-in-white arrived in Sant'Agata it was still very much in an unfinished state, and Lamborghini's artisans would spend many hours sanding and polishing the panels to get it to a standard where the car could be painted.

The body-in-white was then placed on a trolley at the start of the production line. It would actually be more accurate to use the term 'hand-assembly line', as the Diablo was built up through a process quite unlike that found in any conventional car production line. The Diablo went through a series of eight workstations, each of which was manned by two people. Unlike a conventional car factory where one person or one robot does one or only a few tasks, at each of the Diablo's workstations one craftsman might perform as many as fifty different operations.

As the part-finished Diablo slowly trundled down the assembly line, components large and small were progressively attached to it. At different workstations, different components were added on: pipework, the wiring loom, fuel tank, cooling system, suspension, braking system, steering system and, of course, the drivetrain. Inserting the massive V12 engine-cum-gearbox into the close confines of the Diablo bodyshell was a particularly arduous and adrenaline-laced process. Each Bizzarrini-derived V12 engine was built by one person and took twelve hours to assemble. By 1999 Sant'Agata had one woman master engine builder among its staff. Each engine builder was also given additional time to check the quality of their work – Lamborghini's logic being that each master engine builder was best placed to identify a fault in their own work and to then rectify it. As any particular engine that blew up could easily and quickly be identified to the original engine builder, it was in that technician's own

An incomplete Diablo is moved down the production floor on a wheeled trolley.

Building a Diablo was a labour-intensive process. Here three artisans are working on one car.

interest to remedy any defects before any such detonation actually took place. Each V12 engine was run on a dynamometer for eight hours at varying engine speeds to check for leaks, and to ensure that performance and emissions targets were being met, before being installed into a bodyshell.

In the trim area the car would be fitted out with its seats, dashboard, door panels, carpets, instruments and a steering wheel. The last three items were made by outside suppliers, but all of the Diablo's extensive leatherwork was crafted in-house in a dedicated upholstery department. The car would by now have spent about ten days on this hand-assembly line.

The almost finished Diablo would now be transferred to the new Chrysler building located behind the original hand-assembly line for the final touches. The car would spend

VALENTINO BALBONI

Valentino Balboni was intimately involved with the testing and development of the Diablo, as he was with every Lamborghini model from the Miura SV right through to the Murciélago. He took over from Bob Wallace as Lamborghini's Chief Test Driver in 1975 and remained in that role for an almost unbelievable thirty-three years. During his tenure Valentino is estimated to have personally driven or road-tested 80 per cent of all the Lamborghini cars manufactured between 1973 and 2008. Rival Italian supercar manufacturers have had their own well-known chief test drivers, like Dario Benuzzi of Ferrari and Gerino Bertocchi of Maserati, but none has exhibited anything like Valentino's longevity or his deep and moving passion for the marque.

Valentino was personally recruited to his position by Ferruccio Lamborghini and Paolo Stanzani. Talking to Valentino about either of these, but particularly Ferruccio, almost always brings Valentino close to tears. He is acutely aware of just how lucky he was in getting into Automobili Lamborghini SpA in the first place, and what a substantial part fate played in Ferruccio lending him his patronage. In describing these events in his typically modest and unassuming manner, Valentino always omits to mention the hard graft that first brought him to Stanzani's attention, and the dedication to the company that bought him Ferruccio's unwavering support and backing. And he never talks about his God-given talent in wheelsmanship, or his uncanny ability to identify minute and subtle roadholding and handling characteristics and to then provide concise but accurate feedback to the awaiting chassis engineers.

Valentino Balboni was born on 13 May 1949 in Casumaro, a small town not far from Sant'Agata. Fate intervened in 1968 when he had already left school but had not yet landed a steady job. Casumaro's priest was taking some boys on an outing when they unexpectedly stopped in front of the Lamborghini factory at the precise moment that a lorry from Bertone was delivering some naked Miura bodyshells. In a moment that revealed Balboni's inherent work ethic, the young Valentino leapt out of the priest's car and started to help the factory workers push the trolley-mounted bodyshells into the factory buildings. Once inside, he liked what he saw, asked for a job application form, which he filled in on the spot, and was delighted to receive a job offer a month later.

He started at the very bottom of the Sant'Agata hierarchy, washing workshop floors, cleaning tools and doing whatever menial tasks that he was asked to. He did all this with good grace and genuine enthusiasm and quickly gained the favour of all those he came across. Soon he was tasked with moving the still incomplete and unfinished Lamborghini supercars out of the workshop in the mornings and back into the workshop in the evenings. He was meant to move these cars around by pushing them by hand, but he instead took the liberty of starting them up and driving them in and out. Valentino was forever being threatened with the sack if he didn't stop driving them without permission, but he miraculously charmed his way out after each repeat transgression.

Ferruccio and Stanzani noted Valentino's enthusiasm for driving, and about a year later told him that there might be a vacancy at Sant'Agata for an assistant test driver. Valentino couldn't believe his luck, and of course immediately volunteered for the role, but his two bosses tempered his delight by telling him that his aptitude and ability for the job would be very carefully evaluated before he was promoted to the coveted role of Assistant Test Driver. For over a year Balboni sat at Bob Wallace's feet, assiduously learning everything that the maestro could teach him. Then on 5 September 1973 Wallace, Stanzani and Ferruccio decided that Valentino had earned his spurs and he was given licence to conduct his first independent, unsupervised official test drive of a Lamborghini supercar: a brand, spanking new Miura SV fresh off the production line – just about the most desirable car on the planet. What a way to start a new job!

But not everything was rosy. When Bob Wallace suddenly left Lamborghini in 1975 the Countach LP 400 was a far from perfect car. Over the years Valentino had his work cut out in testing and developing the Countach. Then, together with multiple time World Rally Champion Sandro Munari, Valentino tested and developed the many Diablo variants that Sant'Agata's engineers dreamt up and sent his way. The work was hard and sometimes dangerous. Prototype testing was particularly challenging as the early work was almost always carried out in the middle of the night to keep the new car away from the prying eyes of motoring journalists and rival supercar manufacturers, while the later stages of prototype testing involved high-speed manoeuvres in an as yet incompletely tested vehicle.

Valentino took up the reins of the Murciélago's test and development programme as soon as the development work on the Diablo range finally stopped. At his first meeting with Luc Donckerwolke, the Murciélago's designer, Valentino famously quipped, 'Ah, you are the man who designed the engine cover.' When Donckerwolke patiently tried to explain that he had designed the whole car and not just the engine bonnet, Valentino quickly and gently teased him by saying, 'That's right. We did the engine and you did the bit that covers it.' Valentino's wit was as brisk as his driving.

Standard Italian government employment legislation meant that Valentino Balboni was finally forced to retire from Lamborghini in October 2008, but he was kept on as a brand ambassador and an occasional consultant. In 2009 the company showed just how much it respected Valentino by launching a limited edition model called the Gallardo LP 550-2 Valentino Balboni. This rare two-wheel-drive car was born with inherent provenance, so it comes as no surprise to find that it remains one of the most sought-after Gallardo variants.

Valentino Balboni oozes charisma tempered with humility. It is never anything other than a pleasure to meet up with him and hear his tales of Lamborghini's earlier days. In 2014 Matthias Pfannmüller published a study of Balboni's career called *The Best Job in the World: Lamborghini Test Driver*. If Bob Wallace was Lamborghini's mythical but taciturn first Chief Test Driver, the far more personable Balboni can rightly be called Sant'Agata's legendary Chief Test Driver.

about eighty hours here, most of which was spent correcting paint blemishes so that every Diablo reached its owner boasting a mirror-like bodyshell. Road testing was also headquartered at this new facility, from where Valentino Balboni and his tiny team tested every Diablo on the real-world roads around and far beyond the factory. Each car was road tested for a minimum of 145km (90 miles) and two hours, after which the car was returned back to the finishing facility to correct any final cosmetic blemishes.

At the time it took about twenty-two hours to make a Fiat Punto and 1,200 hours to make a Lamborghini Countach. By comparison, it took Sant'Agata's artisans about 500 hours to make a Lamborghini Diablo.

MEETING THE DEMAND

Following the Diablo's Monte Carlo debut, the list of customers who put their names down for Lamborghini's new flagship car continued to grow. Novaro was determined that speculators should not profit at the expense of genuine Lamborghini enthusiasts, and he felt that the best way to deter these parasites would be to ensure that all orders for the Diablo were delivered quickly. This ambition dovetailed with Lee Iacocca's own desire that Lamborghini rapidly increase its production capacity so that Chrysler's investments in Sant'Agata could be recouped as soon as possible. While a few prototype and pre-series cars were delivered to some dealer franchises in

Under Chrysler's ownership quality control took on a whole new meaning at Sant'Agata.

July 1990, the first series production Diablos were delivered in late August and early September 1990. Dealers in Italy, France, Germany, the United Kingdom, Belgium, Monaco and Spain received their demonstration cars from this batch, while franchises in other countries received their demonstrators in October and November. By the end of January 1991 Sant'Agata had delivered almost 100 cars.

The favoured dealers who had been privileged enough to receive very early cars were tasked with a particularly difficult assignment: they had to drive these demonstrators a minimum of 10,000km within the first six months following delivery and file regular reports on the distance covered, any breakdowns or faults encountered, and the car's fuel consumption in different weather conditions. The German Lamborghini franchise in Landau, Gustav Hoecker, was the first to complete this delightful but arduous assignment, and their reports back to Sant'Agata were highly positive. The Hoecker dossier was particularly valuable to Marmiroli and his engineering team as the vast majority of the driving had been carried out at high speed on Germany's unrestricted autobahns.

Homologation also went apace, with the Diablo getting United States approval in late 1990 and passing the particularly tough Swiss tests (the Swiss noise limits are draconian) in January 1991. Japanese certification was obtained in early 1991 and the first Japanese customer cars were delivered in mid-1991. The Lamborghini Diablo was now seriously chewing tarmac all around the world.

CHAPTER 6

DIABLO VT: RADICAL EVOLUTION

The Lamborghini Diablo VT was not a revolutionary car. It was a direct descendant of the Diablo, and its fundamental elements could be traced back to the Countach, except for one radical innovation. This unique and state-of-the art development was the Diablo's ingenious four-wheel-drive system. Called the Viscous Traction system, and so giving the new model variant its name, this complex mechanism was introduced to improve the Diablo's driveability, road-holding, handling and safety profile, especially at the outer limits of its performance envelope.

The Diablo VT was launched in March 1993 at the Geneva Motor Show, alongside Ford's new Mondeo. Lamborghini's parent company Chrysler and Ford had been longstanding and fierce rivals, but the US$6 billion that Ford had spent developing the Mondeo did not allow it to overshadow Sant'Agata's latest offering. Not even the Ferrari 348 Spider and the brand-new Aston Martin DB7, both of which debuted at this Geneva show, could steal the VT variant's limelight.

The Diablo VT was much more than just its new all-wheel-drive system. Almost 1,500 of the original Diablo's 6,000 components were either modified or entirely replaced with the introduction of the Diablo VT, and the Viscous Traction system, and the nine other major developments, demanded many totally new parts.

The Countach and the original Diablo both suffered from a tendency to oversteer. Sant'Agata had known of this defect

The Diablo VT, the first model variant of the range, was launched in March 1993.

since the mid-1970s, and each new Countach derivation had incorporated further suspension geometry alterations to try to quell this unwanted tendency of the car to tuck its nose into the apex of a curve. Sandro Munari, the acclaimed World Rally Champion, was employed by Lamborghini in 1987 to tame the new 25th Anniversary Countach's tail, a task he partly succeeded in. Munari asked for changes to the 25th Anniversary's Pirelli tyre construction and made many small but significant alterations to the car's suspension layout, after which he declared the 25th Anniversary to be more 'Sincera' than its predecessors. By this he meant that the car was now not only less prone to oversteer, but that when it did break away it did so progressively and only after giving an attentive driver plenty of warning that it was about to do so. But even this last iteration of the Countach had a tendency to oversteer under high cornering forces, and one of Marmiroli's key design briefs for the Diablo was to make it more driveable.

Immediately after his work on the 25th Anniversary was done Munari started work with Marmiroli on the dynamics of the original Diablo, and again his brief was to make Sant'Agata's new flagship more neutral in its roadholding and more driveable in its handling. Most of Sant'Agata's customers were not blessed with the seat-of-the-pants sensitivity of a rally champion or the blink-of-an-eye reflexes of a racing driver, but many would want to test the performance and handling claims that Lamborghini made for its latest supercar. Since the days of the Miura, Sant'Agata had enjoyed the custom of many whose wallets were deeper than their driving talents. To illustrate this point consider an entirely true story centred around the 1969 film *The Italian Job*, the opening scene of which shows a Lamborghini Miura being tossed over the edge of a cliff. When the film's producers approached Lamborghini for a Miura for this spectacle, Sant'Agata told them that their budget would not stretch to a new car, but they could have their choice of one of the many bashed-up Miuras that had been returned to the factory after their wealthy owners had run out of genius, flair and luck on the roads. Ferruccio Lamborghini grew so tired of Miura owners sending back accident-damaged Miuras that his original plan was that the Countach would only be sold in very small numbers, and then only to previously vetted customers who he knew could handle its very high performance. Accident-prone Miuras and Countachs were great for the profits of the factory's repair and restoration division, but were very bad news for Lamborghini's reputation for building safe and driveable supercars.

The VT variant's radical innovation was its unique and state-of-the art four-wheel-drive system, which Lamborghini called the Viscous Traction system.

VISCOUS TRACTION

Chrysler too were keen to ensure that the Diablo was a safe and useable car, especially as a key market was the litigious United States. Right from its conception, Lamborghini under the stewardship of the Mimran brothers had anticipated that its new flagship would need an all-wheel-drive system to keep up with its forthcoming rivals. The original 1990 Diablo should have been launched with a four-wheel-drive option, but the technology was simply not ready in time. Motoring magazine reviews of the original 1990 two-wheel-drive Diablo confirmed Patrick Mimran's and Luigi Marmiroli's assessment that the Diablo would benefit from an all-wheel-drive system: journalists found the Diablo to be more stable and driveable than the Countach in high-speed turns, but power oversteer was always only an injudicious throttle pedal stab away, particularly in the damp. Sant'Agata's Viscous Traction system could not come a moment too soon.

Marmiroli once described the Viscous Traction system as 'so simple that it could have been designed by a boy'. While that statement was clearly a gross exaggeration, incorporating an all-wheel-drive system into the Diablo was made infinitely easier because of the car's south-north engine-gearbox orientation. Yet again, the Countach was acting as a pathfinder for Sant'Agata's flagships, a role that it would effortlessly continue to perform for the Murciélago and the Aventador in due course. Stanzani's revolutionary idea for the Countach of placing the gearbox ahead of the engine and allowing the drive to first go forwards to the gearbox before returning backwards to the differential (courtesy of a set of drop-gears and an in-sump driveshaft) meant that the forward-placed gearbox was beautifully positioned to also provide drive to the front axle.

Sant'Agata intensively investigated the various engineering options for a four-wheel-drive system before settling on the Viscous Traction system. Marmiroli's team also researched a fully mechanical permanent all-wheel-drive system and a hydraulic part-time all-wheel-drive system, and got as far as building prototypes of each before rejecting these two alternatives. Marmiroli was keen on a part-time system because it afforded the best of both worlds, as he said, 'It gives you two cars – one two-wheel drive, one four'. Of the two part-time systems that he investigated, Marmiroli found the Viscous Traction system to be superior to the hydraulic part-time system.

The red VT lettering on this Diablo's rump advertises its all-wheel-drive technology

With the Viscous Traction system very little torque is directed to the front wheels for the vast majority of the time. The Diablo wears very wide rear tyres (Pirelli P Zeros measuring 335/35 ZR 17), which do not break traction very easily. This is particularly so as the Diablo has a front-to-rear weight distribution of 41.3 per cent and 58.7 per cent respectively. Even with these extra wide tyres and this advantageous weight distribution, however, the rear tyres might lose grip and start to spin under certain conditions, such as during hard cornering, in the damp, or when unexpectedly encountering mud or spilt oil on the road. Marmiroli stated that one of his principal aims with the VT variant was to eliminate traction problems when the driver was trying to put down a lot of power on a damp road with the car in first or second gear. Sant'Agata claimed that the viscous coupling system 'unifies the functions of torque differential and anti-slip, offering superb traction in all conditions'. Lamborghini also repeatedly emphasised that no mud or snow tyres would be available for the Diablo VT, and that this variant would not feature any electronic safety devices such as traction control or anti-skid technology that might compromise 'the driver's sensitivity'.

Once the rear tyres did break traction, the Viscous Traction system allowed for up to 25 per cent of the Diablo's torque to be directed almost instantly to the front axle, thereby enabling the front tyres to play their part in deploying more of the car's torque onto the tarmac without fuss or incident. Additionally the Viscous Traction system improved the Diablo's active safety profile by improving stability and by reducing the car's tendency to oversteer. Even

Almost 1,500 of the original Diablo's 6,000 components were either modified or entirely replaced with the introduction of the Diablo VT.

with four-wheel drive the Diablo could be provoked into oversteer, in fact almost at will in damp conditions, but the VT variant resisted this tendency for far longer, gave more warning when the car was about to go into a spin, and was a little easier to catch once that threshold had been breached, compared to its two-wheel-drive counterpart.

One of the dangers of neutering any car with a four-wheel-drive system is that the engineers overstep the fine dividing line between reducing the tendency to oversteer and the proclivity to remorseless understeer. Marmiroli's team took great care to avoid falling into this trap as persistent understeer would have been a very undesirable trait in such a focused supercar. Instead they designed the VT variant so that a moderately talented driver could incite the car into controlled oversteer, without kicking off an embryonic accident from which only a Senna or Schumacher could recover. Sandro Munari elaborated on the Diablo VT's dynamics: 'The VT feels different on the road. When you enter a bend you can get help from the front. So if you get oversteer you can stop it by accelerating or keeping the power on.'

The Diablo's Viscous Traction system consisted of a viscous coupling integrated into the forward-placed gearbox. An additional casing positioned in front of the gearbox housed a carbon fibre driveshaft taking torque to the limited-slip front differential and the front half-shafts driving the front tyres (245/40 ZR 17). The rear differential and the rear tyres (335/35 ZR 17) were driven in conventional Countach and early Diablo fashion, utilising the drop-gear sets and an in-sump driveshaft. Alongside the VT variant's centre differential with viscous coupling, this new car boasted a bevel gear-type front differential with a 2.81:1 ratio and a 25 per cent limited slip, and a bevel gear-type rear differential with a 2.41:1 ratio and a 45 per cent slip. The front transfer ratio was 0.8:1 and the rear transfer ratio was 1.59:1.

The car still used a dry single-plate clutch and its gear ratios were also unchanged :

	Ratio	*Maximum speed*
1st	1: 2.312	97km/h (60mph)
2nd	1:1.524	148km/h (92mph)
3rd	1:1.125	200km/h (124mph)
4th	1:0.888	255km/h (158mph)
5th	1:0.676	325km/hg (202mph)
Reverse	1:2.125	106km/h (66mph)

Despite the additional frictional forces and the extra weight of the VT variant's four-wheel-drive system, Sant'Agata claimed the same fuel economy figures and the same performance statistics for the VT variant as for its two-wheel-drive predecessor. The official performance figures released by Lamborghini for the Diablo VT were a top speed of 325km/h (201.9mph) and 0–100km/h and standing kilometre times of 4.09 and 20.7 seconds respectively. The factory stats for fuel economy were 20.21ltr/100km (14mpg) for the standard EPA highway cycle dropping down to 31.44ltr/100km (9mpg) for the standard EPA city cycle. Expressed according to speed, this translated to 13.3ltr/100km at 90km/h and 15.2ltr/100km at 120km/h. Factory literature quoted the Diablo as having a kerb weight of 1,625kg (3,579lb), with a front-to-rear weight distribution of 41 per cent/59 per cent.

The VT variant carried over the original Diablo's engine pretty much unchanged.

One of the key objectives of introducing the Viscous Traction system was to quell the Diablo's tendency to power oversteer.

Sandro Munari's brief was to make Sant'Agata's latest flagship more neutral in its roadholding and more driveable in its handling.

POWER-ASSISTED STEERING

The second major advance that the Diablo VT pioneered was power-assisted steering. Lamborghini customers had been complaining of the Countach's heavy and unwieldly steering since its 1974 debut, and these protestations only increased in volume and frequency as the Countach grew in weight and front tyre width. From its conception, Marmiroli and his development team had planned for the Countach's successor to have the luxury of power-assisted steering. But there were also dissenting voices that put forward the very legitimate argument that any power-assisted steering system would rob the Diablo of the tactility and sensitivity that can only be found with a pure, non-assisted, manual steering system. The authors, for instance, believe that the criticism levelled at the Countach's non-assisted system is grossly exaggerated. It is undoubtedly true that the steering in any Countach and the first version of the Diablo requires both serious muscle and dedication at very low speeds, particularly during parking manoeuvres. In both cars, however, the steering weight lightens up greatly once travelling at more than 5mph (8km/h), and is perfectly exploitable once past 15mph (24km/h). In return for some physical effort and minimal inconvenience, the driver is compensated with an unparalleled level of communication about the road's surface texture through the steering wheel, as well as superlatively detailed feedback about the asphalt's undulations.

The original 1990 Diablo should have been launched with a four-wheel-drive option, but the technology was simply not ready in time.

For many people this would be a perfectly desirable trade-off in an exotic, highly specialised performance car that 99 per cent of owners would only use on high days and holy days. But Lamborghini's new customers were anticipated to want a more usable and more driver-friendly car, so Marmiroli never had any realistic alternative but to bow down before market expectations and design the Diablo with power steering. The assisted rack-and-pinion system that eventually manifested in the Diablo was designed by TRW and had 3.2 turns lock-to-lock, while affording the car a kerb-to-kerb turning circle of 13 metres (42.7ft).

A key design brief was that the power assistance should not corrupt the messages coming from the road surface through to the steering wheel, particularly at high speed. Power-assisted steering systems of that era were sometimes classic sensory deprivation ordeals. Assisted steering systems are by their sheer nature filters that siphon off kick-backs over road bumps, creating barriers that subtract from the natural feedback sent from the front tyres through the steering column to the driver, and too often they have little or no self-centring, particularly from the almost straight ahead steering position.

Incorporating an all-wheel-drive system into the Diablo was made infinitely easier because of the car's south-north engine-gearbox orientation.

Sant'Agata claimed that its Viscous Coupling system 'unifies the functions of torque differential and anti-slip, offering superb traction in all conditions'.

TRW and Sant'Agata therefore decided upon an arrangement in which the degree of power assistance decreased with increasing speed and with the degree of angulation away from the straight-ahead position of the steering wheel. Essentially the driver had to exert more steering effort in direct proportion to the car's speed, and in direct proportion to the arc through which the steering wheel had been turned – so more muscle at high speeds and in tight corners. The VT variant's new steering system was a great success, receiving much praise from customers and motoring journalists alike for offering easy manoeuvrability at parking speeds, but accurate and sensorial control at high speeds.

SMOOTHING THE RIDE

The third key innovation seen with the VT variant was the introduction of electronic damping. In their glossy 1992 news communiqué, Lamborghini described this innovation as an 'intelligent suspension system' that would contribute towards optimum driver and passenger comfort and safety at all times without compromising on driveability or driving dynamics. Designed and built by Koni, this new damping system featured electronic shock-absorber control with an automatic setting as well as four different levels of shock-absorber hardness settings that the driver could set from within the cockpit. In fully automatic mode stiffness of the VT variant's shock-absorbers was governed by the car's speed and predetermined electronic maps that had been derived from extensive road testing on different road surfaces and in different conditions. In manual mode the driver could select his or her preferred shock-absorber stiffness setting from a console-mounted switch. This manual arrangement incorporated an automatic safety override feature, overruling the driver's selection whenever necessary, whereby the shock absorbers progressively assumed an ever stiffer bias as the car passed through the 130km/h (81mph) barrier, the 190km/h (118mph) barrier and finally the 250km/h (155mph) barrier. For example, if the driver manually chose the 'soft ride' program, but then drove at unduly high speeds, the

Should the rear tyres break traction, the Viscous Traction system allows for up to 25 per cent of the Diablo's torque to be almost instantly directed to the front axle.

Even with its four-wheel-drive system the Diablo VT could be provoked into oversteer, in fact almost at will in damp conditions, but the Viscous Traction technology resisted this tendency for far longer.

onboard computer would automatically dictate that the shock absorbers assume a stiffer bias. The shock absorbers would only revert to the driver's chosen 'soft ride' program setting once the car's speed had dropped below the safety threshold set by the pre-programmed computer maps. The VT's suspension system was otherwise unchanged from the original two-wheel-drive Diablo's suspension with the same independent front and rear layout featuring double wishbones all around, gas shock absorbers, coil springs, anti-roll bars and anti-squat and anti-dive technology.

The innovative but unsuccessful two-and-a-half-tier dash binnacle found in the original Diablo was abandoned for

The second major advance that the Diablo VT pioneered was power-assisted steering. The degree of power steering assistance in the Diablo VT decreased with increasing speed, and with the degree of angulation away from the straight ahead position of the steering wheel.

A key design brief for the power-steering system was not to corrupt the messages coming from the road surface through to the steering wheel, particularly at high speed.

the VT variant and a more conventional instrument panel took its place instead. The supposed visual physiology principles underpinning the original Diablo's dash as espoused by Renato Meduri were always very suspect, and the vast height of the binnacle blocked the driver's view of the road ahead and was totally impractical for street driving. Customers and journalists alike complained about the slit-like visibility forced upon them by the towering dashboard and Sant'Agata therefore abandoned Meduri's monolithic dash at the first opportunity for an altogether shorter and simpler affair. The VT variant's redesigned instrument binnacle was about 2 inches (5cm) lower, and the speedometer and tachometer now resided in the centre of the dashboard with the secondary gauges surrounding them. With white markings on a black background and orange gauge needles, the new dash was a great success, aiding readability, outwards visibility and therefore passive safety. Sadly the dash binnacle was now fixed and its angle could no longer be altered, though that was a small price to pay all things considered.

Unusually for a cutting-edge 1993 supercar, the Diablo VT did not have ABS. At its debut Lamborghini had not yet developed a reliable anti-brake-locking system, but Sant'Agata's engineers had not been totally idle on the braking system front. The VT variant was launched with new four-piston Brembo alloy brake calipers, which were much better at dissipating heat. To further enhance the airflow to the front brakes, the air inlets mounted on the front air dam-cum-spoiler were enlarged to allow for greater inflow of ambient temperature air. Thus cooled, the VT variant's modified braking system shortened the car's braking distance, and also decreased the brake fade seen after repeated, vigorous high-speed braking manoeuvres.

The 1990 Diablo had developed an unwanted reputation for its dog-leg gear lever snapping in half during forceful gear changes. Lamborghini addressed this problem in the VT variant by altering the composition of the metal alloy used for the gear lever. The new four-wheel-drive car also boasted improved cabin ventilation courtesy of two new air extractor vents in the rear of the cockpit, and enhanced occupant comfort through the indulgence of a pair of all important coat hooks! Of more concern to most owners was Sant'Agata's upgrading of the Diablo's electrical system in the search for greater reliability, and an enlargement of the car's sill air inlets/scoops to allow in more air to ensure that the car's oil coolers did not overheat in hot climes or on the track. The VT variant's engine bay was also finished in carbon fibre, both for aesthetics and also for better noise insulation. On the noise front, a change to the car's ignition timing drew a mixed reception from customers: some liked the resultant muted engine note, but many lamented that the VT was a trifle emasculated, having now lost a little of its vigorous and strident shriek.

Other than the enlarged sill and front spoiler air scoops, the VT variant's bodywork and interior and exterior dimensions were unchanged compared to its 1990 predecessor. The same went for the car's drivetrain (except for

At the first opportunity Sant'Agata abandoned Meduri's monolithic tri-level dashboard for an altogether shorter and simpler affair.

The third key innovation seen with the Diablo VT variant was the introduction of electronic damping.

Unusually for a cutting-edge 1993 supercar, the Diablo VT did not have ABS.

Symmetrical gorgeousness, but also an illustration of form following function, in this case to vent copious amounts of hot engine bay air efficiently.

its modified ignition timing, a very slightly redesigned but considerably strengthened bottom-end, and a beefed-up valvetrain), its square-section steel alloy tubular space-frame chassis with carbon fibre bracing, its wheel dimensions (OZ Racing three-piece aluminium alloy 8.5x17 fronts and 13x17 rears) and its tyre sizes (Pirelli P-Zero 245/40ZR 17 fronts and 335/35ZR 17 rears). Sant'Agata claimed the same 492bhp (362kW) at 6,800rpm and 428lb ft (580Nm) at 5,200rpm from the VT's 5707cc all-alloy, naturally aspirated, 48-valve, quad cam, fuel-injected, Bizzarrini-derived V12 engine. Contrary to some internet speculation and forum reports, a large rear wing was not standard on the VT variant, and a rear wing is not a differentiating feature between the earlier two-wheel-drive car and the later four-wheel-drive car. The rear wing was an expensive optional extra that a customer could specify, along with a fitted luggage set and an upgraded stereo system with a compact disc player.

A total of 529 Diablo VT units were produced between 1993 and 1998.

Apart from enlarged sill and front spoiler air scoops, the Diablo VT's bodywork and interior and exterior dimensions were largely unchanged compared to its 1990 predecessor.

Enough space for a toothbrush and a credit card.

A Diablo VT and a 88 ½ Countach 5000 QV in the grounds of their designer's house. Marcello Gandini styled both.

CHAPTER 7

DIABLO SE30: THE ANNIVERSARY ROAD RACER

Sant'Agata designed the Lamborghini Diablo SE30 to be a number-plate-wearing, road-legal racing car. It was designed to compete in the Italian Supercar GT Championship where it would go head-to-head against the likes of the Ferrari F40 and the Porsche RSR, but equally it would have to compete for sales against pure road cars like the street versions of the Bugatti EB110 and the Jaguar XJ220. At the farthest reaches, it would even have to count the iconic McLaren F1 as a rival. The SE30 met the challenge of its very wide brief through a three-pronged approach: weight reduction, increased power and new suspension technology. This limited edition supercar cost about £175,000 at its launch during 'Lamborghini Day 3' festivities at the factory in Sant'Agata Bolognese on 23 September 1993. This meant that it cost about £16,000 more than a regular Diablo VT. For this additional outlay the lucky new owner lost 176kg in the car's kerb weight, gained an additional 28bhp, and acquired a car with acres of Alcantara, lashings of carbon fibre, and a much more dramatic and aerodynamic bodyshell.

The Lamborghini Diablo SE30 was remarkable because it was the second variant of the Diablo that Sant'Agata launched in 1993. Never before had Lamborghini launched two flagship variants within a single calendar year. This feat was made necessary due to a rare combination of factors that threatened Lamborghini's long-term viability. It is impossible to write a comprehensive account of the Diablo, or to appreciate the SE30 in its entirety, without understanding the contemporary social and political situation and the economic challenges then facing the factory.

The Diablo SE30 was a limited edition supercar designed to uphold Sant'Agata's honour against rivals through a three-pronged approach: weight reduction, increased power and new suspension technology.

The early 1990s was a turbulent time for Lamborghini and its finances. Ubaldo Sgarzi, its Sales Director, had survived through some of the company's most challenging times and was delighted with the financial security that Chrysler brought with it. He was not going to squander this precious opportunity. Together with Emile Novaro, the Chairman, and Sandro Munari, Lamborghini's Test Driver and Public Relations executive, Sgarzi had engineered the 'Lamborghini Day 2' festivities in Monte Carlo with great care and precision to attract the most promising potential Diablo customers to the event. Their hard work in showcasing Lamborghini's new flagship paid off handsomely, and by the end of that launch weekend Sgarzi had secured enough orders to keep the Diablo production line in work for many months. Chrysler's Lee Iacocca was keen to see a quick return on his investment, and Novaro was keen to ensure that speculators did not profit through the scarcity of this new much sought-after bauble, so these two men shared a common goal in maximising the factory's output of Diablo cars. Lamborghini sent many Diablos out through the factory gates in 1990 and 1991, and in return money poured into Sant'Agata's coffers. Lamborghini had never had it so good. There was financial security through Detroit's largesse, and for once the company was actually earning its own way through sales: in 1991 Lamborghini's financial balance sheet actually showed a profit.

THE IMPACT OF RECESSION

The company's optimism was soon broken by the approaching storm clouds. In the middle of 1990 the United States of America went into recession. There were three underlying reasons for this recession, all of which directly impacted the sort of people who might have been thinking about buying a Lamborghini Diablo. First, the Federal Reserve enacted a restrictive monetary policy to curb rising inflation, and this meant that potential Diablo customers had far less ready cash in their pockets. Second, a collapse in American property prices made would-be Diablo buyers less confident about spending money on a depreciating asset. Finally, there was an oil price shock following Saddam Hussein's invasion of Kuwait on 2 August 1990 as the average price of a barrel of oil rose from US$17 in July to US$36 in August.

Supercar owners still vividly remembered the strict driving restrictions that followed the 1973 oil crisis caused by OAPEC's oil embargo after the start of the Yom Kippur War. They also readily recalled the general public's anti-supercar

The Diablo SE30 variant lost 174kg in kerb weight and gained 28bhp relative to its VT counterpart.

sentiment that followed the 1979 oil crisis, which was caused by the drop in oil production following the Iranian Revolution and the overthrow of the pro-Western Pahlavi dynasty. The Pahlavis had been some of Sant'Agata's best and most celebrated customers. Mohammad Reza Pahlavi, the Shah of Iran, purchased a Miura P400, a Miura S, a Miura SV and an ultra-rare Miura SV/J, which was later sold at auction to the Hollywood actor Nicholas Cage. The Shah's son, Ali-Reza Pahlavi, shared the same birthday as Ferruccio Lamborghini (28 April) and inherited his father's passion for cars, particularly Lamborghinis. The Shah also owned a Lamborghini Espada and two Lamborghini Countachs. It is ironic that this decadent monarch, who loved his flagship Lamborghinis, would later play an indirect part in Sant'Agata's financial misfortunes.

The aphorism 'When America sneezes, the world catches a cold' remained true in 1990 and directly impacted upon Lamborghini. Canada suffered an even deeper recession than the United States, while other major Diablo markets like the United Kingdom, Germany, France, Sweden and Japan were all badly affected. Orders for the Diablo started stuttering before coming to an abrupt halt. It really was as sudden as that.

In his 1992 end-of-tenure report as Chairman of Chrysler, Lee Iacocca wrote:

> *While the past year has not been a good one for Lamborghini and its competitors in the exotic sports car business, and the recession continues to prevent us from resuming the growth of production, nevertheless I am sure that the future for Lamborghini continues to be bright, and that the company will be prepared and able to take advantage of the return of the market when it comes.*

At the same time Emile Novaro wrote: '1992 was made of twelve very difficult months of hard work whilst an exceptional recession was hitting worldwide, weighing very heavily on the automotive industry.' Novaro went on to elaborate that factors as diverse as the Yugoslavian war, the imminent American presidential elections, and the far-reaching implications of the

The Diablo SE30 was a very different car to the Diablo VT. The VT was a road car in the Lamborghini mould, while the SE30 was designed for customers who wanted to go racing.

Maastricht Treaty were all weighing heavily on market sentiment and indirectly impacting on orders for the Lamborghini Diablo. Gianfranco Venturelli, Lamborghini's General Manager, echoed the same sentiments when he wrote:

> *A crisis of major proportions hit all those manufacturers who produce, like us, exotic supercars, deploying a very high level of engineering, technology and knowhow, but producing vehicles in limited series. During the last quarter of 1992 a survey of the market niche to which we belong showed a drop in sales equal to 50% of the average sales of the previous years. Our first and most immediate reaction was to keep production to a minimum level. This is because of a combination of low market demand and heavy stock in some of our markets. 1993 will be a year of great changes and hard work. If we want to survive in a world where competition is fierce we must be able to adapt ourselves to an everchanging world.*

RACING AND THE DIABLO SE30

The Lamborghini Diablo SE30 was the first manifestation of this determination to adapt. Taking as an excuse the thirtieth anniversary of Ferruccio Lamborghini's inauguration of his eponymous supercar company, Sant'Agata launched its second Diablo variant of 1993, the first time that Lamborghini had brought out two wedge-shaped flagship cars within a calendar year. It was a move forced by financial need, but it was also canny.

The Diablo SE30 was a very different car to the Diablo VT. The VT was a road car in the Lamborghini mould while the SE30 was designed for customers who wanted to go racing. The original 1990 Diablo and the VT variant were series production cars, but the SE30 was a limited edition run limited to just 150 units.

The SE stood for Special Edition and the 30 stood for Automobili Lamborghini SpA's Pearl Jubilee. The SE30 was no minor facelift: it was cosmetically very different to its two predecessors, its drivetrain was an amalgam of the original Diablo's and the VT variant's with some added spice thrown in, and its suspension was substantially modified.

The SE30's aggressive aesthetics immediately marked it out. It was much more arrow-shaped, even compared to the already extreme wedge shape of the regular Diablos. In the search for improved aerodynamic efficiency, the lower edge of the front spoiler was made more protuberant, and this, together with a more angular front air dam, lent the SE30 a combative and bellicose air. New slatted brake cooling ducts with three horizontal bars on either side of a broad central pillar now took up residence between the front spoiler and the front air dam. The gold-on-black Lamborghini Raging Bull emblem, which in earlier variants was raised and positioned towards the base of the front bonnet, was now relocated into a recessed triangular depression in the forward-sloping front air dam. The front three-quarters view of the SE30 was notable for the modified air scoops located just ahead of the rear wheels in the car's lower sills. The previous variants had featured quadrilateral scoops with three horizontal blades, but this latest variant showcased an altogether different look with two diagonal and backward-sloping blades forming three almost vertical air inlet vents. These fed air at ambient temperature to two redesigned and enlarged oil-coolers.

The SE stood for Special Edition and the 30 stood for Automobili Lamborghini SpA's Pearl Jubilee.

The rear of the SE30 was also subject to considerable alteration to improve engine-bay cooling and aesthetics. The engine compartment bonnet was redesigned with a slatted Venetian blind-type carbon fibre lid as first seen in the Lamborghini Miura. The rear bumper-cum-spoiler unit was redesigned to incorporate the reversing and rear fog lights and the rear grille now featured a Raging Bull emblem at one end and a thirtieth anniversary wreath logo at the other. For the first time in the Diablo's history a rear aerofoil came as standard equipment. This massive rear spoiler had

The SE30 was a limited edition run of just 150 units. This Hong Kong-based car is Chassis 0001.

The SE30's aggressive aesthetics mark it out immediately. It is much more arrow-shaped, even compared to the already extreme wedge shape of the regular Diablos.

The SE30's new rear wheel arch air scoops showcased an altogether different look, with two diagonal and backward-sloping blades forming three almost vertical air inlet vents.

The SE30's engine compartment bonnet was redesigned with a slatted Venetian blind-type carbon fibre lid as first seen in the Lamborghini Miura.

two backward-sloping vertical struts, ran the full width of the car, and its end-plates curved downwards dramatically, almost but not quite touching the rear bodywork. This rear aerofoil featured a central trim tab whose angle of attack could easily and readily be adjusted by the driver to suit his or her driving style, or to best accommodate the characteristics and peculiarities of any given race circuit.

The Diablo SE30's cabin was also racetrack oriented with thinly padded carbon fibre racing buckets taking the place of sumptuous leather seats. Four-point racing harnesses instead of three-point inertia-reel seat belts now came as standard, while crotch straps and a full roll cage were available as optional extras. Carbon fibre and Alcantara trim dominated the cockpit. Parts of the sills, inner door skins, central tunnel and centre console were all encased in carbon composite. In lieu of leather, swatches of the grippy Alcantara covered the seats, the headrests and the remaining parts of the central console, the dashboard and the binnacle. For a princely sum Sant'Agata would oblige track-oriented customers with an inbuilt fire extinguisher system for their new quasi-racing car.

Mass is always the enemy of performance, and to optimise the SE30's acceleration, braking and turning capabilities, Lamborghini saved considerable weight by specifying the SE30 with two-wheel drive and manual rack and pinion steering only. Power steering was available as an SE30 optional extra, and the factory produced a supplementary booklet for owners, except those in Switzerland and North America, detailing the availability of power steering as well as the exact sequence to be followed to check the power steering fluid level. This was quite a complicated process because the power steering fluid reservoir was hidden behind a composite panel on the right-hand side of the engine compartment that had to be removed to access the reservoir. Lamborghini also rejected many previously standard luxury items such as air-conditioning, a high fidelity sound system (although a pair of now redundant speaker grilles remained) and electric windows for its hardcore SE30.

Instead of conventional glass side windows the SE30 had lightweight, fixed Plexiglass panels. At the bottom rear corner of each Plexiglass panel there was a tiny manually operated window. Electric windows motors are heavy, and in the previous Diablo variants these motors were placed high up within the guillotine doors. Eschewing electric windows for the SE30 not only eliminated all this weight, but as a bonus helped lower the SE30's centre of gravity. Another welcome bonus of losing the window motor and its associated mass was that it was now much easier to open and close the scissor doors. In a pragmatic nod to the fact that a potentially very hot V12 engine was housed within inches of the cockpit, and that many SE30s would be sold to and driven in warm climes, Sant'Agata relented and allowed air-conditioning to be specified as a no-cost option.

The Alcantara-clad racing buckets were great at holding the driver and passenger firmly in position during hard cornering but afforded little adjustability, so it was fortunate

The lower edge of the SE30's front spoiler was made more protuberant in the search for improved aerodynamic efficiency.

The SE30's bodyshell was more sensuous, more dramatic and more aerodynamic.

For the first time in the Diablo's history a rear aerofoil came as standard.

The Diablo SE30's cabin was race-oriented with thinly padded carbon fibre racing buckets.

that the SE30's steering column remained fully adjustable through a wide range for both reach and rake. In keeping with its racing ambitions, the SE30 had drilled foot pedals and a smaller diameter flat-bottomed steering wheel, as seen in some contemporary track cars. The dashboard gauges were racy in design with orange needles contrasting against white dial faces carrying red markings. The SE30 variant had a carbon fibre gear knob to save every last gram, but it suffered from a significantly heavier clutch pedal than its VT sibling. This discrepancy was explained by the fact that, although the SE30's clutch plate measured the same 10-inch diameter as the VT's clutch plate, it was thicker and so more effort was needed to move its increased mass.

The SE30 retained the same Bizzarrini-derived, naturally aspirated, water-cooled 5707cc, 48-valve, quad-cam V12 running a compression ratio of 10:1, but the engine had now been modified with larger diameter inlet valves, a reprogrammed LIE electronic fuel injection map, a more free-flowing exhaust system, and a 7kg lighter crankshaft. The lower inertia and frictional losses that accompanied the crankshaft's lower mass, together with the engine's more free-breathing induction and exhaust systems, liberated an additional 28bhp, taking the SE30's maximum power output to around 520bhp (386kW/525cv) at 7,100rpm. The car's maximum torque output remained unchanged at 580Nm (428lb ft), but this was now delivered higher up the rev range at 5,900rpm instead of at 5,200rpm as in the case of the VT variant. The SE30's increased power output demanded bigger water radiators to keep the powerplant cool, and its faster acceleration and higher top speed dictated harder brake pads, so these items came as standard.

The SE30 could also be ordered with a racing-style crash gearbox in which the luxury of synchromesh was only available on first and reverse gears. This was entirely in keeping with the SE30's design brief as a road-legal racing car. Even the engine bay now looked more purposeful with magnesium (instead of aluminium) intake manifolds and cam covers. The top surface of the engine was finished in a gold colour, with a central spine in silver, while two massive black air ducts dominated the nethermost region of the engine compartment. The central spine carried a gold Raging Bull

Note the steering wheel has a squared-off bottom segment.

An incredibly low mileage icon. Note where the yellow and red segments start on the rev counter.

The interior of SE30 Chassis 0001.

emblem, below which was the word 'Diablo' in red, and below that again was the engine's firing order, also in the same bright red.

For the first time in Lamborghini's road car history, traction control made its debut with the SE30. Sant'Agata's traction control system was very advanced for its day, and much of its technology was derived from Lamborghini's brief involvement in Formula One. The SE30's traction control system could be switched off completely, or the driver could use a console-mounted switch to set the system to only intervene in any one of three intermediate tyre grip versus torque output situations. If the traction control system detected that a wheel was about to spin, it would cut the fuel flow to the injectors and thereby reduce the engine's torque output until full traction was re-established. The traction control system essentially ensured that grunt never triumphed over grip.

The SE30 also set another first in offering wholly in-cockpit adjustable anti-roll bars. The anti-roll bars could be set to one of three positions. To adjust the suspension so that it could best absorb large bumps, the anti-roll bars had to be set to their highest mounting point, so softening the suspension and allowing the rear tyres the best possible traction on undulating surfaces. As the anti-roll bars were adjusted to their remaining two settings, they adopted ever lower mounting points and became ever stiffer, and in the process minimised the car's tendency to roll while also optimising the rear axle's dynamic response. There was common agreement among the contemporary motoring press that, compared to the original 1990 two-wheel-drive car's set-up, the SE30's modified suspension was much more precise, neutral and consistent in hard cornering, while also being more refined and composed during less aggressive driving manoeuvres.

Lamborghini's latest flagship still did not have an anti-brake-locking system, and it retained the same ventilated

Headlights up as it's party time at the Museo Ferruccio Lamborghini.

Who can blame the owner?

If you've got it, flaunt it!

front and rear brake discs measuring 330mm in diameter and 32mm in width, and 284mm in diameter and 22mm in width, respectively. But it did feature the aforementioned harder brake pads, which were clamped by four-pot alloy brake calipers. The SE30 also had subtly altered shock-absorber and spring rates to take into account its lower mass. To further improve handling and roadholding Sant'Agata's engineers lightened some components of the SE30's double wishbone suspension, and used cast magnesium alloy wheels instead of the aluminium alloy wheels used in the earlier Diablo variants. Even the SE30's wheel nuts were put on a diet as they were now made of titanium. The new one-piece magnesium OZ Racing wheels were a visual delight, deeply cupped but with slightly convex faces, and with five almost circular holes in the Lamborghini Bravo tradition. They had the words 'Special Edition' printed on them. By using these special magnesium wheels and titanium wheel nuts, Sant'Agata saved almost 25 per cent in weight over its aluminium equivalents. As this was all unsprung mass, it contributed massively to the SE30's improved handling and roadholding.

To keep the SE30's prodigious power output under control its rear wheels were increased in diameter. The car's front wheel size remained unchanged at 8.5 x 17 inches in diameter but the rear wheel size was increased by an inch to 13 x 18 inches. Both front and rear tyre sizes were changed to 235/40 ZR 17 and 335/30 ZR 18 respectively.

The SE30 looked more sleek and mean than its predecessors because it was longer at 4,550mm (179.1in), and had a larger front overhang at 1,010mm (39.7in). All its other bodyshell dimensions were unchanged. Its maximum power of 520bhp at 7,100rpm and maximum torque of 428lb ft at 5,900rpm propelled it from a standing start to 100km/h in 3.9 seconds, and to the standing kilometre in 20.7 seconds en route to a top speed of 333km/h (207mph). Sant'Agata claimed a kerb weight of 1,449kg for the SE30 against a kerb weight of 1,625kg for the VT variant – the prize for abandoning heavy power-steering and four-wheel-drive systems, and using lots of expensive but lightweight magnesium, carbon fibre and Alcantara. Gordon Murray, the designer of Brabham Formula One cars and the iconic McLaren F1, has claimed that 'I've never driven a car that weighed more than 1,400–1,500kg that I could honestly say was a true sports car'. Well, the V12-engined Lamborghini Diablo SE30's weight fell just within Murray's target range for delivering truly sporting driving dynamics.

Diablo SE30 fuel consumption

90km/h	15.1ltr/100km	18.7mpg
120km/h	16.6ltr/100km	17.0mpg
City	29.7ltr/100km	9.5mpg

At its launch the limited edition SE30 was the pinnacle of Sant'Agata's offerings. The first Diablo SE30 was delivered to its owner in June 1994, and the last SE30 passed through the factory gates in late November 1995. Especially in its signature fluorescent metallic purple, the SE30 remains one of the most exclusive and most desirable Diablos ever built.

Instead of conventional glass side windows the SE30 had lightweight, fixed Plexiglass panels. Within that there was a tiny manually operated window.

Swatches of Alcantara everywhere. Note the perforated accelerator pedal.

The SE30's engine was modified with larger diameter inlet valves, a reprogrammed LIE electronic fuel injection map, a more free-flowing exhaust system, and a 7kg lighter crankshaft.

The SE30's maximum power output was a substantial 520bhp at 7,100rpm, and an equally respectable 580Nm at 5,900rpm.

LAMBORGHINI DIABLO SE30 JOTA

But even within this highly desirable limited edition, there was something even more exclusive, something even more covetable: the Lamborghini Diablo SE30 Jota. The Jota name, together with the Super Veloce (SV) appellation, remain the most hallowed terms in the Lamborghini lexicon, reserved for Sant'Agata's most special cars.

The Jota edition was a further development of the standard Diablo SE30. This upgrade took the form of a factory-supplied set of bodywork and mechanical parts developed by a sideshoot of Automobili Lamborghini SpA called Lamborghini Engineering SpA. When Chrysler and Lamborghini pulled out of Formula One, Lamborghini Engineering SpA suddenly had spare capacity in terms of

The Jota edition was a further development of the standard Diablo SE30, and this upgrade took the form of a factory-supplied set of bodywork and mechanical parts.

personnel, talent and factory floor space to design, test and build these Jota upgrade kits.

A total of only twenty-eight Jota upgrade kits were ever built. As the Jota upgrade option became available only fairly late in the SE30's life cycle, only twelve of these were fitted at the factory before delivery to customers. For these twelve cars, standard SE30 units were pulled off the production line and sent off to the specialist Lamborghini Engineering SpA division where the upgrade kits were fitted. Just as with cars built in the motor sport divisions of Porsche and Lotus, the SE30 gained extra kudos for having been built in a facility that had only recently been constructing Lamborghini V12 Formula One engines. A further fourteen upgrade kits were offered to SE30 owners who had already taken delivery of their cars for installation by the local Lamborghini franchises. As the Jota edition's engine had been significantly modified over the standard car's engine, its emissions profile was also quite different. These fourteen upgrade kits were therefore only sold to owners in countries where the SE30 Jota would pass emission regulations. Sant'Agata kept back two Jota kits as spares.

LAMBORGHINI ENGINEERING SpA

Lamborghini Engineering SpA was set up by Chrysler's Lee Iacocca for the sole purpose of developing a 3.5-litre Formula One engine so that both Lamborghini and Chrysler could have a presence in the very highest echelon of motor sport. The project was based in Modena and Lamborghini employed former Ferrari team manager Daniele Audetto to oversee it, with Mauro Forghieri brought in as Technical Director.

The company supplied several Formula One teams with engines, notably Larrousse, Lotus, Ligier, Team Modena and Minardi. This powerplant was called LE 3512 (Lamborghini Engineering 3.5 litres 12-cylinder), and it made its Formula One debut in 1989. It was a 3493cc, double overhead camshaft, four-valve per cylinder, dry sumped, direct fuel injection, naturally aspirated 80-degree V12 engine. It weighed 150kg and produced between 600 and 750bhp (447–559kW) and between 285 and 330lb ft (386–447Nm) torque depending on its state of tune. This engine quickly became known as the best-sounding engine on the 1989 Formula One grid. Aguri Suzuki driving for Larrousse gave Lamborghini its first ever Formula One podium finish at the 1990 Japanese Grand Prix, and the Larrousse team finished sixth in the 1990 Constructor's Championship using this engine.

By 1992 Diablo road car sales had dried up, and Lamborghini was once again in financial difficulties. Bob Eaton was by now Chairman of Chrysler and he decided that Chrysler should no longer subsidise Lamborghini's Formula One adventure and steal all the limelight. Instead Eaton pronounced that Chrysler would essentially take over Sant'Agata's motor sport programme and would rebadge the Lamborghini Engineering SpA engines as Chrysler engines. To complement this ambitious takeover Eaton entered into negotiations with Ron Dennis for Chrysler to supply engines for the McLaren Formula One Team. These negotiations progressed so well that in the autumn of 1993 both Ayrton Senna and Mika Hakkinen tested a McLaren-Lamborghini prototype, only for Ron Dennis to pull the plug on the Lamborghini/Chysler deal at the last moment and choose Renault as McLaren's engine supplier instead. By this stage Larrousse had already gone bankrupt, so with no Formula One team wanting its engines, Chrysler and Lamborghini Engineering SpA pulled out of Formula One. Shortly after, in November 1993, Chrysler sold Lamborghini to Megatech, and this Indonesian-led consortium had no appetite for any involvement in the Formula One circus. With this Lamborghini's brief twentieth-century excursion into the dizzy and ultra-expensive world of Formula One came to an abrupt end. Diablo SE30 owners were the ultimate and unsuspecting beneficiaries of this ill fortune.

The SE30 Jota kit was developed by Lamborghini Engineering SpA, an offshoot of Automobili Lamborghini SpA that was originally set up by Chrysler's Lee Iacocca for the sole purpose of developing a 3.5-litre Formula One engine.

The SE30 Jota was essentially a privateer's race car. It was designed with the BPR Global GT Endurance Series in mind – a grand tourer-based sportscar endurance racing series. The upgrade kit therefore aimed to transform the standard SE30 car into the leanest, meanest version possible while staying within the BPR series' racing regulations.

The most striking of the Jota's cosmetic modifications was its new engine compartment bonnet, which now incorporated two massive air snorkels that towered over the car's roofline. These gave the car's roof a 'double-bubble' appearance, reminiscent of Zagota's signature double-domed cupolas. The front half of the original Venetian blind-style bonnet had to be sacrificed to accommodate these new intakes, but this was a small price to pay for the additional induction air needed for the Jota's modified engine to deliver its maximum power and torque outputs. The redesigned engine bonnet further reduced the already poor rear visibility, but this too was deemed acceptable for a car that was always meant to be in the lead, and for a car that would never be threatened or slighted by another car attempting the ultimately futile task of trying to overtake it. These air snorkels also gave the SE30 Jota an even more aggressive and purposeful appearance, which was entirely in keeping with its racing ambitions. A small 'Jota' emblem was also affixed to these upgraded cars' rear grille, the speedometer was substituted with a new one that now read to 400km/h, and the rear view mirror was jettisoned to save weight and because the newly redesigned engine compartment bonnet rendered it completely useless.

The SE30 Jota had an M-Mec breathing system bolted onto the top of the engine's cam covers, a pressure plate to redirect the air snorkel air into the induction system, racing cams, two additional throttle bodies, lighter cranks to reduce rotational inertia, and a reprogrammed and even more aggressive LIE electronic fuel injection map. The SE30 Jota featured a completely new, more free-breathing, open exhaust system as standard, and almost all the car's sound deadening material was jettisoned to save weight. The SE30 Jota therefore had a particularly rough and raw roar at idle that transmuted into a truly howling shriek at high revs, and its induction and exhaust music would be yet another of this ultra-exclusive car's defining features.

With all these modifications the SE30 Jota's 5707cc naturally aspirated V12 engine produced 595bhp at 7,300rpm and 471lb ft torque at 4,800rpm, making it the most powerful Bizzarrini V12 road engine produced to date. With all this power and torque the car was able to post 0–100km/h and 0–1,000 metre times of 3.9 seconds and 20.1 seconds respectively, and claim a maximum speed of 339km/h (211mph).

Sant'Agata sold the SE30 Jota as track-only cars, but several owners modified their cars such that they were able to pass local legislation and become road legal, and are today being enjoyed on public roads.

The most striking of the Jota's cosmetic modifications was its new engine compartment bonnet, which now incorporated two massive air snorkels that towered over the car's roofline.

CHAPTER 8

DIABLO SV: THE LIGHTWEIGHT LEGEND

The Lamborghini Diablo SV brought back to life the hallowed Super Veloce moniker that had laid dormant for more than two decades. The SV label was an appellation that Sant'Agata used very sparingly, and not a single Countach variant had been deemed worthy of this epithet. The Lamborghini Miura SV, the only Lamborghini that previously held this name, had represented the highest pinnacle of its model range. So it was with the Diablo, provided one chooses to ignore the almost mythical Jota cars, which were almost as rare as unicorns. The Miura SV had introduced pivotal and far-reaching engineering solutions to the earlier Miuras' powertrain defects and was a legend in its own lifetime. The Diablo SV on the other hand did not bring any revolutionary innovations, but earned its epithet by virtue of subtracting all that was unnecessary and judiciously adding only the barest of essentials, to make the Diablo SV the ultimate driver's Diablo.

The Diablo SV was presented in March 1995 in the Palexpo Halls at the sixty-fifth Geneva International Motor Show. There it had to battle for attention with the Ferrari F50, which was also making its debut. While the F50 featured a carbon-Kevlar monocoque and radical aerodynamic-led styling by Pininfarina, the SV picked up the gauntlet by being, in Sant'Agata's own words, 'The quickest and most responsive road car Lamborghini has ever produced'. Lamborghini explicitly stated that they were happy for the SV to sacrifice top speed for the ultimate in acceleration, braking, roadholding and handling, and what they wanted most from this model variant was superlative driver feedback and the absolute best in responsiveness to driver input. The Diablo SV was aimed squarely at driving enthusiasts.

The SV could be considered as a much pared-down SE30 Jota, in that it took some of the best bits of the highly exclusive SE30 and made it more readily available to the general public. While the SE30 was a limited edition car restricted to a maximum of 150 units (and only twenty-eight SE30 Jota upgrade kits were ever made), the Diablo SV was a standard series production car with factory supply limited only by customer demand.

Customer demand was a key consideration for Lamborghini's management when the SV was being conceived. The early 1990s had been a financially turbulent time for all exotic car manufacturers, as detailed in the previous chapter, but Sant'Agata had to contend with an additional obstacle in the form of a change in ownership. Lee Iacocca's enthusiastic purchase of Lamborghini in 1987 had paid early dividends with Sant'Agata balancing its books for the first time in years, thanks to exceptionally strong demand for the original Diablo at its launch. The global recession and the oil crisis that followed had brought all this to a premature end, with Diablo sales suddenly evaporating. Chrysler, now headed by Bob Eaton, could no longer afford to subsidise Lamborghini and put the company up for sale in late 1993. Megatech, an Indonesian-led consortium, which itself was part of an oil and energy conglomerate called Group SETDCO, bought Lamborghini in January 1994. Group SETDCO was run by Setiawan Djody, but his main financial backer was Tommy Suharto, the youngest son of Indonesia's second president. Both these men imposed tight fiscal restraint upon Sant'Agata, while simultaneously demanding that Sant'Agata actively stimulate demand for its flagship car.

Lamborghini uses its hallowed Super Veloce moniker very sparingly. The two-wheel-drive Diablo SV was an appropriately special car.

In Sant'Agata's own words, the Diablo SV was 'The quickest and most responsive road car Lamborghini has ever produced'.

Weighed down by these two constraining and almost contradictory factors, Lamborghini took the only realistic avenue open to them. While the Diablo VT variant had catered to the safety-conscious and comfort-oriented customer, the SE30 variant had fed those Lamborghini clients looking for the ultimate in exclusivity, and the Diablo Roadster had accommodated the attention-seeking patron and those looking for the full al fresco experience. The monomaniac driver still remained uncatered for, and Sant'Agata decided to fill this void with the Diablo SV variant.

Megatech did not have the same appetite for extravagantly lavishing funds upon Lamborghini in the way that Lee Iacocca had done when Chrysler first bought the company. In fact Megatech did the opposite and vigorously tried to cut costs, as best exemplified by almost immediately withdrawing Lamborghini from any Formula One involvement, and then following this up in June 1994 by closing down Lamborghini Engineering SpA, its specialist motor sport subsidiary. Mike Kimberley was poached from General Motors and installed by the Indonesians as both President and Chief Executive Officer of Automobili Lamborghini SpA, with the specific brief of reinvigorating the company's model line-up and guaranteeing that strict financial prudence would be observed at all times. The Diablo SV was designed and developed under these budgetary constraints.

LIGHTER AND CHEAPER

Happily, Sant'Agata's concept for its next flagship variant fitted in perfectly with these restraints. A driver-focused car could best be delivered by jettisoning mass, and Lamborghini

Lamborghini explicitly stated that they were happy for the SV to sacrifice top speed in the search for the ultimate in acceleration, braking, roadholding and handling.

Diablo SV was a standard series production car with factory supply limited only by customer demand.

had already been through this learning curve when designing the SE30. Since the days of Paolo Stanzani Lamborghini had adhered firmly to Colin Chapman's famous adage: 'Adding power makes you faster on the straights. Subtracting weight makes you faster everywhere.' Mike Kimberley had been under Colin Chapman's tutelage at Lotus during his formative years as a young engineer, and readily subscribed to the idea that Sant'Agata's next model variant should be a stripped-out, lightweight car.

Kimberley was further attracted to the SV concept because Lamborghini already possessed the basic bodywork and mechanical ingredients necessary to put this car into series production. With only minor modifications to existing components needed, huge development costs could be neatly sidestepped. Furthermore, abandoning unnecessary and expensive luxury niceties in the name of weight-saving brought additional financial savings. All this meant that the Diablo SV could be priced very competitively: in fact it would be the cheapest Diablo in the range. Being significantly more affordable also meant that the SV could attract new customers to the Lamborghini brand. All of which was exactly what Setiawan Djody and Tommy Suharto had demanded of Kimberley and Sant'Agata.

To keep the sales and marketing teams happy, the Diablo SV combined a modest increase in power with genuine weight saving. A further 18bhp was released through more aggressive cams and a more free-breathing exhaust system to take the car's maximum power output to 510bhp (380kW) at 7,100rpm, accompanied by a maximum torque output of 428lb ft (580Nm) at 5,900rpm. With a weight of 1,530kg, this gave a highly respectable power-to-weight ratio of 333bhp per tonne.

The 46kg weight saving was achieved principally by employing a two-wheel-drive system instead of a four-wheel-drive

The Diablo SV combined a modest increase in power with genuine weight saving: it weighed 1,530kg and had 510bhp at its disposal.

system, and also by shunning a traction control system. Lightweight composites were used for parts of the doors, sills and centre console, and lightweight Alcantara-covered seats complemented the Alcantara-swathed dashboard and centre console armrest. But the SV was no horse-hair mobile monastery. Self-flagellation was renounced in the name of pragmatic road usability, and the SV had power steering, air-conditioning and even a hi-fi system. The last was a curious choice as a standard factory fitment, not only because it went against the SV's governing principle of ditching all unnecessary mass, but also because the SV's modified exhaust system was very loud and wonderfully musical, thus rendering any sound system instantly redundant and annoyingly intrusive.

For its exterior the SV adopted a lightly modified version of the SE30 Jota's engine compartment bonnet featuring two roof-mounted air intakes. Huge italicised SV logos adorned the sides of the car, swooping across the whole length of the doors and over the rear flanks. Self-conscious customers could ask the factory to delete these logos, in which case the factory would send these unmounted logos to the customer in a box in case they ever had a change of mind, or had a

Lightweight composites were used for parts of the doors, sills and centre console, and lightweight Alcantara covered the seats, dashboard and centre console armrest.

The SV adopted a lightly modified version of the SE30 Jota's engine compartment bonnet featuring two roof-mounted air intakes.

Note the carbon-fibre weave on the steering wheel.

mid-life crisis and developed an acute need for attention. In any case these orange bodywork logos fitted well with the car's interior styling, which featured black Alcantara seats with orange stitching and orange Raging Bull and SV headrest emblems.

The SV had a single-plane rear spoiler with an adjustable centre trim tab, which allowed the driver to tailor the car's high-speed aerodynamics depending on the tab's chosen angle of attack. This standard-issue rear wing could be colour-matched to the car's body or be ordered in black carbon fibre. The tail lamp surrounds were changed to black, and the rear fog and reversing lights were now incorporated into the rear bumper-cum-diffuser following in the style of the SE30. The front spoiler-cum-air dam was modified and two fog lamps now took over from the previous quad set-up, and the shield-shaped gold on black Raging Bull front emblem now reverted back to its usual position at the base of the front compartment bonnet.

Redesigned front brake cooling ducts led to 10mm larger ventilated front brake discs made by Brembo. These brake discs measured 330mm in diameter, while their rear counterparts measured 310mm. ABS was not available on the Diablo SV. New, rather fussy alloy wheels with coloured centres and silver rims were employed, and these were enveloped by Pirelli P-Zero tyres measuring

The SV had a single-plane rear spoiler with an adjustable centre trim tab.

The Diablo's front spoiler-cum-air dam was modified for the SV variant, and two fog lamps now took over from the previous quad style set-up.

235/40/ZR 17 and 335/35/ZR 18 on the fronts and rears, respectively.

The SV had a shorter final drive ratio, and this altered gearing was critical to the car's accelerative capability. The SV was just able to crack through the critical 4 second barrier for the 0–100km/h dash with a time of just 3.9 seconds. This was important for bar-room banter and to attract new customers into the Lamborghini fold. The downside of adopting this shorter final drive ratio was the inevitable trade-off in the car's top speed, but a maximum speed of 300km/h (187mph) was nothing to be ashamed of. Most people would regard this as a fair trade-off, especially when the SV's vivid acceleration was accompanied by the unadulterated engine and exhaust symphony that now freely entered the cockpit because most of the car's sound-deadening material had been thrown overboard to save weight.

The SV's redesigned front brake cooling ducts led to 10mm larger ventilated front brake discs made by Brembo.

At its launch the stripped-out Diablo SV had a list price of £125,000 in the United Kingdom. At this time the standard two-wheel-drive Diablo variant was priced at £143,932, while the four-wheel-drive VT variant cost £159,000 and the limited edition SE30 was £175,000. The SV was the cheapest car by far, but many immediately considered this stripped-out, minimally assisted, highly responsive, driver-oriented variant to be one of the finest of the breed. Like the Miura SV, it too became a legend in its own lifetime.

In 1999 Sant'Agata, now under the ownership and engineering influence of the VW-Audi conglomerate, produced a facelifted Diablo SV. This second-generation Diablo SV is covered in Chapter 10.

An expensive load: two early Diablo SV supercars.

Still only five forward gears, but what glorious gears.

LAMBORGHINI DIABLO SV MONTEREY EDITION

In 1998 the factory produced a limited edition Diablo SV run called the Monterey Edition. Only twenty of these cars were built, and all were sold into the United States market. They were named after the Monterey Car Week, held in Monterey, California, each August, the highlight of which is the Pebble Beach Concours d'Elégance. These cars sold out almost as soon as they were announced. The most striking feature of the Monterey Edition cars was that they adopted the SE30's modified lower sill air scoops. Located just ahead of the rear wheels in the car's lower sills, these air scoops were now reconfigured with two diagonal and backward-sloping blades forming three almost vertical air inlet vents. The Monterey Edition cars also featured twin air scoops mounted on the roof. These were some of the last Diablos that Sant'Agata manufactured with pop-up headlights.

LAMBORGHINI DIABLO SV-R

In 1995 Automobili Lamborghini SpA established its own one-make race series called the Lamborghini Philippe Charriol Super Trophy and built a lightweight racing adaptation of the Diablo SV road car specifically for this championship. This Super Trophy series and the SV-R are of historical motor sport importance for two reasons. This was the first time that Sant'Agata officially went against Ferruccio Lamborghini's 1963 resolution that Lamborghini was exclusively a road car company that had no interest whatsoever in indulging in motor racing. The second reason was that this single-make championship and its attendant SV-R racing cars were the forerunners of the modern GT3 racing series.

One of the prime movers and shakers behind this project was Stéphane Ratel, who had previously set up the highly successful BPR GT1 and GT2 race series. Ratel enticed Sant'Agata into setting up their Lamborghini Super Trophy race series by promising them extensive media exposure through radio and television motor sport channel coverage. Ratel also assured Sant'Agata that there would be increased sales of Diablo race cars to gentlemen racers who could convert their cars back to road car specification at a later date, if they so desired.

Ratel and Lamborghini set up a partnership with a finance company called LeasePlan France through which any aspiring

Monterey Edition: note its rear wheel arch air intake with two diagonal and backward-sloping blades forming three almost vertical air inlet vents.

The Diablo SV-R's *raison d'être* was racing.

supercar racing driver could lease or buy a Diablo SV-R car, together with a package containing everything needed for a full season of racing. To keep things affordable and to capture as many customers as possible, Ratel and LeasePlan France offered a payment scheme whereby the car and factory support, and a maintenance and repair package, were paid for on a monthly schedule. This finance package also included a crateload of components to make the cars road legal at the end of the car's racing career, should its owner so choose.

automobili Lamborghini

Press Information Press Information Press Information

PRESS RELEASE

PHILIPPE CHARRIOL SUPER SPORT TROPHY

HAS ITS DEBUT ON THE OCCASION OF THE 24 HOUR LE MANS

Le Mans, 13th June 1996.

After its launch only three months ago at the Geneva Motorshow, the Lamborghini One-Make Trophy, which is being organized by Stéphane Ratel Organisation Ltd (S.R.O.), has become a reality.

27 Diablo SV-Rs will fight for victory. Amongst the competitors are professional drivers, gentlemen drivers, amateurs and beginners, and for each category there will be a separate classification.

World Class 1 Offshore Champions 1994 POWERED BY automobili Lamborghini

Thanks to Lease Plan-France, who have offered three different leasing schemes, the lucky drivers can obtain a "package" comprising the Diablo SV-R and the entry to 7 races in 1996 and 7 in 1997.

The SV-Rs which are production GTs, homologated to EEC regulations, can easily be returned to their original version at the end of the championship: i.e. to Diablo SVs.

All races will be "semi-endurance" of between 50 minutes and 1 hour 10 minutes. They will be broadcast on Eurosport, ESPN in Asia and other TV networks throughout the world.

It will also be possible to follow the races in real time on the Internet: Pictures of the circuits and classifications will be transmitted live on web-site **http://www.speednet-pro.com/supersport/.**

Official Trophy sponsors are Dunlop, Lease Plan-France and Philippe Charriol Watches. Major car equipment companies who have assured their co-operation as technical sponsors are AGIP, Brembo, OMP, OZ Racing, SEAL Carbon Fabrics, Magnetti Marelli, Eibach and Koni.

Automobili LAMBORGHINI S.p.A.
Via Modena, 12 - 40019 Sant'Agata Bolognese (BO) - ITALY - Tel. (051) 68.17.611 - Tlx. 510278 LAMBOR I - Fax (051) 68.17.644

A treat awaits.

This fitted in exactly with what Setiawan Djody, Tommy Suharto and Mike Kimberley wanted. They were happy to consider and get involved with any scheme that increased Diablo sales and kept Lamborghini in the black. Writing in 1996, in his role as Lamborghini President, Kimberley said of the Super Trophy: 'This entry into GT Racing is another first for Automobili Lamborghini.'

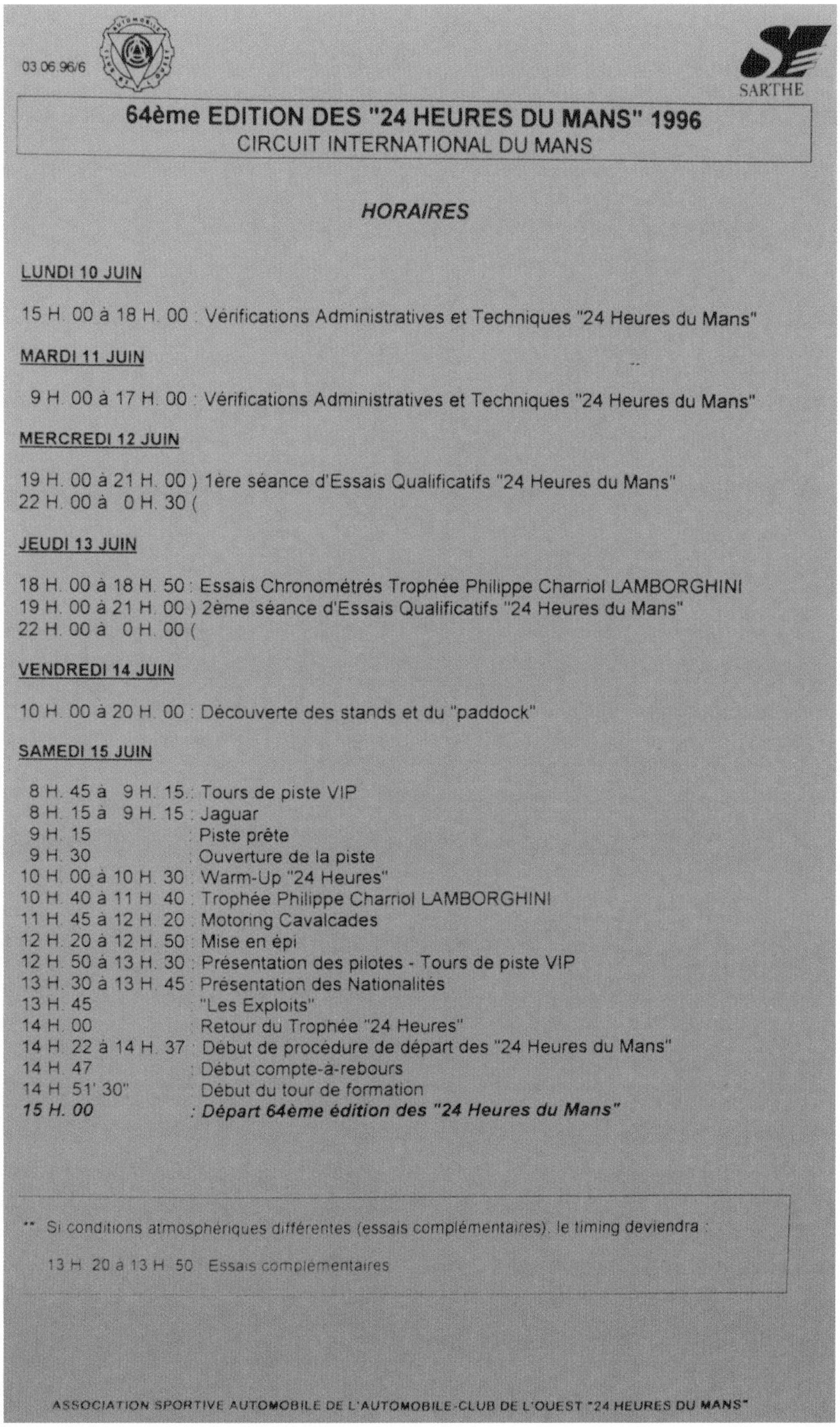
03 06 96/6

SARTHE

64ème EDITION DES "24 HEURES DU MANS" 1996
CIRCUIT INTERNATIONAL DU MANS

HORAIRES

LUNDI 10 JUIN

15 H. 00 à 18 H. 00 : Vérifications Administratives et Techniques "24 Heures du Mans"

MARDI 11 JUIN

9 H. 00 à 17 H. 00 : Vérifications Administratives et Techniques "24 Heures du Mans"

MERCREDI 12 JUIN

19 H. 00 à 21 H. 00) 1ère séance d'Essais Qualificatifs "24 Heures du Mans"
22 H. 00 à 0 H. 30 (

JEUDI 13 JUIN

18 H. 00 à 18 H. 50 : Essais Chronométrés Trophée Philippe Charriol LAMBORGHINI
19 H. 00 à 21 H. 00) 2ème séance d'Essais Qualificatifs "24 Heures du Mans"
22 H. 00 à 0 H. 00 (

VENDREDI 14 JUIN

10 H. 00 à 20 H. 00 : Découverte des stands et du "paddock"

SAMEDI 15 JUIN

8 H. 45 à 9 H. 15 : Tours de piste VIP
8 H. 15 à 9 H. 15 : Jaguar
9 H. 15 : Piste prête
9 H. 30 : Ouverture de la piste
10 H. 00 à 10 H. 30 : Warm-Up "24 Heures"
10 H. 40 à 11 H. 40 : Trophée Philippe Charriol LAMBORGHINI
11 H. 45 à 12 H. 20 : Motoring Cavalcades
12 H. 20 à 12 H. 50 : Mise en épi
12 H. 50 à 13 H. 30 : Présentation des pilotes - Tours de piste VIP
13 H. 30 à 13 H. 45 : Présentation des Nationalités
13 H. 45 : "Les Exploits"
14 H. 00 : Retour du Trophée "24 Heures"
14 H. 22 à 14 H. 37 : Début de procédure de départ des "24 Heures du Mans"
14 H. 47 : Début compte-à-rebours
14 H. 51' 30" : Début du tour de formation
15 H. 00 : Départ 64ème édition des "24 Heures du Mans"

** Si conditions atmosphériques différentes (essais complémentaires), le timing deviendra :

13 H. 20 à 13 H. 50 Essais complémentaires

ASSOCIATION SPORTIVE AUTOMOBILE DE L'AUTOMOBILE-CLUB DE L'OUEST "24 HEURES DU MANS"

The calendar and the timetable.

An unlikely setting for a race car. Note the tiny opening aperture set within the sidescreen.

The Diablo SV-R made its debut in March 1996 at the Geneva Motor Show. The first production Diablo SV-R car was only completed in May 1996, but a further twenty-eight cars were built very quickly and all of these were ready to race by the opening weekend of that year's Le Mans 24 hour race, which started on 13 June 1996. The twenty-eight cars were entered for the inaugural round of the Lamborghini Super Trophy Championship, which was held as a support race to the main event. The seven races of the 1996 season were run at Le Mans (France), Nürburgring (Germany), Anderstorp (Sweden), Brands Hatch (Britain), Spa (Belgium), Nogaro (France) and Vallelunga (Italy). Lamborghini's accompanying press release stated that 'participants include beginners, amateurs, gentlemen drivers and professional drivers'. Each race was classed as a 'semi-endurance' race lasting between fifty and seventy minutes, depending on the circuit, and was televised on Eurosport and ESPN. Technical sponsors included AGIP, Brembo, OMP, OZ Racing, SEAL Carbon Fabrics, Magnetti Marelli, Eibach and Koni. A total of thirty-one SV-R cars were produced and the Lamborghini Super Trophy Series ran from 1996 to 2000.

Lamborghini comprehensively updated and modified the SV road car for racing by changing almost 250 components. The SV-R's 5707cc naturally aspirated engine boasted variable valve timing and a revised fuel system. It produced 540bhp (397kW) at 7,100rpm and 441lb ft (598Nm) torque at 5,800rpm. All this power and torque was put down onto the tarmac through a dog-leg five-speed manual gearbox.

The car's interior was stripped down and spartan, with only a roll cage, Sparco racing seats with full racing harnesses, a detachable steering wheel, a few gauges and a fire extinguisher system. The Diablo's signature pop-up headlights were either ditched for lighter fixed units, or more commonly the headlight apertures were left unfilled and altered to take on a new role as NACA duct shaped inlets for front

In 1995 Automobili Lamborghini SpA established its own one-make race series called the Lamborghini Philippe Charriol Super Trophy.

Lamborghini comprehensively updated and modified the SV road car for racing by changing almost 250 components.

brake cooling. In a similar vein the electrically powered side windows were abandoned in favour of fixed Plexiglass plates containing small manually opened sliding sections.

The front spoiler was enlarged and deepened and the massive new rear carbon fibre wing was altered so that it became more adjustable, thus allowing for finer tuning of the spoiler's angle of attack. Side skirts that barely skimmed the tarmac optimised the SV-R's aerodynamic efficiency, but were so low that conventional manually operated trolley jacks could no longer fit underneath the car, so the SV-R came with built-in pneumatic jacks as standard. The rear bumper was removed and two gargantuan vertical diffuser fins took its place.

Early cars used lightweight, multipiece centre-lock OZ wheels, but these proved too fragile in the bitter heat of competition and later cars used stronger, monoblock Speedline wheels. These measured 8.5x17 inches at the front and 13x18 inches at the rear. Sticky, Pirelli P-Zero slick tyres measuring 240/645 and 326/640, respectively, were wrapped around these wheels. The SV-R had a modified and more robust Brembo braking system, and new stiffer springs and Koni shock absorbers. The SV-R weighed 1,385kg, a highly significant 191kg less than a standard Diablo SV road car. Sant'Agata claimed that the SV-R could sprint from rest to 100km/h in 3.7 seconds and reach a top speed of 330km/h (205mph).

The SV-R's 5707cc naturally aspirated engine boasted variable valve timing and a revised fuel system, and produced 540bhp at 7,100rpm and 598Nm of torque at 5,800rpm.

The SV-R's headlight apertures were left unfilled and altered to take on a new role as NACA duct-shaped inlets for front brake cooling.

CHAPTER 9

DIABLO ROADSTER: A SANT'AGATA FIRST

Until the Diablo Roadster made its debut Lamborghini had never put into series production an open-top version of any of its flagship cars. Touring had shown a convertible version of the Lamborghini 350 GT called the GTS at the 1965 Turin Motor Show, but despite garnering much admiration the GTS never made it into production and only two cars were ever made. Similarly, Bertone had showcased its one-off Lamborghini Bertone Miura Roadster at the 1968 Brussels Motor Show. This unique car became known worldwide after it was bought by the International Lead Zinc Research Organization and used to extol and promote the potential benefits of zinc alloy in car manufacture. Ferruccio Lamborghini continued to resist the desperate supplications from those demanding a production Miura Roadster, just as he, together with Paolo Stanzani, Giampaolo Dallara and Giulio Alfieri, was never tempted by the idea of an open-top Countach.

Chrysler, however, had a very different plan for Sant'Agata, which involved a different marketplace and a different type of customer. The Detroit giant badly needed to expand its new acquisition's customer base, and an open-top version of the Diablo was the perfect route to achieving this aim. Europe had been a prime market for Lamborghini since the company's inception, but new money was now also to be found in the warmer climes of North America, the Middle East, Japan and South-East Asia. Sunny blue skies, balmy temperatures and dry roads all screamed out for a convertible version of Lamborghini's flagship car.

The earliest patricians of the Italian motoring industry, including Fiat in its earliest incarnation, Alfa Romeo, Maserati and Ferrari, had all boasted the most exquisite open-top cars through the 1920s and into the 1950s. Lamborghini, which had already gained a reputation for being the most avant-garde of supercar manufacturers, was late to the party in this respect and Chrysler was very anxious to remedy this deficiency.

Lee Iacocca championed the development of a Diablo Roadster. Marcello Gandini is credited with designing this model variant: inscribed on a small silver plaque low down on every Roadster's flanks, just ahead of the rear wheels, are the words 'disegno Marcello Gandini'. Gandini, helped by the stylists at Chrysler's Detroit design studio, certainly had to work hard to transform the hard-top Diablo into its open-top sibling.

The first fruit of their labour was presented as the 'Lamborghini Diablo Roadster Prototype' at the 1992 Geneva Motor Show. Among the most prominent of the many changes that the Prototype showcased was a removable single-piece hard-top, a completely redesigned engine compartment bonnet, and a very shallow, almost non-existent, windscreen. Mounted in the centre and at the very top edge of this vestigial windshield was a large box-like rear view mirror, and Gandini had modified the Prototype's cockpit and engine bonnet to allow a straight-through view backwards. Other changes included a revised dashboard, wing mirrors painted in body colour, specially designed five-hole OZ wheels with painted centres, and an enlargement of the two air vents on either side of the car's flanks. The Roadster Prototype was a foretaste of the production Roadster, but much more midnight oil was to be burnt before homologation, legislation and reliability and performance targets could be met. Once again Lamborghini's choice of Puccini's 'Nessun dorma' for the Diablo's original 1990 launch was being vindicated: Princess Turandot and Chrysler would not allow Sant'Agata any rest until a series production Roadster hit the market.

The Lamborghini Diablo Roadster Prototype was presented at the 1992 Geneva Motor Show.

Until the Diablo Roadster made its debut Lamborghini had never put an open-top version of any of its flagship cars into series production.

DIABLO ROADSTER: THREE CARS IN ONE

The Lamborghini Diablo Roadster made its worldwide debut at the Bologna Motor Show in December 1995 and was an instant sensation. There were simply no other V12 convertibles with such high performance available on the market, especially in the Roadster's price range, and with its knock-out, crowd-pulling looks. From twenty paces the car was immediately recognisable as a Diablo, and yet it featured many differences in its close-up detailed appearance. There were a few trifling changes to this new car's interior, a few necessary modifications to its chassis, minimal adjustments to its suspension, and almost no alterations to its drivetrain. This car was all about outward show, style and image.

Contemporary Lamborghini sales brochures described the Diablo Roadster as three cars in one, depending on whether the detachable roof was on, completely off, or removed but affixed over the engine compartment. With the roof on, many observers considered the car awkward-looking, if not downright ugly, but with it off the car was the last word in glamour. Perhaps that should be 'almost the last word', however, because the third option of affixing the roof over the engine compartment made the car look even sleeker and it then became the epitome of sophisticated style.

The detachable hardtop was made of lightweight carbon fibre and could be removed and replaced by one person, although having a helper made these activities a lot easier and safer, with less risk of inadvertently scratching the car's expensive paintwork. The detachable roof was secured over the cockpit by four latches: two at the extreme right and left sides of the forward end of the hardtop adjacent to the windshield, and two similarly positioned latches at the rear. To detach and remove the carbon-fibre roof panel these latches had to be manually undone, after which the panel had to be lifted vertically upwards, which took some muscle. It then had to be carefully manoeuvred out of the way or, more arduously, into its other affixing position above the engine compartment bonnet. Negotiating the roof panel over the rear bulkhead and aligning it perfectly onto the rear bonnet without incident or accident required strength, delicacy and dexterity.

The Lamborghini Diablo Roadster made its worldwide debut at the Bologna Motor Show in December 1995 and was an instant sensation.

Many observers considered the car awkward-looking with the roof on, if not downright ugly, but without it the car was almost the last word in glamour.

The bonnet had four matching latch holes and tabs, and the removable roof panel studs locked securely into place using these fixing points. Since the latches and studs were hidden away from view and touch once the roof panel was mounted on the bonnet, and so could not be accessed, Lamborghini devised an ingenious way of releasing these latches and studs. Within the cockpit, high up on the centre console and between the seats, was a small black cube housing a push-button switch. Pushing down on this button released the latch studs through a complex vacuum-operated mechanism, thereby enabling the roof panel to be lifted off the rear bonnet. To ensure that this button was not pressed inadvertently when the Roadster was travelling at speed, which would be catastrophic for any vehicles following behind, the black cube had a transparent opening flap, and the release button was held in protective custody behind this shield.

The detachable hardtop was made of lightweight carbon fibre and could be removed and replaced by one person.

The hardtop was secured over the cockpit by four latches: two at the extreme right and left sides of the forward end of the hardtop adjacent to the windshield, and two similarly positioned latches at the rear.

The car's transmutation from a fixed-head coupé to a detachable roofed cabriolet also meant adopting a differently raked windscreen and losing the small side windows behind the doors. This area was now replaced by a fixed body-coloured panel carrying the Raging Bull emblem. The loss of the side windows further restricted the driver's already poor rearwards visibility, making reversing and exiting junctions just that much more challenging and dangerous. The Roadster's bodywork alterations also demanded entirely new frameless doors. More theatre accompanied these doors: whenever the car's exterior or interior door handles were pulled, an electrical signal was sent from the handle mechanisms to the side window motors, activating the motors and thereby lowering the side glass by a couple of centimetres. This elaborate sideshow was necessary to allow the glass to clear the detachable roof panel. Once the guillotine doors were firmly locked into their closed positions, the side glass would automatically elevate into its fully raised position.

The car's transmutation from a fixed-head coupé to a detachable roofed cabriolet also meant adopting a differently raked windscreen and losing the small side windows behind the doors.

Other exterior bodywork changes included a restyled front bumper-cum-spoiler, a new engine compartment bonnet, and the SE30's modified lower-sill air scoops with two diagonal and backward-sloping blades forming three almost vertical air inlet vents. The front spoiler assembly now featured two rectangular lights and two circular lights instead of the four identical square units seen in earlier model variants, and carried two central air intakes to channel ambient temperature air to the front brake discs. The two large upper-body air intakes above the rear flanks were also substantially modified, and now boasted a totally different shape and appearance to that seen in previous Diablo incarnations. These air intakes had to be greatly enlarged to compensate for the inevitable restriction in airflow through the engine compartment once the detachable hardtop was secured over the engine bonnet. The more posterior of these two air scoops was the larger and more prominent, and was shaped like a fighter jet's ram duct air intake. This particular duct looked like a more modern and more aerodynamic version of the Countach's infamous elephant-ear ram duct intake.

New logos, reading Diablo in red, and Roadster in silver, were embedded into the most unusual of places. Buried into the horizontal, rearmost part of the engine compartment bonnet, these logos were almost invisible except from a bird's eye view of the car. The car's rear grille carried only a VT logo, so denying any following driver the knowledge that they were driving behind a particularly special Diablo. Furthermore the optional rear wing, if specified, almost completely obscured this identity emblem. It was surprising that this most extrovert of supercars would choose to appear so incognito. Sitting below this grille was the rear bumper carrying reversing and rear fog lights. Subtly redesigned and

Other exterior bodywork changes included a restyled front bumper-cum-spoiler, a new engine compartment bonnet, and the SE30's modified lower-sill air scoops.

Cabin modifications included minimally redesigned seats draped in specially chosen leather. The Roadster's seats and backrest also enjoyed a unique stitch pattern.

The hide covering the Roadster's seats and parts of its cockpit were specially treated with a variety of chemicals to resist better the ravages of prolonged sunlight exposure and raindrops.

specially commissioned three-piece 17-inch alloy wheels with a five-hole telephone dial design further distinguished the Roadster from its more pedestrian brethren.

Cabin modifications included minimally redesigned seats draped in specially chosen leather. This hide had been specifically treated with a variety of chemicals to better resist the ravages of raindrops and prolonged sunlight exposure. The Roadster's seats and backrests also enjoyed a unique stitch pattern. Most unexpected, however, and probably unique to the Roadster, was its quirky but very practical dual-size sun visor. Each sun visor had a triangular tab sticking out of its lower lateral corner. Pulling this tab outwards brought forth a mini sun visor extension that shielded the driver or passenger from any bright sunlight assaulting them from the upper-outer extremities of the windscreen. This elaborate design was needed because the detachable hardtop's latch mechanism ate into the space that a full-length sun visor would normally occupy. Adopting this novel design allowed space for the latch mechanism, while also protecting the Roadster's occupants from annoying and potentially dangerous sunlight or headlight glare.

Losing the fixed roof might have compromised the Roadster's torsional rigidity and crash protection. Lamborghini compensated for this by strengthening the A-pillars and adding additional bracing in the sills, between the pillars, and around the small rear windscreen. The chassis's box sections were also significantly reinforced, so much so that Lamborghini was able to claim that the Roadster's torsional and flexional rigidity actually bettered that of its closed-roof counterpart. Contemporary road-testers independently confirmed this, stating that the car was unusually rigid, stable, and unjelly-like for a convertible.

The Diablo Roadster represented the pinnacle of the Lamborghini pyramid, at least from the retail pricing point. In March 1996 the Roadster carried a list price in the United Kingdom of £174,995, at a time when the Diablo VT cost £161,995, the standard two-wheel-drive Diablo cost £147,995, and the Diablo SV retailed at the bargain basement price of £124,995. Even the optional extras for the Roadster cost significantly more than their equivalents in the various Diablo hardtop cars: a standard optional rear wing, for example, cost £2,204, while a Roadster's rear wing cost £2,840. Special interiors for the Diablo coupé cars cost £1,714, but special interiors for the Roadster were priced at £2,204. Glamour, indulgence and theatrics have never come cheap.

This decapitated Diablo maintained the same 5707cc, 48-valve V12 engine, producing 492bhp at 7,000rpm and 428lb ft (580Nm) torque at 5,200rpm. The Roadster retained the VT variant's four-wheel-drive system unchanged. Sant'Agata claimed that this convertible weighed 1,625kg, and could accelerate from rest to 100km/h in 4.0 seconds before reaching a top speed of 323km/h (201 mph). These performance figures allowed Lamborghini to claim that the Diablo Roadster was the world's fastest four-wheel-drive convertible, and also the world's fastest production convertible.

The Roadster was all about show. There were a few trifling changes to the car's interior, a few necessary modifications to its chassis, minimal adjustments to its suspension, and almost no alterations to its drivetrain.

CHAPTER 10

THE SECOND-GENERATION VT, VT ROADSTER AND SV: AUDI FACELIFTS THE 1999 MODEL YEAR DIABLO

In 1996 Lamborghini was poorly placed to respond to the gauntlet thrown down by Ferrari in the form of its new V12-engined 550 Maranello. Lamborghini was at this point yet again in the financial doldrums, and furthermore was burdened by disinterested and inexperienced owners. The Indonesian-Malaysian consortium made up of V Power and MyCom Bhd had no prior expertise in supercar manufacturing before buying Lamborghini, and acquiring Sant'Agata was for them largely a trophy purchase. They did not invest much at all in their new acquisition, and did not bring any genuine enthusiasm for the marque with them, all of which hampered Sant'Agata's riposte to the 550 Maranello.

Sant'Agata's engineers, however, were quick to recognise that while the Ferrari 550 Maranello represented a threat to the Diablo, it was also an opportunity that could be exploited. By abandoning the classic mid-engined, wedge-shaped, thrusting format of its earlier Ferrari 512M in favour of the front-engined, rounded, anodyne, grand tourer 550 Maranello, Ferrari was abandoning the caricature big-banger, arrow-shaped, aggressive supercar field completely to Lamborghini. Sant'Agata did not have the money to design and put into production a wholly new flagship to rival the 550, but it parried Maranello's thrust in three different ways. First, Sant'Agata streamlined its Diablo range by eliminating the base two-wheel-drive Diablo (the 1999 Model Year Diablo SV took over the role of the cheapest, simplest and most accessible variant), second, it facelifted and modernised the Diablo VT, the VT Roadster and the SV models, and third, it launched a series of limited edition cars.

With limited funds available, none of the 1999 Model Year Diablo variants were dramatic departures from their earlier counterparts – rather they were refinements and modernisations of the originals.

All these Diablo variants had two things in common, which makes it sensible to consider them together in a single chapter. First, with the limited funds available, none of these cars were dramatic departures from their earlier counterparts – rather they were refinements and modernisations of the originals, with the basic mechanical ingredients retained largely unchanged. Second, almost all the changes seen in these facelifted cars were forced upon Sant'Agata either by government legislation or by customer expectation. Another Ferrari product, the V8-engined 355 had made its debut in 1994, and it had genuinely revolutionised the supercar market. Although it was four cylinders short of the 550 and the Diablo, contemporary motoring magazines portrayed the 355, correctly, as more than a match for the Diablo in terms of real-life performance and beauty. The 355 was packed with modern technology, had great visibility and offered unprecedented levels of occupant safety and comfort. It is difficult to overemphasise the effect the technically advanced 355 had on later Diablo variants and the Murciélago. In September 1998 Volkswagen AG would buy Lamborghini through its subsidiary, Audi AG, and would immediately invest heavily in, and expertly guide, Lamborghini through the next chapter of its history. In the meantime, however, the 1999 Model Year Diablos would have to keep the company afloat.

Introducing the 1999 Model Year Diablo line-up in September 1998, Vittorio Di Capua, Lamborghini Automobili's President and Managing Director, gave credence to these assertions when he said:

> *The bodyline of our supercar is still absolutely unique, making it instantly recognisable in the automotive world. All the same, Lamborghini customers are not the sort who will be satisfied with distinctive body styling alone; they want the top-grade technology that the marque has always been able to offer. Our Research and Development centre is at the leading edge not only in mechanical engineering, but in the field of electronic control systems too – a fact amply demonstrated by this year's innovations: ABS, electronic inlet valve timing control and more generally the improved engine control system, which has ensured compliance with the new and extremely stringent United States standards.*

Di Capua went on to say that he was immensely proud when the engineers at the US Environmental Protection Agency not only homologated the 1999 Model Year cars, but also singled out and congratulated Lamborghini 'for the level of excellence displayed in Lamborghini's technical solutions'.

The single most striking new aesthetic of the 1999 variants was the replacement of the earlier Diablos' retractable headlights with fixed, faired-in, glass-covered headlamps.

The most concise way to present the 1999 Model Year variants would be to discuss each of the major bodywork and mechanical innovations common to all the models, and then to discuss the details of how each model differed from the generic. The three 1999 variants had more similarities between them than they had differences. They were first presented at the Paris Auto Show in October 1998.

COMMON FEATURES OF THE SECOND-GENERATION DIABLOS

The single most striking aesthetic of the 1999 variants was the replacement of the earlier Diablo's retractable headlights with fixed, faired-in, glass-coved headlamps. Pop-up headlights had been a signature feature of Lamborghini's flagship cars since the prototype Miura P400 made its sensational debut in the Palexpo Halls of the thirty-sixth Geneva Motor Show in March 1966. Part of the Countach's impact, of course, was down to its pod-mounted retractable headlights. In the early 1970s the Countach's pop-up headlamps were almost as much of a stylistic talking point as its guillotine doors or its extreme wedge-shaped profile. The Countach's successor could not afford to lose such a key design feature and no one was surprised or horrified that the Diablo was launched with retractable headlights.

Pop-up headlights are particularly well suited to supercars. The truth is that these special and very expensive cars are generally brought out of their glorified, heated and dehumidified cages and released into the wild and unkind outside world only when the weather is good and during daylight hours. Headlights are generally not much needed under such circumstances, and by flipping the headlight pods down into their retracted position, the car's aesthetics and aerodynamics are immensely improved and optimised, respectively. The headlights can then be flipped into their raised position on those few occasions when ambient light conditions call for additional illumination. Headlight design and technology in the latter part of the twentieth century was considerably less advanced than it is today, and adequate lighting demanded larger light bulbs and bigger light pods than are commonplace today. Any such fixed, raised headlight would act as a permanent and substantial aerodynamic barrier, and greatly worsen a car's drag coefficient. A key selling point of any supercar is its ability to travel at very high speeds. Since, at its most simplistic, aerodynamic drag increases with the square of velocity, every automotive aerodynamicist adored the idea of retractable headlights. The first retractable headlight appeared on the Cord Model 810 in 1936, and its designer Gordon Buehrig advocated the car's revolutionary roll-up headlights for its supposed aerodynamic advantage. Marcello Gandini bought into this thinking for the Miura, Countach and Diablo, although the aesthetic opportunities made possible by adopting pop-up headlights were also a major incentive here.

The standard MY1999 Diablo VT coupé sold in most markets, and all the second-generation Diablo SV cars, featured the usual quadrilateral air scoops with three horizontal blades located just ahead of the rear wheels in the car's lower sills.

The second-generation MY1999 Diablo VT and VT Roadster sold in the United States featured the modified lower-sill air scoops first seen in the Diablo SE30 with two diagonal and backward-sloping blades forming three almost vertical air inlet vents.

Pedestrian safety legislation, however, soon made retractable headlights essentially illegal. The U.S. National Highway Traffic Safety Administration's Standard No 108 imposed strict rules on 'Headlight Concealment Devices', and European Commission laws regarding cars' front end deformability made it very difficult to make retractable headlights that complied with these regulations. As a result the 1999 Model Year Diablos were forced to sacrifice their pop-up headlights.

Lamborghini, though, was able to retain the Diablo's wedge-shaped profile through the clever use of a new flush-fitting, fixed, glass-covered, headlight unit and the car's aerodynamics were not compromised, even if its beauty and theatre were. Headlamp homologation is a hugely expensive business, and Lamborghini and Audi neatly sidestepped this financial ravine by using the Nissan 300ZX Z32's headlights under a licensing agreement with the Japanese automotive giant. This headlight glass had a Nissan engraving on it, so Sant'Agata designed a special carbon-fibre lip to overlie this logo and thereby hide it from view. In a September 1998 press release Lamborghini tried to soften the blow of losing the Diablo's signature pop-up headlights by claiming that the 1999 Model Year's new fixed headlights were an 'aesthetically pleasing modification, lending more strength to the front end, and also very important technically since fixed lamps guarantee better beam alignment and optimized visibility'.

The second-generation Diablo VT and VT Roadster sold in the United States featured the special front and rear bodywork first seen in the original VT Roadster. All these North American market cars also sported the modified lower-sill air scoops first seen in the Diablo SE30 with two diagonal and backward-sloping blades forming three almost vertical air inlet vents. Second-generation Diablo VT coupés sold in other markets could be ordered with these highly desirable cosmetic modifications as optional extras, albeit at considerable additional cost. The standard Diablo VT coupé sold in most markets and all the second-generation Diablo SV cars featured the more usual quadrilateral air scoops with three horizontal blades located just ahead of the rear wheels in the car's lower sills.

In another first for Lamborghini, the 1999 Model Year Diablos were fitted with driver and passenger airbags. These cars also received a comprehensive interior facelift with a completely new dashboard. The driver's airbag was easily housed behind the steering wheel's central boss, but Lamborghini were forced to redesign the Diablo's dashboard, and in particular the dashboard's shape, to properly accommodate a fully integrated passenger airbag system. With the old dashboard design the passenger airbag housing would have been located so far forward that in an accident the inflated airbag could not offer any cushioning protection to the passenger. The new dashboard swept forwards much closer to the passenger, thereby resolving the airbag housing problem. On the driver's side, this new dashboard featured an upper row of indicator and warning lights hidden behind a thin strip of black glass, which was inspired by the design

The MY1999 cars received a comprehensive interior facelift with a completely new dashboard. The key reason why Lamborghini had to redesign the Diablo's dashboard was because the original dash could not properly accommodate a fully integrated passenger airbag system.

language of the contemporary Danish Bang & Olufsen high-fidelity sound systems. Below this avant-garde panel were quite conventional analogue gauges with standard dial faces, but these instruments were now electronically controlled. The interior also featured minimally revised, thinly padded leather seats, and there were now two additional air vents in the centre console.

Another major electronic innovation seen in the 1999 variants was the Lucas Varity/Kelsey Hayes anti-brake locking system. Lamborghini's Research and Development Department collaborated closely with this Anglo-American conglomerate to develop a new-generation system best suited to the demands of a heavy, four-wheel drive, mid-engined supercar. The system they came up with for the Diablo was a cutting-edge, four-channel, double-microchip arrangement, with speed sensors on each wheel. Sant'Agata insisted on a system featuring full self-diagnosis and also prioritised minimal weight, diminutive size and low noise on activation. A particularly important part of this new system was its electronic Dynamic Rear Proportioning (DRP) control. DRP had the capacity to recognise road surface conditions, as well as instances when braking was initiated in a bend. It could then optimally and precisely distribute the available braking force between the front and rear axles, with the ultimate aim of stopping the car within the shortest possible distance while simultaneously allowing full steering control. Sant'Agata and Lucas Varity/Kelsey Hales claimed that this ABS arrangement also reduced brake pedal effort and brake fade. Further improvements to the Diablo's braking system included new aluminium brake assemblies, upgraded brake calipers and a modified brake servo. A larger brake master cylinder was fitted to keep the brake pedal travel as short as possible.

In keeping with this thorough revision of the Diablo's braking system, the front brake discs were enlarged to 355mm, and the rear discs to 335mm. The front discs were cross-drilled. Larger wheels were needed to house these larger brake discs and to clear the new brake caliper assemblies. All four corners of all 1999 Model Year

A major electronic innovation seen in the MY1999 variants was the Lucas Varity/Kelsey Hayes anti-brake-locking system.

Diablos therefore received 18-inch OZ Racing wheels: 8.5 x 18 fronts and 13 x 18 rears. These split-rim aluminium alloy wheels were draped in 235/35 ZR 18 front tyres and 335/30 ZR 18 rear tyres.

The 1999 variants also featured several major engineering innovations. Foremost amongst these was a brand new, state-of-the-art, electronically controlled variable valve timing system. A whole new electronic control system featuring full diagnostic and data-acquisition functions was developed to coordinate this variable valve timing system. This new ECU could act as a black box recorder, logging the running parameters of the engine, and data about the car's performance. These latest Diablo engines boasted larger diameter valves, revised valve cam profiles to give increased lift, an upgraded fuel-injection system, and the words 'Valve Timing Management' embossed on the intake manifold covers. The new inlet valve camshafts significantly improved the engine's volumetric efficiency and hence power and torque outputs. Lamborghini successfully modified the engine's three-way catalytic converters and lambda sensors and their associated emissions control systems, as well as the car's OBD II systems, to compensate for these altered parameters. All the 1999 Model Year cars effortlessly passed the strict new US and Californian noxious pollutant legislation that came into force in 1999.

The MY1999 variants all featured a brand new, state-of-the-art, electronically controlled variable valve timing system.

These latest Diablo engines boasted larger diameter valves, revised valve cam profiles to give increased lift, an upgraded fuel-injection system, and the words 'Valve Timing Management' embossed on the intake manifold covers.

The 1999 Model Year Diablo VT, Diablo VT Roadster and Diablo SV all featured a 5707cc double overhead camshaft, 48-valve, naturally aspirated engine with electronically controlled variable intake valve timing. A generous maximum power output of 530bhp (390kW) at 7,100rpm and an equally lavish maximum torque output of 446lb ft (605Nm) at 5,500rpm allowed Lamborghini the luxury of altering these cars' transmission ratios. Additionally these more than adequate engine performance parameters even allowed Sant'Agata the opportunity to offer customers the option of bespoke gear ratios. Customers with deep enough pockets could either choose shorter gear ratios for faster acceleration, or they could opt for long gear ratios if their priority was higher top and cruising speeds and comfort. Sant'Agata quoted identical performance parameters for the VT and VT Roadster variants: top speeds of 335km/h (208mph), 0–100km/h acceleration times of 3.95 seconds and standing kilometre times of 20.5 seconds. The equivalent figures for the SV variant were 320km/h (199mph), 3.85 seconds and 20.1 seconds.

All 1999 Model Year variants retained the Diablo's usual rectangular tube spaceframe chassis with carbon fibre composite reinforcements, independent front and rear double-wishbone suspension with electronically controlled shock absorbers, power-assisted rack and pinion steering, Lamborghini's LIE engine management system with electronic static ignition and multipoint sequential fuel injection, and a five-speed manual gearbox. The 1999 Diablo VT and the Diablo VT Roadster had permanent four-wheel-drive systems with a front differential limited slip ratio of 25 per cent, and a rear differential limited slip ratio of 45 per cent. These cars' weight distributions

The 1999 Model Year Diablo VT, Diablo VT Roadster and Diablo SV all featured a 5707cc double overhead camshaft, 48-valve, naturally aspirated engine with electronically controlled variable intake valve timing.

All four corners of all 1999 Model Year Diablos received split-rim 18-inch aluminium alloy OZ Racing wheels, with 8.5 x 18 fronts and 13 x 18 rears. Note that this Roadster's hardtop is affixed over the engine compartment lid.

The 1999 Model Year Diablo SV took over the role of the cheapest, simplest and most accessible variant.

Lamborghini was able to retain the Diablo's arrow-sharp nose and wedge profile through the clever use of a new, highly angled, flush-fitting, fixed, glass-covered headlight unit.

Twin high-pressure gas struts hold up the front bonnet lid.

The new dashboard swept forwards much closer to the passenger, thereby resolving the airbag housing problem. On the driver's side, this new dashboard featured an upper row of indicator and warning lights hidden behind a thin strip of black glass. Below this were conventional analogue gauges, but these were now electronically controlled.

were 43–57 per cent front to rear. The SV was rear-wheel-drive only, with a rear differential slip ratio of 45 per cent and a weight distribution of 41–59 per cent front to rear. The VT and VT Roadster weighed in at 1,625kg, while the SV weighed a relatively waif-like 1,530kg. The 1999 Model Year variants were fundamentally modifications and upgrades of their respective ancestors – their key ingredients were basically unchanged – but these latest cars had more power and torque, improved drivability, modernised aesthetics, enhanced safety and stability equipment, and were fully compliant with all forthcoming emissions legislation and could be homologated throughout the world. Sant'Agata had picked up Maranello's gauntlet.

1999 MODEL YEAR DIABLO ALPINE EDITION COUPÉ

Exclusively for the United States market, Sant'Agata produced a highly limited run of just twelve 1999 Model Year Diablo VT coupés called the Diablo Alpine Edition. Alpine and Sant'Agata had a deep and long-standing association dating back to the early Countach days, as evidenced by the joint Lamborghini-Alpine posters that adorned the bedroom walls of many teenage boys in the late 1970s and the 1980s, while their more mature counterparts would lust after collecting the joint Lamborghini-Alpine brochures.

To celebrate the long-established collaboration between the two companies, the Italian supercar manufacturer decided to make a Diablo variant that would showcase the best of Alpine's high-fidelity in-car entertainment products, while also demonstrating the progress that Sant'Agata had made with on-board automotive electronics. These twelve cars featured Alpine's latest and most expensive multimedia entertainment system, the CVA-1005 model, which included a stereo FM/AM tuner, a 6-disc CD changer, an optional DVD, cassette or Minidisc player, an amplifier with a Lamborghini logo, a bevy of subwoofers, midrange drivers and tweeters, and a rear-mounted camera that fed into a console-mounted 165mm (6.5in) colour monitor screen. Most importantly and impressively, it incorporated an integrated satellite navigation system and an anti-radar speed detector system.

These cars ran exactly the same drivetrain components as the standard 1999 Model Year Diablo VT coupés, but had additional, specially commissioned carbon fibre trim in the cockpit and on the exterior, including composite lower-sill air scoop blades, headlight eyebrows and tail-light panels. Their seat headrests and floormats carried the Alpine logo, and they all ran on specially designed 18-inch OZ Racing wheels finished in chrome with gold-plated screws. Each car came with a bespoke car cover with an Alpine logo, and each carried a numbered plaque detailing the car's vehicle identification number and its place in the build sequence of the twelve Alpine Edition cars.

All the MY1999 cars had split-rim aluminium alloy wheels draped over with 235/35 ZR 18 front tyres and 335/30 ZR 18 rear tyres.

Guillotine doors did not get the chop during the MY1999 revisions.

MOMO EDITION DIABLO ROADSTER

To complement the limited edition Diablo Alpine coupés, Sant'Agata also produced a limited run of just twelve MOMO Edition Diablo Roadsters, again exclusively for the United States market. These cars were simply cosmetically enhanced 1999 Model Year VT Roadsters, with identical drivetrain components to the standard Roadster variant. Again, Lamborghini had an established and coveted relationship with its fellow Italian styling company, and had used MOMO components extensively in the past. The MOMO Edition Diablo celebrated this friendship and association, and gave Sant'Agata the opportunity to market yet another variant of its flagship car. All twelve of these ritzy cars had upgraded cockpit upholstery, MOMO four-point harnesses, chrome MOMO wheels, and seat headrests and floor mats with the MOMO logo.

These Momo Edition cars received excellent marketing exposure as they were launched at the 1999 'Running of the Bulls' charity event in California from North Rodeo Drive, Beverly Hills, to Monterey. Mario Andretti, the Italian-born American Formula One, NASCAR and Indycar winning racing driver, and serial Lamborghini supercar owner, was present for the MOMO Edition Diablo's debut, which was followed by a spirited drive to Monterey. This event was also attended by many well-heeled current and aspiring Lamborghini owners, so it was no surprise that all twelve cars were sold very quickly.

Purposeful. Note the twin wiper blades mounted on a single wiper arm.

Two MY1999 Diablo Roadsters on the Automobili Lamborghini stand at the 1998 NEC Motor Show in Birmingham.

CHAPTER 11

DIABLO GT: SCION OF A RACING LINEAGE

Lamborghini's fastest, lightest, most advanced and most expensive series production flagship to date was misnamed. The GT moniker stood for Gran Turismo, a direct and literal translation from the English term Grand Tourer. The Grand Tour was a pan-European expedition that young men (and latterly women) undertook during the seventeenth to nineteenth centuries, often immediately after graduating from Oxford or Cambridge, to further their world-view by exploring the sites of Classical Antiquity. Large distances were covered during this voyage, and as these travellers were well-heeled, the likes of James Boswell and Lord Byron travelled across the continent in great comfort. In the same vein Gran Turismo cars were designed for long-distance journeys, carried out at high speed, all while cossetting their occupants.

Lamborghini's Diablo GT certainly fulfilled one of these criteria – it could travel at very high speeds. At its debut at the Geneva Motor Show in March 1999, Sant'Agata once again made the claim that its latest flagship, this time the Diablo GT, was the world's fastest production car. Although the GT, like almost any motor vehicle of the late twentieth century, was capable of travelling long distances, it was not especially good at doing so, and most certainly any sense of pampering its driver or passenger was not part of the contract.

The Diablo GT was Lamborghini's fastest, lightest, most advanced and most expensive series production flagship to date. It had a huge, shield-shaped extrusion that dominated the car's front bonnet.

At its debut at the Geneva Motor Show in March 1999, Sant'Agata claimed that the Diablo GT was the world's fastest production car.

The series production Diablo GT could trace some of its ancestry to the racing Diablo SV-R, the very limited production motor sport Diablo GT1 Stradale (2 units) and the unique competition-oriented Diablo GT2 (1 unit). In time the road-going production Diablo GT would itself spawn the racing Diablo GTR, which entered battle in the 2000 Supertrophy season. All these cars were stripped of cockpit luxuries to save weight, and carried extensive bodywork modifications to optimise aerodynamics and increase downforce, and thereby increase straight line and cornering speeds. Their drivetrains and braking systems were also altered for enhanced engine power and torque and braking power, respectively, and their chassis adapted for trackwork. The street-legal Diablo GT would follow this method and pattern, adopting some of this DNA, even though it was always designed to be strictly a road car. The Diablo GT was not a grand tourer in the classic mould.

By the time the Diablo GT made its debut in early 1999, the VW-Audi conglomerate had already been sole proprietors of Lamborghini for some months. The Diablo GT was the last Lamborghini conceived and designed in the pre-Audi era. Audi had elaborate plans for a brand new flagship to take over from the Diablo, and unlike some of Lamborghini's previous owners the Germans had the money and the know-how to realise this ambition. But it would take time to design and build a worthy successor to the Diablo, and the Diablo GT was the first model to come out of Sant'Agata while waiting for something truly new to appear.

The rear-wheel-drive only Diablo GT's claimed top speed of 340km/h (211mph) genuinely allowed Lamborghini rightful claim to the title of the world's fastest production car against some pretty fearsome competition. Porsche modestly only claimed a top speed of 320km/h (199mph) for its high-tech 959, while the Ferrari F40 had a claimed maximum speed of 323km/h (201mph). Admittedly the Jaguar 220, Bugatti EB110 and McLaren F1 were all faster than the Diablo GT at 343km/h (213mph), 349km/h (217mph) and 388km/h (241mph) respectively, but none of these cars was in series production in 1999 when the Diablo GT made its debut.

To complement its 211mph top speed, the GT boasted equally startling acceleration: it could sprint from 0–60mph in just 3.7 seconds. These prodigious performance figures were achieved courtesy of the strict weight-reduction programme that the GT had been put through, as well as to the substantial powertrain modifications carried out by Sant'Agata's talented engineers, which resulted in mammoth power and torque outputs.

The Diablo GT's relatively waif-like kerb weight of 1,490kg (3,285lb) was achieved through stripping the car of some luxuries, and by the abundant use of lightweight materials like carbon fibre and Alcantara. The GT's guillotine doors were made from aluminium and its roof panel from steel, but the vast majority of the rest of its bodyshell was made of

Lamborghini claimed that the rear-wheel drive Diablo GT could reach a top speed of 340km/h (211mph).

carbon composite material. Additionally its roof-mounted engine air intake scoop, transmission tunnel, floorpan, sills, door trim panels and lacquered cockpit adornments, including the dashboard instrument panel, were all made of carbon fibre. Alcantara-covered winged racing bucket seats were accompanied by a matching Alcantara-swathed dashboard and central console. Lightweight alloy foot pedals were also part of the diet that the GT was subjected to. Standard four-point racing harnesses added to the GT's quasi-racer feel, although this was somewhat undone by the optional, very non-racing, console-mounted rear-view colour television monitor. Hugely helpful for city-centre parking and reversing manoeuvres, this Alpine LCD screen was fed by a video camera mounted on the GT's rear wing, and was part of a state-of-the-art Alpine high-fidelity and satellite navigation system. The GT's carbon fibre body parts alone supposedly saved 70kg (154lb) from the car's kerb weight, relative to using conventional, non-composite materials.

The GT boasted equally startling acceleration, sprinting from 0–60mph in just 3.7 seconds.

The Diablo GT boasted a maximum power of 575bhp (423kW) at 7,300rpm and 465lb ft (630Nm) torque at 5,500rpm from its 5992cc naturally aspirated, aluminium-magnesium, four-valve per cylinder V12 engine. This expansion of the engine's cubic capacity to almost 6 litres was achieved through a bore and stroke of 87mm and 84mm respectively. The new engine had a redesigned longer throw but lighter-weight steel billet crankshaft, reprofiled intake and exhaust camshafts, a state-of-the-art one-throttle-per-cylinder intake manifold, and an advanced engine management system. The engine's twenty-four intake valves were electronically controlled for variable valve timing to maximise engine performance and efficiency, particularly in the mid-to-high rev range. The car's exhaust system was modified to further reduce back pressure and so increase the engine's power and torque output. Much of this engine and lightweight bodyshell technology and knowledge was derived from experience with the prototype Diablo GT2 race car.

Advanced aerodynamics dictated the GT's radically new and dramatic aesthetics. At the front, a new bumper and splitter incorporated three gaping wide air intakes, partly to feed the new front-mounted oil cooler. This new nose was finished in carbon fibre and had redesigned driving and fog lights. Its black carbon weave lent the GT an aggressive air. Fixed, faired-in, glass-covered headlights, as already seen in the 1999 Model Year Diablo VT, Diablo VT Roadster and Diablo SV, featured on the GT.

The most aggressive and striking feature of the Diablo GT, however, was the huge, shield-shaped protrusion that dominated the car's front bonnet. Curved on all three sides, with the Raging Bull emblem at its lowest point, the upper edge housed an outlet scoop that vented air just below the base of the windscreen. Ambient temperature air scooped up by the nose intakes was first channelled past the oil cooler, then through a carbon fibre moulding underneath the front bonnet and thence to the outlet duct at the upper edge of the front bonnet and the windscreen. Routing the air through this aerodynamically designed pathway created a venturi effect and thereby produced downforce over the GT's front axle.

Aerodynamic improvements also dominated the Diablo GT's side and rear bodywork. The single large roof-mounted air scoop featured a carbon-weave leading edge. It had a triangular profile when viewed from above, and it integrated smoothly with the engine compartment bonnet. New black carbon fibre sill extensions running from the front wheel arch to the rear wheel arch increased the GT's effective undertray area, and thereby increased the overall downforce the car produced, especially at high speeds. This development was carried forward into the Diablo's successor, the Murciélago. Further back a new carbon fibre rear wing with downturned end plates dominated the rear and gave the car's side profile a more arrow-like and aggressive appearance. The central part of the trailing edge of this wing was adjustable. The factory set this flap in a raised position (elevated at 15 degrees from the horizontal) for medium-speed stability. For a high-speed attempt, the driver could set the flap at 0 degrees, so that it sat flush with the wing's upper surface. With aerodynamic drag thus minimised, and with the highest of the three available rear differentials fitted, a brave pilot could shoot for the GT's infamous 211mph claimed top speed.

The Diablo GT and its racing sibling, the Diablo GTR, achieved their prodigious performance courtesy of a strict weight-reduction programme, as well as to the substantial powertrain modifications.

Chassis improvements included increasing the GT's front track by 110mm and the rear track by 30mm, as well as a total revision of the car's suspension geometry. These changes enhanced front-end grip as well as overall high-speed stability. The increased aerodynamic downforce that the GT's new bodywork appendages generated at high speed was compensated for by using uprated springs. As stiffer, more unyielding springs normally worsen ride composure, the GT's shock absorbers were softened off in bounce (the rebound rate was kept unchanged) to compensate for these new springs. Front tyre section was also increased to improve front-end bite. The GT's three-piece OZ Racing alloy wheels therefore wore Pirelli P-Zeros measuring 245/35/ZR 18 at the front, and standard 335/30/ZR 18 tyres at the rear. The Diablo GT owner could select either an airbagged or non-airbagged steering wheel, and depending on their personal priority of acceleration or top speed, could choose one of the three different gear set options that Sant'Agata offered. Even with the shortest of these the GT could reach a maximum speed of 300km/h (186mph). ABS-assisted Brembo brakes, power-assisted rack and pinion steering, electronically controlled shock absorbers and air-conditioning all showed that Sant'Agata were paying attention to their customers' safety and comfort, and that the GT had brought the Diablo into the digital age.

The limited edition Diablo GT was both rare and expensive. All these cars were left-hand-drive only. Sant'Agata only homologated the Diablo GT for the European market, although with time some cars made their way to the United States and Japan through the grey market. Only eighty cars were ever built. The GT's launch price in the United Kingdom in October 1999 was £195,461.25, making it the most expensive production Lamborghini to date.

DIABLO GTR

The Lamborghini Diablo GTR was the proud successor to a long line of single-make championship racing cars. Launched at the Bologna Motor Show in December 1999, the Diablo GTR was the immediate descendant and heir of the motor sport-focused Diablo SVR, but it also owed some of its mechanical, aerodynamic and carbon composite technology to other predecessor Lamborghini racers: the 1995 Japan-specific dry-sumped 5707cc Diablo Jota PO track car, the 1996 646bhp, 1,050kg Diablo GT1 Stradale, and the 1998 6-litre, twin-roof scooped, skirted and rear-winged Diablo GT2 prototype. Just as the SVR had been a heavily modified, race-oriented version of the Diablo SV, the GTR was a redesigned and reconfigured track-biased variant of the road-legal Diablo GT, as well as an updated development of the Diablo SVR.

The SVR had been designed for, and competed in, the one-make Lamborghini Super Trophy Championship, which was inaugurated in 1996 (see Chapter 8). Four years on, and ready for the 2000 Lamborghini Super Trophy Championship season, Sant'Agata showed that it had not been resting on its laurels by building thirty Diablo GTR race cars. Lamborghini made these, the ultimate production race cars, in just six months, between the end of 1999 and May 2000.

The GTR had a simple and classic rear-wheel drive set-up, and a minimally modified V12 engine. It was a spartan car, stripped of all the road-going GT's creature comforts, so there was no air-conditioning, no heat- or sound-deadening material and no stereo system. Lightweight fixed Plexiglass side windows with sliding sections took the place of the usual electrically operated glass windows. The 5992cc naturally aspirated engine featured an uprated engine management system, a lighter crankshaft, titanium conrods, Dellorto throttle bodies, and a more free-flowing exhaust system. This exhaust system had no catalytic convertor, and featured

Launched at the Bologna Motor Show in December 1999, the Diablo GTR was the immediate descendant and heir of the motor sport-focused Diablo SVR.

The GTR had a simple and classic rear-wheel-drive set-up, and a minimally modified V12 engine.

The GTR was a spartan car, stripped of all the road-going GT's creature comforts.

The GTR had lightweight fixed Plexiglass side windows with sliding sections.

a new exit pathway with the primary outflow feeding into four separate three-into-one pipes at the manifold. These modifications allowed the GTR to boast 590bhp at 7,300rpm and 472lb ft torque at 5,500rpm. The standard five-speed gearbox was retained, and only a single set of gear ratios was available. This gearbox and the differential each had an oil cooler.

Koni double adjustable shock absorbers, adjustable front and rear anti-roll bars, lightweight, hollow, centre-lock Speedline forged magnesium wheels, racing brakes with Ferodo or Performance Friction carbon metallic pads, a racing fuel cell instead of the standard fuel tank, a carbon fibre MOMO seat, a MOMO six-point racing harness, a bigger front splitter, and a truly massive, trackside-adjustable single-element rear wing formed the rest of the package. In true race car fashion this rear wing was attached directly to the GTR's modified chassis. The car also had pneumatic air jacks and an emergency fuel cut-off switch. This racer had a

The GTR's 5992cc naturally aspirated engine featured an uprated engine management system, a lighter crankshaft, titanium conrods, Dellorto throttle bodies, and a more free-flowing exhaust system.

The GTR boasted 590bhp at 7,300rpm and 472lb ft torque at 5,500rpm.

pressed steel roof panel, aluminium guillotine doors, an integrated roll cage with X-door bars constructed from hefty 45mm-diameter tubing, and a body made almost exclusively of carbon fibre or composites.

The two-wheel-drive GTR weighed in at just over 1,400kg, with a front-to-rear weight distribution of 40 to 60 per cent. This, together with its rear mid-engined configuration and the car's south-north engine gearbox orientation, meant that the GTR had a very low polar moment of inertia, making this track car very responsive during hard and abrupt cornering manoeuvres. Despite its enhanced aerodynamic appendages, which inevitably carried the unwanted price of additional aerodynamic drag, Lamborghini claimed that the two-wheel-drive Diablo GTR could still reach a top speed of 340km/h (211mph), and could sprint from rest to 100km/h in just 3.5 seconds.

In true race car fashion the GTR's rear wing was attached directly to its chassis.

Advanced aerodynamics dictated the GT's radically new and dramatic aesthetics. Note the new front bumper and splitter, the massive rear wing and the huge air snorkel.

The GTR had pneumatic air jacks and an emergency fuel cut-off switch.

The two-wheel-drive GTR weighed in at just over 1,400kg, with a front-to-rear weight distribution of 40 to 60 per cent.

The GTR had a very low polar moment of inertia, making this track car very responsive during hard and abrupt cornering manoeuvres.

Closing time at the 2000 Geneva Motor Show.

The reception foyer in the Sant'Agata factory: the racing GTR looks so much more aggressive than the sensuous road-only Murciélago behind it.

CHAPTER 12

DIABLO 6.0 VT: VW-AUDI REIGN SUPREME

Sant'Agata's launch brochure for the Diablo 6.0 VT introduced its new flagship car as 'the Lamborghini Diablo of the third millennium' and went on to stress that it featured both 'new technology and new design'.

The VW-Audi conglomerate's acquisition of Lamborghini was led by its chairman, the formidable Ferdinand Piech. Piech's grandfather, Ferdinand Porsche, had designed the Volkswagen Beetle and established his world-famous eponymous sports car company. Piech, however, was not one to bathe in reflected glory. He was a very serious engineer in his own right, and first made his mark by designing the Porsche 906 and 917 racing cars, the latter of which gave Porsche its first overall win at Le Mans in 1970. Piech was an equally successful businessman and saved the Volkswagen Group from bankruptcy, before aggressively pursuing and acquiring Bugatti, Bentley and Lamborghini.

The Diablo 6.0 VT was Piech's baby and the first real opportunity for the VW-Audi conglomerate to put its stamp on Sant'Agata. They would have preferred to have launched a completely brand new replacement for the Diablo at the point that the 6.0 VT made its debut, but designing and developing a worthy successor to the Miura, Countach and Diablo was taking much longer than expected. To keep up with the ever more fierce competition from rival supercar manufacturers, and to demonstrate to potential customers and the outside world that Lamborghini was still alive and kicking and properly resourced, as well as to bring in VW-Audi design and technology know-how without undue delay, Piech, VW-Audi and Sant'Agata decided to launch the Diablo 6.0 VT as a transitory flagship before the Murciélago finally made its debut.

This temporary replacement was immediately and widely acclaimed as the most accomplished series production Diablo ever made. And no small part of this was due to Ferdinand Piech's intimate involvement with its design and development. Piech regarded Lamborghini as a trophy acquisition, and his delight in having bought this renowned supercar manufacturer was reflected in his animated conversations about Sant'Agata at social and business meetings. It was also noted that Piech often sported a Raging Bull emblem on his jacket lapel. Piech spared nothing for the Diablo 6.0 VT. He gave Sant'Agata clear directions as to what he expected of a Lamborghini flagship car, made available Luc Donckerwolke, a promising young designer, and even personally took on the role of occasional test and development driver for this forthcoming crown jewel supercar.

The 6.0 VT, which was launched in January 2000 at the Detroit Auto Show, had a smoother, less adorned exterior. The Diablo had been following in the footsteps of the Countach, with the addition of an ever-growing profusion of ducts, vents, wings and air scoops with each new iteration, thereby progressively diluting the purity of the original. The 6.0 VT reversed this trend with Luc Donckerwolke's much more restrained bodywork. The car's exterior panels were almost exclusively made of carbon fibre, except for the aluminium guillotine doors and the steel roof panel. Marcello Gandini had always aimed for a swooping, wedge shape for the Diablo, but Donckerwolke's treatment of the 6.0 VT's nose and rear bumper, in particular, meant that the car now looked even more arrow-like in profile than its predecessors.

The Diablo 6.0 VT was the first real opportunity for Ferdinand Piech and the VW-Audi conglomerate to put their stamp on Sant'Agata.

The 6.0 VT was immediately acclaimed as the most accomplished series production Diablo ever made.

The 6.0 VT, which was launched in January 2000 at the Detroit Auto Show, had a smoother, less adorned exterior.

The car's exterior panels were almost exclusively made of carbon fibre, except for the aluminium guillotine doors and the steel roof panel.

The front of the car featured new clear-lens headlights and indicators, and a simpler, less cluttered, more rounded bumper with just two, almost rectangular, air intakes for brake cooling. The Diablo's successor, the Murciélago, adopted this twin air intake front bumper design. A revised air dam and smoother, more rounded wheel arches also tidied up the Diablo's previously fussy aesthetics. Donckerwolke got rid of the air scoops on the top surface of the front wings just below the base of the windscreen, which all previous Diablo models had featured, and instead redesigned the front bonnet area as a simple and plain flat surface.

The rear of the 6.0 VT was also very simple in comparison to its predecessors, with new body-coloured tail-light panels surrounding classic round lamps and sandwiching a black oblong central panel. This black panel bore two emblems in silver: on the left was 'Lamborghini' in italics, and on the right 'VT' in capitals. The fog and reversing lights were integrated into the tail-lights, so there were no messy little lights littering the back of the car. The massive upward-slanting rear bumper-cum-diffuser integrated beautifully with the two large, upward thrusting, centrally placed exhaust pipes, and with the car's overall shape: the front and back ends were now in flowing harmony. The large air intakes in the 6.0 VT's side sills just ahead of the rear wheels were tidied up, and now married up well with the car's extended undertray. The air intakes above the rear wheels were similarly simplified and smoothed out. The engine compartment bonnet sported eight vents, but was otherwise completely flat. The car did not come with a rear wing as standard, but customers could specify one as an optional extra.

Luc Donckerwolke also treated the 6.0 VT to a thorough interior redesign. Contemporary Lamborghini press releases stated that 'The interior is completely new incorporating carbon fibre technology', and indeed the cockpit was a carbon fibre fetishist's dream. The new sweeping and crescent-shaped dashboard design was pure Audi, with seven clear, alloy-rimmed instrument gauges contrasting beautifully against the blue-black tinged carbon fibre dash panel. Similarly, the gleaming, spherical aluminium gear knob, gear stick stem, and Ferrari-like open slot gear gate all contrasted

The rear of the 6.0 VT was also very simple in comparison to its predecessors, with new body-coloured tail-light panels surrounding classic round lamps and sandwiching a black oblong central panel.

well with the carbon fibre central console and the simple, round, black, airbagged steering wheel. A passenger airbag was standard fitment, and the passenger airbag compartment was now much better integrated into the overall dashboard design, no longer protruding into the cockpit like a sore thumb. Ergonomics was a key Donckerwolke-Audi consideration. The dashboard gauges could now actually be read from the driver's seat, and the minor and major switchgear were more logically and more conveniently placed. The upgraded switches themselves had a precision and tactility that screamed Audi rather than Lamborghini, and they also lifted the cockpit ambience.

New leather seats, now with movable backrests, boasted lumbar and rake adjustment. These seats sat on longer seat runners, allowing longitudinal adjustment over a wider range, so that drivers of all heights and body shapes had a better chance of getting comfortable. The seats themselves were also moved inboard towards the car's centre axis to tackle the Diablo's longstanding and notorious problem with hugely offset foot pedals. The steering column was adjustable for height and reach, a feature already present in the Countach, and this helped with driver comfort and therefore passive safety. A new automatic climate control system with more cooling capacity kept the 6.0 VT's occupants cool and composed, and a new windscreen wiper arrangement afforded improved visibility when the clouds decided to unload their contents. Donckerwolke's ergonomically designed cockpit, which took driver and passenger comfort and security very seriously, increased this latest Diablo's passive safety profile by a significant margin.

The 6.0 VT's new 5992cc, 60-degree V12 engine borrowed heavily from the limited edition Diablo GT's powertrain. It had an aluminium-alloy cylinder block and cylinder heads, used lighter but stronger titanium conrods, and had a lightened crankshaft. This naturally aspirated, 48-valve, twin cams per bank, engine with electronically controlled variable intake valve timing produced 550bhp (405kW) at 7,100rpm and 457lb ft (620 Nm) torque at 5,500rpm.

A more powerful 32-bit microprocessor replaced the previous model's 16-bit microprocessor within Sant'Agata's Lamborghini Iniezione Elettronica (LIE) engine management system. This controlled the engine's sequential multipoint fuel injection system, the static electronic ignition system, and Lamborghini's latest and elaborately named Exhaust Noise Control System, which was more conveniently abbreviated to ENCS. The ENCS was designed to allow the 6.0 VT's engine to bellow in true Lamborghini fashion, while still meeting the ever more stringent noise legislation that many countries were now insisting on for homologation. The ENCS worked in tandem with a new, reduced back-pressure exhaust system, and it was sufficiently sophisticated not to compromise the powertrain's power and torque outputs. The ignition system featured individual coils fitted directly on the spark plugs, and Sant'Agata integrated an engine diagnostic system, which it called the Lamborghini Data Acquisition System (LDAS), into the pre-existing but now modernised and upgraded LIE engine management system.

A 6.0 VT powertrain and car at the Geneva Motor Show. This latest flagship boasted a revised 5992cc, 60-degree V12 engine with stronger titanium conrods and a lightened crankshaft.

The 6.0 VT coupé was initially offered only as a viscous-coupled four-wheel-drive system car. Its tubular spaceframe chassis was extensively modified, and carried

On display at the Sant'Agata factory museum.

additional carbon fibre reinforcement inserts to increase torsional rigidity. Its front track was widened by 60mm and its rear track was widened by 30mm. The car featured revised suspension geometry with front and rear independent wishbones, anti-roll bars, coil springs and electronically controlled shock absorbers. The 6.0 VT's braking system was based on the 1999 Model Year Diablo systems. A Lucas-Varity designed ABS system worked in tandem with a double hydraulic braking circuit operating on 355mm ventilated front discs and 335mm ventilated rear discs. The car had power-assisted steering. It also had new five-hole, monoblock, lightweight magnesium alloy wheels measuring 8.5 x 18 inches at the front and 13 x 18 inches at the rear. These were clothed in 235/35 ZR18 and 335/30 ZR18 Pirelli P Zero tyres respectively. These massive tyres, together with the car's not inconsiderable kerb weight of 1,625kg, demanded power-assisted steering, and

Luc Donckerwolke treated the 6.0 VT to a thorough interior redesign. Ergonomics was a key Donckerwolke-Audi consideration.

Lamborghini obliged with a variable-assistance rack and pinion system.

At launch the 6.0 VT carried a manufacturer's suggested retail price of £155,000 in the United Kingdom and $260,000 in the United States. Sant'Agata claimed that the Diablo 6.0 VT could accelerate from rest to 100km/h (62mph) in just 3.95 seconds and could reach a top speed of 330km/h (205mph). As important as these devastating performance statistics were to Ferdinand Piech, he was even more delighted that the 6.0 VT almost immediately gained a reputation for being dynamically polished, safe at the limits of its performance envelope, and more user-friendly than any previous Lamborghini flagship. Not bad for a temporising stand-in.

LAMBORGHINI DIABLO 6.0 VT SE

The Diablo 6.0 VT SE made its debut at the Geneva Motor Show on 3 March 2001. It was the final series production Diablo, albeit a model made in relatively limited numbers. The SE stood for Special Edition and only forty units were ever built.

The 6.0 VT SE came in two different colours that Sant'Agata claimed symbolised the two extremes of the day. Oros Elios, a metallic gold shade, represented the sunrise, while Marrone Eklipsis, a metallic maroon-bronze that changed shade depending on the angle of incident light, portrayed the sunset. Twenty cars in each colour were built.

Each car featured the latest Alpine stereo DVD-based audio system with integrated satellite navigation, and electrically adjustable seats. These seats and the cockpit interior were lavishly draped in an exclusive, high-grain leather with a special contrast stitching pattern. The hue of the interior's leather was colour coordinated with the exterior finish. The SE's cockpit ambience was further lifted over that of its more standard 6.0 VT brethren by boasting special titanium-threaded carbon fibre parts that had a more lustrous and silky metallic appearance. This special titanium-laced composite was also used on the SE's external carbon fibre components. The gearshift knob, gearshift slot plate and the dashboard instrument bezels were all made of titanium.

Mechanically the 6.0 VT Special Edition was almost identical to the standard 6.0 VT, except for gold-coloured, lightweight magnesium cylinder heads, covers and intake manifolds. The engine bay surrounds were also made of titanium-threaded carbon fibre. The Special Edition cars were fitted with shorter gear ratios to enhance acceleration, and these cars could supposedly reach 100km/h from rest in about 3.85 seconds. In the United States the SE version of the 6.0 VT would command a price premium of slightly more than 15 per cent over the standard car.

DIABLO VT ROADSTER MILLENNIUM

The Lamborghini Diablo VT Roadster Millennium and the Diablo 6.0 VT coupé were both presented for the first time at the Detroit Auto Show in January 2000. The Roadster Millennium, however, was a throwback as it employed the earlier 5707cc engine, rather than the 6.0 VT's 5992cc engine, and retained the previous model's nose treatment instead of the 6.0 VT's modernised frontal air dam and bumper. The Roadster was Sant'Agata's jubilee celebratory gesture to the beginning of the next 1,000 years. It was a limited edition and only thirty units were built, with twenty units going to Europe and the Middle East, and ten units going to the United States.

European and Middle Eastern customers could specify their cars in either Yellow or Titanium Metallic, but American customers were only offered the bespoke Titanium Metallic finish. Every Yellow Millennium Roadster boasted a yellow and black leather interior, while the Titanium Metallic Millennium Roadsters came with a two-tone grey and black interior. A black carbon fibre rear wing was a standard fitment, although owners could choose to forego this as a no-cost option. The Diablo VT Roadster Millennium produced 530bhp at 7,100rpm and 446lb ft torque at 5,500rpm, and weighed in at 1,625kg. All thirty cars came with the Diablo SV's shorter geared rear differential for the fastest possible acceleration, and Sant'Agata claimed that the 0–100km/h dash took just 3.95 seconds.

The 6.0 VT did not come with a rear wing as standard, but customers could specify one as an optional extra.

Marcello Gandini had always aimed for a swooping, wedge shape for the Diablo, but Luc Donckerwolke's treatment of the 6.0 VT's nose in particular meant that the car now looked even more arrow-like than its predecessors.

CHAPTER 13

MURCIÉLAGO: THE NEXT IN LINE

The Lamborghini Murciélago was the natural result of the Diablo coming to the end of its evolutionary cycle. Over the course of the Diablo's production run rival supercar manufacturers had not only been pushing the performance envelope of their own ultra-expensive and hyper-exclusive vehicles, but had also been making these cars more driver- and passenger-focused, safer, more fuel-efficient and more environmentally friendly. Ferrari, Bugatti, Pagani, Porsche, Aston Martin and McLaren had all either already produced supercars, or had pragmatic and sedulous designs on the drawing board, all of which showed up the Lamborghini Diablo's shortcomings. Just as the iconic Countach had to give way to an entirely new model in 1990, the Diablo had to do the same in 2001.

Another pressing reason for replacing the Diablo was because of Lamborghini's new owner. The Volkswagen conglomerate owned Audi, which in turn owned Lamborghini, and Volkswagen's ferociously ambitious Chief Executive Officer, Ferdinand Piech, was very protective of his company's standing. He had spent years building up the reputation of Volkswagen, Audi and its other subsidiary companies for mechanical reliability, up-to-date engineering, and top-notch interior and exterior design. In particular the Volkswagen group had become famous for its highly tactile and eye-pleasing switches, toggles, seats, steering wheels, gear levers and other user interfaces with which the driver and passenger would often interact directly. Piech found that the final pre-Audi Diablo variants did not meet his exacting standards in any of these respects, and the first Diablos developed under the Audi umbrella were designed to address these issues urgently to the limited extent that it was possible to do so. Volkswagen's quality control standards and avant-garde design and engineering objectives, however, could only really be fully met by replacing the ageing Diablo with an entirely new model.

This new model was the Murciélago. Just like the Diablo, and unlike the Miura and the Countach, the Murciélago was an evolutionary car and not a revolutionary one. It did feature new technology, with genuine engine, gearbox, suspension, bodywork and cooling innovations, but in essence it was simply a Countach with a dash of Diablo. The Murciélago retained the Countach's wedge shape, albeit smoothed over to reduce aerodynamic drag, kept the rear mid-engine south-north engine-gearbox layout, held on to the longitudinal orientation of the naturally aspirated Bizzarrini-derived V12 engine, maintained the tubular spaceframe chassis, and of course retained the spectacular signature guillotine doors. The Murciélago also retained the Diablo's innovative Viscous Traction four-wheel-drive system and electronically controlled shock-absorbers.

While the Lamborghini Murciélago was first launched to a select group of motoring journalists and franchised dealers on the foothills of a still-smoking Mount Etna in Sicily, its real public release was carried out a few days later at the factory in Sant'Agata. Lamborghini were keen to get as many historic cars as possible assembled at the factory for the Murciélago's debut and, courtesy of owning Countach chassis 12399, the authors were lucky enough to be invited to the event, which was held over the weekend of 8–9 September 2001. Rumours of a totally new and startling innovation spread around the guests well before a striking Murciélago in Verde Ithaca (a sparkling metallic green) was driven onto the elevated platform that formed the centrepiece of the gala dinner setting.

This much touted innovation turned out to be yet another Lamborghini party piece, set to rival the Countach's and Diablo's guillotine doors and retractable headlights. The Murciélago boasted a variable airflow cooling system that Sant'Agata called VACS. This was an arrangement whereby

The Murciélago was an evolutionary car, not a revolutionary one. Its essence was simple and straightforward Countach with a dash of Diablo.

The Murciélago retained the Countach's wedge shape, albeit smoothed over to reduce aerodynamic drag.

The Murciélago's party piece was its Variable Airflow Cooling System. VACS automatically elevated electronically controlled air intakes located high up on the car's rear bodywork when a preset engine coolant temperature was reached.

The Murciélago VT 6.2 featured the L535 engine: a 6192cc Massimo Ceccarani fettled dry-sump all-aluminium 60-degree Bizzarrini V12. It produced 571bhp at 7,500rpm and 479lb ft torque at 5,400rpm.

electronically controlled air intakes located high up on the car's rear bodywork would automatically rise to face the on-coming airstream when a preset engine coolant temperature was reached. At other times these ram ducts would retract into their lowered position to keep the Murciélago's aerodynamic drag as low as possible. It was a neat solution to cooling the Murciélago's rampantly hot engine while also optimising aerodynamic efficiency, and took its inspiration from the 1987 Project 150 Countach Restyling Prototype. Other innovations included a dry-sump lubrication system for the engine, a new six-speed gearbox, bodywork almost exclusively made of carbon fibre (the doors and the roof panel being the exception) and a totally redesigned cockpit interior in keeping with the Volkswagen conglomerate's famed cabin furniture quality, composition and construction.

The Murciélago was named after a famous fighting bull from Navarre, which fought on with vigour, spirit and passion against the matador Rafael Molina Sánchez ('Lagartijo') at Córdoba on 5 October 1879, despite suffering twenty-four stab wounds from Lagartijo's sword. (Murciélago was spared and retired to stud.) The Murciélago name translates from Spanish into English as 'bat', which was appropriate as the car looks like a bat with outspread wings when the VACS air inlets are in their raised position. This car was the first all-new Lamborghini model produced under the ownership of the Volkswagen-Audi Group, and it was designed by an Volkswagen-Audi designer, Luc Donckerwolke. He had already successfully refashioned the last of the Diablo variants, the 6.0 VT, but the Murciélago was his masterpiece – and he readily admitted that he drew inspiration for the Murciélago's exterior configuration from the Miura and the Countach, particularly the Countach's trapezoidal design language.

The Murciélago carried the internal codename L147. The first variant was the Murciélago VT 6.2 coupé, which featured the L535 engine, an all-aluminium 60-degree Bizzarrini V12 engine that had been fettled by Massimo Ceccarani. This powerplant had a bore of 87mm and a stroke of 86.6mm for a total displacement of 6192cc, and boasted four camshafts, four-valves-per-cylinder, revved to 7,800rpm and produced 571bhp at 7,500rpm and 479lb ft torque at 5,400rpm. This engine was the first dry-sump Lamborghini production engine since Bizzarrini's original prototype engine of 1963. In another first for a production Lamborghini, it was mated to a new gearbox with six

The Murciélago's optional E-Gear robotised manual gearbox dispensed with a clutch pedal and a conventional gear lever.

The Murciélago had excellent ergonomics. Note the steering column-mounted gear-shift paddles.

forward gears. This CEEMA-made gearbox was also used in a modified form in the Gumpert Apollo and the Pagani Zonda, two cars that were even more bespoke, exclusive and expensive than the already hand-made, rare and ruinous Murciélago. Using this same gearbox certainly did not hurt the Murciélago's provenance or reputation at all. Lamborghini claimed that the Murciélago could accelerate from rest to 100km/h in 3.8 seconds, and reach a top speed exceeding 330km/h (205mph).

The year 2004 was pivotal for the Murciélago and Lamborghini. The optional E-Gear robotised manual gearbox was introduced that year, and the first production

Convertibles have always, as a general rule, claimed the top position within their model range, and the Murciélago Roadster immediately became Lamborghini's flagship car.

Murciélago Roadster was also launched in 2004. The E-Gear transmission featured contemporary Formula One-style steering column-mounted paddles instead of a conventional gear lever, and brought the Murciélago straight into the twenty-first century. Convertibles have always, as a general rule, claimed the top position within their model range, and the Murciélago Roadster immediately became Lamborghini's flagship. Spectacular in every aesthetic, it was not without its faults. Its soft-top, for example, was difficult and time-consuming to fit. The authors have designed their own bespoke Murciélago tonneau, which can be attached and detached in about ninety seconds, but this contraption will only stay on at very low speeds. This is very useful in rainy England, however, where a sudden summer shower can hit unannounced at any moment. The Murciélago Roadster's only real rival at launch, certainly for its aesthetics if not outright performance, was the Pagani Zonda Roadster, which also debuted in 2004, albeit at almost double the price.

In 2006 the Murciélago LP640 was launched with a lightly restyled body and a 6496cc engine featuring a completely new cylinder head, crankshaft, camshafts, and intake and cooling systems. The LP640's 631bhp at 8,000rpm and 486lb ft at 6,000rpm allowed it to accelerate from rest to 100km/h in 3.4 seconds on the way to a top speed of 340km/h (211mph). Nine months after the launch of the LP640 coupé a Roadster version made its debut.

In 2007 Lamborghini produced the very exclusive and very, very expensive Lamborghini Reventon coupé and Roadster. Essentially a styling exercise, both these limited edition Reventon variants took their cue from the F-22 Raptor jet fighter and had very angular bodywork and a futuristic dashboard display. Their engines produced 650bhp and 661bhp for the coupé and Roadster variants, respectively. Both Reventon versions could accelerate from rest to 100km/h in 3.4 seconds, but the coupé had a higher top speed (340km/h or 211mph) than the Roadster (330km/h or 205mph) because of its superior aerodynamics.

In 2009 Sant'Agata presented the stripped-down Murciélago LP670-SV, which weighed 100kg less than the LP640. This, the last car to employ Lamborghini's stalwart Bizzarrini V12 engine, was laden with carbon fibre and tuned for 661bhp. It could sprint from 0–100km/h in just 3.2 seconds and had a top speed of 342km/h (212mph).

The Murciélago was the last of the classic Lamborghini flagship cars. It was the last Sant'Agata model to boast the classic combination of the Bizzarrini V12 engine, a tubular spaceframe chassis and genuine vertically opening guillotine doors. The passing of the Murciélago represented the end of an era for Lamborghini.

The Murciélago Roadster had a glaring fault: its soft-top was difficult to fit. The authors designed their own bespoke Murciélago tonneau, which can be attached and detached in about ninety seconds.

Luc Donckerwolke drew inspiration for the Murciélago's exterior configuration from the Miura and the Countach, particularly the Countach's trapezoidal design language.

The Murciélago was the last of the classic Lamborghini flagship cars. The classic combination of Bizzarrini V12 engine, a tubular spaceframe chassis and genuine vertically opening guillotine doors ended with the passing of the Murciélago. It was the end of an era for Lamborghini.

CHAPTER 14

RANDOM MUSINGS OF A DILETTANTE

The Lamborghini Diablo will always shine bright in the supercar firmament, even if it never glows with quite the same intensity as its two immediate predecessors, the Countach and the Miura. Those were revolutionary cars – aesthetically and technically – while the Diablo was an evolutionary car. This should not, however, in any way diminish the Diablo's significance. As Lamborghini's flagship car from 1990 to 2001, the Diablo ensured Sant'Agata's financial survival through multiple company ownership changes, it introduced several important engineering, safety and environmentally conscious innovations, and it set the stage well for its successor, the Murciélago.

The Diablo, like any other senior league supercar, is more than mere transportation. It is clearly an *objet d'art* and a collector's trophy as well. Some might object loudly to this characterisation, saying that the Diablo is just another car, but any such sanctimonious and feigned censure would surely recall Queen Gertrude's response to the Player Queen's insistence on her fidelity in Shakespeare's *Hamlet*: 'The lady doth protest too much, methinks.'

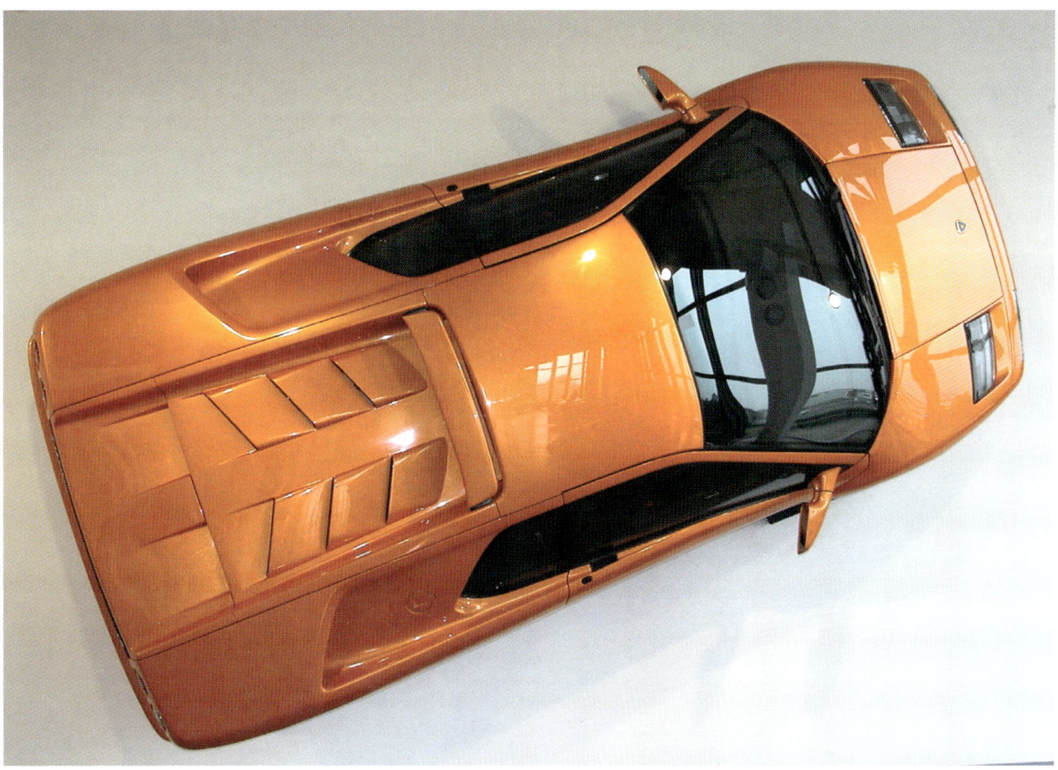

The Diablo is more than mere transportation. It is clearly an *objet d'art* and a collector's trophy as well.

It is particularly important that any owner or potential owner acknowledges this uncomplicated and patently true fact, simply because the jewel-like Lamborghini Diablo needs an exceptional degree of care and attention, and if deprived of this cosseting and nurturing will quickly perish and die.

The early Diablos are not much different to the later Countachs, and the later Diablos are very similar to the early Murciélagos. Drawing on many discussions with specialist Diablo mechanics and experienced owners, and pairing this with almost three decades of personal experience – both the pleasure and the pain – in caring for the two Lamborghini V12 flagships that sandwich the Diablo, here are some important and immediately relevant general principles that translate directly to the Diablo, and indeed any supercar.

PROVENANCE

Vigilance and prudence need to be exercised even before the purchase of a Lamborghini Diablo. Every Diablo now on sale is more than twenty years old, and some may be more than thirty. With proper and timely care and attention, any Diablo, whatever its vintage, should still be fighting fit and in peak condition, even now. Sadly, however, many Diablos will have been neglected, some very badly mistreated, and a few run down to the point of being derelict.

A shiny exterior and a sweet-smelling cockpit are no indication of the true health of a Diablo. Touch-up paint, wax polish, body-filler and an in-car deodorant sachet can quickly disguise a multitude of underlying sins. This is not to say that the cosmetic condition of the car is unimportant – in fact quite the opposite. An outwardly tarnished car may be impossible to restore to its former glory. Technicians who can repair carbon fibre and aluminium properly are not readily found in every street corner bodyshop, and the same goes for specialist leather upholsterers and expert carpet fitters.

Replacement carbon fibre parts are almost always absurdly expensive, and hand-beaten aluminium parts may simply no longer be available: anything made of 'unobtanium' is always literally priceless. Getting bespoke parts made in very small volumes is often prohibitively expensive, which is where specialist car clubs might come to the rescue, as having several club members order the same replacement part from the same supplier at the same time might make that part marginally more affordable. Although still in its infancy in the car restoration industry, 3D printing might one day be an important tool to keep small-volume, bespoke supercars running.

Provenance is all important with jewel-like cars such as the Diablo. Ideally the car's bodywork and interior colours should be unchanged from its original factory specification. Replacement body parts should have just the right carbon fibre weave or twill, the correct aluminium gauge, the exact grade and thickness of hide, and the original texture and thread-count of carpet. Putting matters of cost to one side, getting the car's cosmetic provenance right is also expensive

Vigilance and prudence must be exercised before the purchase of any supercar. Provenance is all important with jewel-like cars such as the Diablo.

in terms of time and emotion. It is a matter of blood, sweat and tears finding just the right component parts, and then the same again finding someone expert enough to assemble all these parts correctly and well.

That is why many experts say that any prospective owner should always buy the best Diablo that they can afford, as restoring an uncared-for car is almost always significantly more expensive than buying a decent car in the first place. They also often advise waiting a bit longer, and collecting more money first, if the funds currently available do not allow the immediate purchase of a good-quality car.

These matters of care and provenance apply equally to any supercar's mechanical systems. Matching engine and gearbox numbers, meaning that the car currently has the same engine and gearbox with which it originally left the factory, are among the first things that classic car collectors and non-owning connoisseurs alike look for. Factory-sanctioned replacement parts are the next best thing if the factory no longer has original stock on its shelves. Lamborghini has recently set up a factory-based restoration and certification department very similar to Ferrari's Classiche Department. Called Lamborghini Polo Storico, this in-house centre opened in the spring of 2015 and is dedicated to the preservation of classic Lamborghinis. As well as offering ground-up, bare-metal restorations, Polo Storico is also tasked with supporting classic Lamborghinis like the Diablo by maintaining a stock of original spare parts, thereby keeping older examples of Lamborghinis in as original and authentic a state as possible. Polo Storico also issues Certificates of Authenticity and maintains Lamborghini's Heritage Archives.

BUYING A DIABLO

A Diablo sold by Polo Storico, or fresh from a Polo Storico restoration with all the accompanying certification, must be one of the simplest and most straightforward ways of getting a top-quality, fully provenanced Diablo. But there are not many such cars available on the market at any given time, often none at all, and all Polo Storico cars will carry a very substantial price premium.

Franchised Lamborghini dealers are probably the next most reliable, but not necessarily the best, source for Diablos, as they too seldom stock Diablos anymore. When the authors bought their 88 ½ Countach 5000 Quattrovalvole in May 2001, they did so from H. R. Owen, then the only franchised Lamborghini dealer in the whole of the United Kingdom. H. R. Owen had supplied F920OYR to its first and only other owner on 1 August 1988, and had serviced it for him throughout his ownership tenure. But when we asked H. R. Owen about servicing the car going into the future, they were honest enough to tell us that they now sold very few Countachs, and that their technician who specialised in Countachs, and who had cared for F920OYR for many years and had just carried out its pre-sale inspection, was about to leave the company. H. R. Owen also stated, that while their remaining technicians were totally competent with assessing and servicing Diablos, they were less experienced with the Countach. H. R. Owen instead recommended an independent Countach specialist called Mike Pullen, who worked solo in his own company called Carrera Sports in Haywards Heath, for the pre-purchase inspection and further maintenance of ZA9COO5AOJLA12399 (Sant'Agata's internal factory code for F920OYR). Over the twenty-two years that have passed Mike Pullen's work on our Countach can only be described as impeccable and unimpeachable, so H. R. Owen's advice and recommendation was perfect for our needs. In the same vein, most of today's franchised Lamborghini dealerships' salespeople and technicians will be very familiar with the Aventador, but they may not have much experience with the Diablo. Therefore, it is incumbent on any aspiring Diablo owner to find a sales team and mechanic who really know their way around the Diablo.

Independent specialist Lamborghini retailers provide a third source of Diablos. Many are brilliant, but some are not. The following story is told in detail as it contains much information from which a potential Lamborghini Diablo buyer may benefit. The authors' Murciélago was bought from an independent trader posing as a specialist Lamborghini retailer. The car looked lovely (remember our cautionary note above about not being taken in by shiny metal) and we fell in love with it immediately, but alarm bells should have rung when this purported specialist repeatedly insisted, including on email, that Murciélagos came with 20-inch wheels as standard (they never did – all the Murciélago variants, including the highly exclusive and very expensive Reventon, left the Sant'Agata production line with 18-inch wheels). The car in question, 921SMA, was a 2005 Murciélago Roadster, stunning in a triple layer, flecked, fluorescent Arancio Atlas (orange) hue, with a full franchised Lamborghini Main Dealer service history, and with only 12,000 miles on the odometer

Monterey Concorso Italiano 1996 factory banner. A Diablo sold by Polo Storico, or fresh from a Polo Storico restoration with all the accompanying factory certification, must be one of the safest ways of getting a top-quality, fully provenanced Diablo.

when we bought her in October 2014. We paid for the car to have a full pre-purchase inspection at a franchised Lamborghini Main Dealer before agreeing to buy the car, and indeed 921SMA passed this inspection. As is the law in the United Kingdom (unless explicitly stated in the sales contract), the car came with a standard consumer protection type warranty.

The car was delivered to us by trailer direct from the independent's premises. When the delivery driver lowered the ramps, however, the trailer floor was covered with a pool of brake fluid. When the delivery driver fired up the car to unload it off the trailer, 921SMA's dashboard lit up like a rainbow, with every conceivable warning light coming on. The delivery driver suggested that we should reject the car and refuse delivery, and that he would take the car back to the independent trader – which is exactly what we had already decided upon. The independent trader fought this rejection, and did so again later when another problem surfaced. Reducing an interminably drawn-out, eighteen-month story into half a sentence, we took the trader to court and won both costs and damages.

It was the first time that either of the authors had been to court, and it was a stressful experience. The United Kingdom consumer protection laws are straightforward. They explicitly state that it is a buyer's statutory right to reject any item that is not fit for purpose, and that includes Lamborghinis. The examples we have given here are of buying a Countach and a Murciélago, but the principles are directly applicable to a Diablo, and it is therefore important that any buyer should be aware of the prevailing laws in their own country that might protect them against unscrupulous motor traders. As we were taking the trader to a Small Claims Court, we studied the basics of law beforehand so that we could represent ourselves without the assistance of an expensive barrister. Doing both these things allowed us to minimise our upfront costs, which is important as it is impossible to be certain which way the judge will decide, however confident you might be in the strength and validity of your case.

The take home messages that I am hoping to convey to the reader are to be extremely careful about who you buy from. In the unusual but unhappy instance of the car not meeting its brief, try very hard to come to an amicable settlement with the vendor in the first instance. Then consider the merits of your case very carefully and objectively, ascertain your legal rights and, if you are still confident that you have been wronged and the trader remains unwilling to compromise, be prepared to fight your corner in front of a judge. We have heard from enough Lamborghini owners to know that our Murciélago buying debacle was not unique, or to believe that the Diablo is immune from suffering this same sort of misfortune.

The whole experience was unpleasant and time-consuming, but it was also a salutary lesson, and we hope that the reader can learn from our bitter experience.

Remember too that you are buying the supercar, not the supercar vendor. If the Diablo is exactly the model you want and to the specification you desire, if it passes an independent inspection, and if it is rare and you are unlikely to find another one like it (we wanted a one previous owner Countach and we wanted a first-generation Arancio Atlas Murciélago Roadster, neither of which was readily available in 2001 and 2014, respectively), you might have to overlook your distaste of the vendor and buy the car. Buying the Countach from Jason Barker of H. R. Owen was a pure delight, while buying the Murciélago from the independent trader was a nightmare, but we are delighted with both cars and still have them after twenty-one and eight years respectively. Again these principles and rules are just as relevant and applicable to a Diablo as they are to a Countach or a Murciélago.

I would like to pass on one last piece of handed-down advice about buying a second-hand Lamborghini. A serial and very experienced Lamborghini owner advised us to only buy from independent dealers who have their own workshop facilities and employ their own factory-trained mechanics. Such establishments are better placed to inspect and assess a car before buying it in as retail stock, and are also better placed to repair any small defects that might surface in the warranty period immediately after purchase. This is particularly pertinent to older Lamborghinis like the Diablo. It is not unusual to find that a Diablo might not have been driven for many months in the period immediately before its owner puts it up for sale. Its enthusiastic new owner then comes along and drives his new toy frequently and vigorously, thereby bringing to light dried-out seals, worn bearings and leaking dampers – none of which are insurmountable problems for a dealership that has its own workshop and its own Lamborghini-trained technicians, but a major headache for one without these facilities.

Buying a Diablo privately direct from its current owner is the fourth, and possibly the cheapest, way of buying a Diablo. It is also the riskiest route, as this approach affords the buyer almost no consumer law protection. It does, however, allow the buyer to quiz the current owner deeply and to see exactly how the car has been garaged. Observing how an owner drives and treats his Diablo, especially if it is a one-owner car, can speak volumes about its mechanical condition.

Whatever the status of the Diablo vendor, the buyer needs to remain objective and alert to the harsh realities that accompany the purchase of such a specialised and complex supercar. It can be very difficult not to be blinded by the bedazzling beauty of a Diablo, but the wrong car can cause untold misery.

PRE-PURCHASE INSPECTION

In order to avoid a similarly miserable experience, I would thoroughly recommend a full pre-purchase inspection by an independent mechanic who is totally conversant with the marque, and deeply experienced with the model in question. It is impossible to overstate the case for a pre-purchase inspection. Such an inspection is never cheap but it is very good value for money. The reader might rightly point out that our Murciélago's pre-purchase inspection did not identify the fault that manifested itself as a pool of brake fluid on the trailer bed, but this was a relatively minor issue that almost certainly happened while the car was in transit. As such it could have been very easily sorted out by the independent trader with a minute amount of goodwill and a modicum of common sense, since 921SMA was fundamentally sound.

Learning all you can before buying will help in landing a decent Diablo. Maurizio Reggiani, Lamborghini's current Technical Director, was very generous with his time.

Not only will a proper pre-purchase inspection warn a potential buyer to walk away from a shiny but essentially bad Diablo, but it will also highlight existing hidden issues that will allow the buyer to have a sensible discussion with the vendor to see if they can come to a compromise sale price that takes into account the cost of any repair work that might be necessary to bring the car up to scratch. A thorough pre-purchase inspection will also give the buyer some notification of upcoming problems that are not yet serious enough to warrant intervention, but which will need attention in the future. The buyer will then be able to plan for these maintenance works and their associated costs.

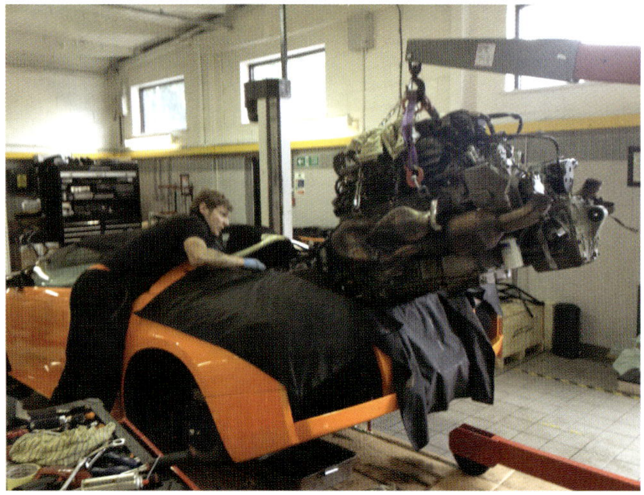

Removing the drivetrain from any mid-engined V12 Lamborghini flagship is an expert, expensive and exacting process.

CAUTIONARY ALERTS

No buyer's guide, or purchasing tips from a motoring author, can begin to compare with having a prospective Diablo high up on a four-poster lift, being carefully and minutely examined by a specialist mechanic with years of Diablo experience behind him. With this caveat clearly stated, it is worth imparting some of the gems that veteran Diablo mechanics have disclosed to us.

Most agree that the stalwart Bizzarrini V12 engine as found in the Diablo is fundamentally strong and reliable, as long as it is correctly serviced. The engine does, however, have its own idiosyncrasies and peculiarities, which means that it should only be worked on by a specialist technician who knows what to look for, and who can exercise preventative maintenance so that potential problems never develop into actual problems.

The Diablo's timing chain tensioners are one such potential weak point, especially the hydraulic tensioners found in the earlier cars. These hydraulic tensioners have a propensity to progressively tighten the cam chains until the chains snap – a catastrophic event. From about 1994 onwards these tensioners were changed to manual adjusters, and these later tensioners are less likely to overtighten the timing chains to the point of snapping. If a car has the earlier hydraulic tensioners, it might be worth changing over to the newer version at the earliest possible moment. At the other end of the spectrum, stretched chains will announce themselves by rattling on the overrun after the engine has been revved. An experienced Diablo mechanic will readily identify these issues and advise on what needs to be done. He will also be able to check that the oil pump belts have not been overtightened, as this can cause the oil pump bearings to wear over time, which can culminate in terminal oil starvation. The sealant between the engine block and sump can gradually perish leading to an oil leak. The posterior end of the head gasket is also liable to perish, and this too can result in an oil leak. Radiators can leak, and it is important to check that the radiator fans cut in at the correct temperature threshold.

The early Diablos had two catalytic convertors, one for each cylinder bank, and they have a tendency to disintegrate. Catalytic convertor particles are then sucked back into the engine, causing major scoring damage to the internals, which can only be repaired by an expensive engine rebuild. Owners might get some warning of such an impending disaster by the dashboard warning lights coming on, and if this happens it is imperative to shut down the engine immediately. Later cars had a more sophisticated engine management system that might shut down the engine automatically in this scenario. Removing the catalytic convertors and replacing them with decat pipes would obviously obviate this problem, but it would be illegal to do so in most countries, and is therefore not a realistic option.

The engine mounts carry a lot of weight and are exposed to high temperatures, and so also tend to disintegrate and need replacement. Engine valve clearances need checking at least every 18,000 miles (29,000km): again follow the instructions in the owner's manual, and take guidance from an experienced mechanic. The Diablo is very sensitive to its engine oil level, so be sure never to over- nor underfill, and always use a lubricating oil of the specified viscosity.

Diablos have strong gearboxes that are generally not a problem as long as they are treated kindly, and the gearbox oil is changed at the specified intervals and mileages. Mechanically unsympathetic drivers can, however, readily inflict severe damage on the gear wheels and the synchromesh mechanisms. It is important to avoid engaging second gear until the transmission oil has warmed up, and to be aware that the transmission oil takes a lot longer to warm up than the engine coolant fluid. Early Diablos used a push rod to the clutch slave cylinder and this rod had a propensity to snap, but it is a relatively easy and inexpensive job to change this for the upgraded replacement part found in later cars.

Clutches on the other hand are eye-wateringly expensive: the centre plate alone will make you weep quietly, while a complete clutch assembly will make you holler aloud in anguish and disbelief. And that is just for the parts alone: the clutch can only be replaced by removing the whole engine-transmission complex out of the car, and the labour charge for this engine-out job is frightening. Treat the Diablo's clutch with plenty of respect: do not indulge in traffic light burn-outs, do not reverse uphill if at all possible, and at traffic lights always disengage the clutch completely and put the gear lever into neutral. All of which is kind to the Diablo's transmission system and the owner's wallet.

A partially stripped-down Bizzarrini V12 engine.

The Countach has a well-deserved reputation for an even more fearsome clutch mechanism and gear change than the Diablo, but F920OYR is still on its original factory clutch at 34,361km (21,350 miles) and thirty-four years after leaving Sant'Agata. It is entirely possible to extract the same sort of longevity from a Diablo's clutch by exercising some mechanical compassion and consideration. Talking of gear changes, the gear lever stems on early Diablos were made of poor quality metal, and quickly developed a reputation for snapping in half during quick and forceful gear changes. Later cars used stems made of sterner material, which cured this problem. Later cars also employed a modified and strengthened primary driveshaft from the gearbox to the differential, because that fitted in the earlier variants had a tendency to break when subjected to the full torque of the Diablo's V12 engine. On the test drive listen carefully for any unexpected noises from the differential, as this may warn of an imminent and expensive bill.

Under normal road use the Diablo's brake pads and discs are adequate and last perfectly well, but when used hard on the track they can crack, and the calipers can seize. All these parts are expensive. The shock absorbers that form part of the later Diablos' front lifting system are particularly expensive and unfortunately they can leak. The rear shock absorbers carry a lot of the car's weight and are exposed to the heat from the V12 engine, so can perish and need replacement. Replacement wheels are not only expensive but are also difficult to find, so it is imperative not to accidentally kerb the Diablo's wheels during parking manoeuvres or to otherwise damage them. Tyre wear is largely dependent on the heaviness of the driver's right foot: injudicious application of a colossal amount of torque in a heavy car generally equates to poor tyre longevity. Lamborghini's four-wheel-drive Viscous Traction system distributes the torque between all four tyres (admittedly not equally), and in doing so helps reduce the number of visits to the tyre depot compared to what would be needed if only the rear tyres had to transmit all that torque to the tarmac.

Chrysler's and VW-Audi's quality control standards meant that Sant'Agata was now forced to produce cars with more reliable electrical systems than it had previously been accustomed to. The Diablo, however, particularly the later variants, had more electronic systems, more electronic control units, and more injection modules than its less technologically advanced predecessor, the Countach. While the electrical systems were ever better designed and ever more

Refurbished parts of a Bizzarrini V12 powertrain waiting to be reassembled.

carefully assembled, there were more of them to go wrong with each passing Diablo variant. Additionally, each system, control unit and module became increasingly more complex with every new Diablo version, which inevitably meant a greater chance of developing a fault.

One of the principal things that can go wrong with the Diablo is the interaction of air, water and salt with the Diablo's complex and intricate steel spaceframe chassis. This tubular lattice is prone to oxidation, and it needs an experienced mechanic to detect the rust as some of the most important structural tubes are hidden away from immediate view by the overlying bodywork. Galvanic corrosion is an additional risk wherever the aluminium body comes into contact with the steel spaceframe chassis. The Diablo's ferrous body panels can also rust, the windscreen can delaminate, and the side windows can crack. The wheel arches, the bottom edges of the doors, the area around the petrol filler inlet, and the boot floor are all particularly susceptible to corrosion and must be carefully examined. The Diablo Roadster's removable hardtop can leak if its locking mechanism wears out. In the earlier Diablo variants, the steering wheel's airbag cover had a tendency to simply fall off, a fault that Audi fixed soon after they took over ownership of Lamborghini.

All of the above simply underlines the need for a thorough pre-purchase inspection and continued periodic maintenance by an expert technician.

PERIODIC MAINTENANCE

Once the right Diablo has been purchased, it needs to be looked after properly. The Owner's Manual sets out the basic servicing requirements – but this might need to be augmented, or sometimes some owners and their mechanics might together decide that a particular scheduled service item is not needed immediately, and can be delayed without risk until the next service.

Most Diablo owners will not be able to service their cars. They will lack the mechanical know-how, the specialist tools, the detailed service manuals and update bulletins, and the workshop facilities to properly maintain their cars. The vast majority of owners are therefore hostage to the small number of specialist garages that have the necessary expertise and facilities to keep their Diablos in fine fettle and on the road.

Finding the right mechanic is vital, and this search should start at the same time as, if not before, the hunt for the car itself. Without the correct periodic maintenance the car will deteriorate very rapidly, and will soon be irretrievably damaged beyond economic repair. Additionally an experienced mechanic will be able to recommend and carry out prophylactic maintenance, since spotting a developing problem and addressing it before it fully manifests itself is always gentler on, and better for, the car – and kinder on the owner's credit card.

Lamborghini

Scheduled Maintenance

Operation:	1.9 2.4 1.2 1.5	12 7.5	24 15	36 22.5	48 30	60 37.5	72 45	84 52.5	96 60	108 67.5	120 75	132 82.5	144 90	156 97.5	168 105
	KILOMETERS IN THOUSANDS / MILES IN THOUSANDS														
Fuel filters					R*			R*			R*				R
Air filters			R*		R		R*		R		R*				
Injection system: lines and connections	I				I				I						
Spark plugs			R*		R		R*		R		R*				
Valve clearance			I-A		I-A		I-A		I-A		I-A				
Cooling system	I		I		I		I		I		I				
Injection / Ignition wiring and wire condition	I							I							I
Camshaft drive chains	I		I*		I*		I*		I*		I*				I
Engine accessory control belts	I-A		I*		I-A		I*		I-A		I*				
Engine oil filter (minimum once per year)	R	R	R	R	R	R	R	R	R	R	R	R	R	R	R
Carburetion, CO/HC concentration								I*							I
Idle speed	I				I*				I*						I
Oxygen sensor															R

I – Inspection and any additional services if required; A – Adjust; R – Replace **ATTENTION:** The * marked operations, although not strictly necessary, are recommended if the car is driven often on dusty roads or in unusual traffic conditions. If these operations are not performed, your warranty will NOT be invalidated.

14

Lamborghini

Scheduled Maintenance

Operation:	1.9 2.4 1.2 1.5	12 7.5	24 15	36 22.5	48 30	60 37.5	72 45	84 52.5	96 60	108 67.5	120 75	132 82.5	144 90	156 97.5	168 105
	KILOMETERS IN THOUSANDS / MILES IN THOUSANDS														
Fuel evaporative emission control system															I
Charcoal carbon trap															R
Crankcase emission control system								I							I
Braking system: pipes and calipers			I		I		I		I		I		I		I
Brake pedal clearance, handbrake adjust.	I		I		I		I		I		I		I		I
Brake fluid (replace every year)	I	I	I	I	I	I	I	I	I	I	I	I	I	I	I
Brakes discs and pads	I	I	I	I	I	I	I	I	I	I	I	I	I	I	I
Clutch reservoir fluid (replace every year)	I	I	I	I	I	I	I	I	I	I	I	I	I	I	I
Front/Rear wheel bearings: clear and lubric.	I		I		I		I		I		I		I		I
Air condit. system (replace Freon every year)			I		I		I		I		I		I		I
Transmission and differential oil	R	I	R	I	R	I	R	I	R	I	R	I	R	I	R
Drive shaft and steering: (joint protection)	I		I		I		I		I		I		I		I
Suspension geometry and shock absorber adjust.	I		I		I		I		I		I		I		I

I – Inspection and any additional services if required; A – Adjust; R – Replace **ATTENTION:** The * marked operations, although not strictly necessary, are recommended if the car is driven often on dusty roads or in unusual traffic conditions. If these operations are not performed, your warranty will NOT be invalidated.

15

The periodic maintenance that needs to be carried out at specified intervals, as stated by the Diablo's Owner's Manual, should be regarded as the bare minimum servicing that a Diablo needs.

24000 km
15000 mls

automobili Lamborghini

- ❑ Replace air filters
- ❑ Check injection system: lines and connections
- ❑ Replace spark plugs
- ❑ Check and adjust valve clearance
- ❑ Check cooling system
- ❑ Check camshaft drive chains
- ❑ Check accessories control belts
- ❑ Replace the engine oil and filter
- ❑ Check braking system; pipes and calipers
- ❑ Check brake pedal and handbrake clearance
- ❑ Check brake fluid
- ❑ Check brake discs and pads
- ❑ Check clutch reservoir fluid
- ❑ Check front/rear wheel bearings: clearance and lubrication
- ❑ Check air conditioning system
- ❑ Replace transmission and differential oil
- ❑ Check steering components, joint protection and gaiters on the steering rack, steering levers and on the drive shafts
- ❑ Check front and rear suspension joints and their tightening
- ❑ Check suspension geometry and shock absorbers adjustment
- ❑ Check battery and connections
- ❑ Check tightening of screws, bolts and clips on body/chassis
- ❑ Check doors, boot, bonnet and engine lid hinges lubrication

When the work have been carried out, check tire pressure and their condition, wheels are correctly tightened, the indicators on the dash-board, the lights and stop lights and then road test the car

24000 km
15000 mls

TAGLIANDO A PAGAMENTO
CHARGEABLE SERVICE
COUPON A PAIEMENT

- ❑ Remplacer les filtres à air
- ❑ Contrôler l'injection: tuyaux et connections
- ❑ Remplacer les bougies
- ❑ Contrôler et régler le jeu des soupapes
- ❑ Contrôler le système de refroidissement
- ❑ Contrôler les chaines de distribution
- ❑ Contrôler les courroies accessoires moteur
- ❑ Remplacer le filtre et l'huile moteur
- ❑ Contrôler le système de freinage, tuyaux/calipers
- ❑ Contrôler le jeu pédal de frein, et frein à main
- ❑ Contrôler le liquide des freins
- ❑ Contrôler les disques de freinage et plaquettes
- ❑ Contrôler le liquide circuit d'embrayage
- ❑ Contrôler le jeu et lubrification roulements roues av./arr.
- ❑ Contrôler le système de conditionnement
- ❑ Remplacer l'huile boîte de vitesses et différentiel
- ❑ Contrôler les organes de direction, la protection des rotules, les soufflets sur la crémaillère, sur le leviers de direction et sur les arbres des roues
- ❑ Contrôler les articulations des suspensions avant et arrière et leur serrage
- ❑ Contrôler la géometrie de la voiture et le réglage des amortisseurs
- ❑ Contrôler la batterie: joints et charge
- ❑ Contrôler le serrage vis, boulons, clips sur la carrosserie/châssis
- ❑ Contrôler la lubrification registres en général, charnières portes et capots

Les travaux étant réalisés, contrôler l'état des pneumatiques, la pression, le serrage des roues, vérifier les indicateurs de changement de direction, les stop puis essayer le véhicule sur route

An experienced Lamborghini mechanic will be able to go beyond the factory recommended service schedule and carry out prophylactic maintenance.

If all of the above makes the case for employing a specialist mechanic, actually finding such a technician is an altogether more difficult matter. There are very few such people around, especially if you live far away from the larger cities. Except for a fortunate few owners who happen to live next door to a Lamborghini Diablo specialist, everyone else will need to travel, sometimes long distances, to enjoy the skills that only an expert can lavish upon their steeds.

Our Countach F920OYR was worked on only by Del Hopkins and Lee Cunningham of H. R. Owen for the first thirteen years of its life, when it was under the custody of its first and only other owner. For the following twenty-one years under the authors' ownership it has only been worked on by Mike Pullen and Roberto Grimaldi. The same goes for our Murciélago Roadster, 921SMA, which under our ownership has only been looked after by David Jenkins, the Master Technician at Lamborghini Pangbourne. Getting these two cars to these three people has required military-like planning as they are respectively 145 miles (233km) and 3½ hours, 228 miles (367km) and 4¼ hours, and 130 miles (209km) and 2½ hours from where we and the cars live. And these are just one-way mileages and times – double them for the round trip! Using these three technicians is therefore a time-consuming and financially demanding commitment, but it is one that we are happy to subscribe to as it safeguards the long-term wellbeing of our cars. The Countach and Murciélago sandwich the Diablo in terms of bloodline and automotive technology, so the thinking outlined above is directly transferable and applicable to the Lamborghini Diablo. In summary, find an experienced and expert Diablo technician and take the car up to him or her whatever the cost.

Finding these elusive specialist technicians can be very challenging, but Lamborghini Car Clubs, specialist internet Lamborghini forums, and meeting and quizzing existing Diablo owners will all throw up some relatively local options. As mentioned above, there are only a scattering of such technicians around, so most Diablo owners are fishing from the same small pool, and the few relevant names will quickly surface. Once you have found such a technician, cling on to them like a limpet and do not let them go. The prophylactic maintenance necessary is best performed by a technician who knows your Diablo intimately.

GARAGING

The truth is that, however loudly non-owning aficionados might object, the classic V12 Lamborghini flagships are simply not suited to daily use. They are wide, temperamental, have poor sightlines, are difficult to park, and only truly come alive at socially unacceptable road and engine speeds. They are really quite unsuited to going down to the supermarket, and why would you want to do that anyway? Honestly, there are cheaper and more reliable ways to play the peacock.

To really experience the Diablo, to really enjoy the roar and performance of a Diablo or Countach or Murciélago

Proper maintenance of a Diablo requires expert mechanical knowledge, specialist tools, detailed service manuals and update bulletins, and expensive workshop facilities.

Finding an able and enthusiastic specialist technician is difficult, and this search should start at the same time as, if not before, the hunt for the Diablo itself.

you need to wind it up to speed, for which you need wide, lightly trafficked roads. An alarm clock is your best friend here: get up at 4.30 on a dry summer's morning and you and your Diablo might be lucky enough to stumble into a parallel universe of driving joy. After all, space and time are among life's, and a Diablo driver's, greatest luxuries. I often tuck my cars back into bed by 6.30, and as a consequence they seldom meet and have to endure other road-users and cars.

The corollary to this is that the average Diablo will cover very little mileage each year, and spend most of its time garaged. I see no shame in this. It is far more important that each mile driven is truly enjoyed in the manner that Sant'Agata designed their machines to be piloted, rather than simply trundling around at Mayfair speeds.

It is very important to garage a Diablo carefully, as this is where it will spend the vast majority of its life. This is especially so because, like many Diablo owners, we never drive our cars in any situation where they might come across salt-infested roads, which in Europe often means an unbroken stretch of enforced idleness between November and April each year. The importance of avoiding salt-laden roads was impressed upon me by Mike Pullen when he refused to accept my Countach for routine servicing one March unless it was sent to him in a fully enclosed transporter. He had just received a Diablo that had been sent to him by trailer wrapped in a tarpaulin-type cover. It arrived at Mike's garage splattered in road salt, but more importantly the salt had readily penetrated under the cover and got into the nooks and crannies of the Diablo's spaceframe chassis. Parts of this lattice are notoriously difficult to access, and once salt gets into these crevices, the risk, no, the certainty, of accelerated corrosion escalates exponentially. Hence, to escape the curse of corrosive brine, many owners of classic Lamborghinis send their cars into hibernation for almost half the year.

Leaving a car unmoved for long periods, however, is bad for the car's mechanical and electrical systems, so every six weeks in the winter our cars are gently woken up and driven. On crisp, dry days I drive them up and down my drive, which is never salted, but only after starting them up and letting them idle until the radiator fans cut in, which can take up to half an hour. At this point the coolant will have reached its normal operating temperature, but the engine and gearbox oils will still be at less than ideal temperature. Some heat would have reached through to these two lubricating fluids, principally through conduction, and a little bit through convection and radiation. It is important not to rev the engine aggressively at this point. Wait at least until the engine oil temperature gauge needle has moved off its stop before revving the engine much above its normal idle rpm.

Never just start up the car and leave the engine running for a few minutes before turning the engine off and walking away from the car for the next six weeks. This is possibly worse than not starting it up at all, and for the following reason. One kilogram of water is produced for each kilogram of petrol combusted within the Diablo's engine. Unless the temperature within the Diablo's drivetrain is sufficiently high to evaporate off all this water, the water will remain trapped within the Diablo's various systems. This water will cause corrosion and will also dilute all the drivetrain lubricating oils, so leading to accelerated wear when the car is next started. The vast majority of engine wear takes place in the first few moments after start-up, when there is unprotected metal-on-metal friction due to little or no lubricating oil being present at the interfaces, and while whatever oils are present are still below their optimal operating temperatures.

Our cars are garaged in a purpose-built brick building with sectional up-and-over doors. Watertight wooden or metal buildings are just as good. The important thing is to keep the elements out, and to have sufficiently good ventilation to keep the relative humidity level within the optimal range for a classic car. I try to approach this magical point by using a heater and a dehumidifier in the garage. An alternative approach is to have a fully sealed garage maintained at just the right temperature and humidity, but achieving this utopian environment in a large garage is difficult to the point of being financially ruinous for most ordinary people. Some people use car cocoons – tent-like insulated sheaths that fully envelop the car and have small in-built fans – in an attempt to recreate this ideal.

Garage security is an important consideration. There is a solid argument for having as few garage openings that thieves can exploit as possible – so no side doors and no windows. The garage doors should be strong and robust, with double or preferably triple locks, and have standalone opening sensors. Sectional doors are said to offer the best security as they offer no obvious points of attack. A garage door defender is also very valuable. This is a two-part anchor bar, one part of which is concreted into the garage floor, and the second part of which is removable and when in use clamps over the raised part of a sectional door, thereby

Classic Italian auto-electrics carry a reputation, and for good reason. Keeping the elements out and controlling the relative humidity level are both critical to any Lamborghini's wellbeing.

preventing its unauthorised opening. In addition to in-car alarms, immobilisers and trackers, in-garage closed-circuit television cameras linked through to the owner's mobile phone via the internet, and in-garage security alarms directly connected to the local police station or the selected private security company's switchboard are all useful security devices. Retractable bollards are brilliant visual deterrents to the casual thief, and genuine physical barriers to the more professional class of criminal. We use stainless steel retractable bollards, 900mm high and 168mm in diameter, made by the same company who make the barriers, bollards and road blockers for the British Embassy in Baghdad.

When garaged, the cars are always hooked up to battery conditioners. Batteries with sub-par voltages can play havoc with a car's electronic modules, causing a multitude of strange and apparently inexplicable starting and running problems. I over-inflate the tyres for the duration of a car's hibernation, and I also hand roll the cars a metre up and down the garage every week or two. Doing these two things prevents the tyres from developing flat spots, and also avoids having all the car's weight pressing down on the same wheel bearings for extended periods. Hand rolling also means that that the car's engine is not started up, thus sidestepping petrol combustion, and thereby evading water accumulation and oil dilution issues.

PREPARING TO DRIVE A DIABLO

Each variant of the Diablo model range has its own peculiarities. I have not driven every one of these different versions so cannot comment on every eccentricity, but they all share many common features, which together make up the essence of, and therefore define, the Diablo. Some of these signature traits are described below.

Both a microsurgical scalpel and a chainsaw can cut, but each was designed for a specific task and it would be unwise to use them interchangeably. We have already discussed that the Diablo was designed as a road car, and although it can be used on the track, this is not what it is best at. The Diablo is too heavy, too wide, and its body panels too precious and too expensive, to be an ideal track car. The perfect track car needs to be exceptionally agile, which in turn demands low mass and very high torque-to-weight and power-to-weight ratios. In the heat of competition accidents happen, so body parts should ideally be cheap and easy to replace in the pit lane or at the trackside. The Diablo does not excel in any of these areas. Where it does excel is as an extravagant, very high-speed, grand-touring road car that will surpass its driver's every expectation, and blow the minds of any bystander lucky enough to catch a glimpse of it.

To experience the full power of the Diablo's ability to astonish as a road car, however, the driver has to first put in some work. Timing is all important, and I have already discussed the virtues of very early morning drives. Preparation is equally important: a Diablo is unlikely to be used daily, so it is important on the evening prior to a drive to check the engine oil and coolant levels, and the tyre pressures and tyre condition. Hopefully the drive will be at least to a moderate speed, so every reasonable precaution needs to be taken beforehand. Loose clothing and narrow thin-soled driving shoes are the best sartorial accessories for a Diablo. I never use driving gloves in a Diablo or any other coupé – the heating system is there for a reason. I do, though, when driving an open-top, open-wheel, quasi-track car without a windscreen like the KTM X-BOW R in the late autumn and early spring, because numb fingers are incompatible with safe car control. Some hard-driving Diablo drivers, however, might find gloves useful to ensure that moist palms and fingers do not compromise their grip of the steering wheel.

Simply approaching any Lamborghini Diablo, knowing you are about to drive it, is intimidating. It is imperative that you know every detail of the car's controls and its systems before you start driving it. Again the Owner's Manual is there for a reason and not simply for decoration, so read it assiduously and thoroughly assimilate its contents. Get comfortable in the cockpit by adjusting the seat, the steering column, the mirrors and the seat belt. I have never understood why a supercar needs a stereo system, or why some owners upgrade their in-car entertainment systems. The previous owner of our Murciélago spent an additional one-twentieth of the car's retail price on an improved aftermarket hi-fi system that I have never turned on. The music from a Bizzarrini V12 is beyond compare, and anyway I don't have the spare mental capacity to appreciate music while driving, as simply piloting a V12 Lamborghini takes up all my attention and concentration and drains all my reserves. The first few times I drive any new car I tell my passengers beforehand that I will not be talking much at all, and will instead be concentrating on the driving. It takes time to know a car, and this is especially true of one as unusual and challenging as a Diablo.

A dedicated track car like this KTM exposes the Diablo as being too heavy, too wide and too expensive for racing. Instead the Diablo excels as an extravagant, high-speed, grand-touring road car.

Simply approaching any Diablo is intimidating. It is imperative that you know every detail of the car's controls and its systems before you start driving it.

When you start up a Diablo it welcomes you with a deep basso profundo roar. Allow time for the fluids to heat up and circulate around the beast. Never rev the engine while the lubricating oils are still cold.

ACTUALLY PILOTING A DIABLO

The moment of truth has finally arrived, and keen anticipation is about to be replaced with long-awaited ecstasy. Before turning the ignition key in its barrel, always depress the clutch. When you do finally start up a Diablo it welcomes you with a deep basso profundo roar. This is almost certainly the same bang and bark with which the Devil wakes the dead, and Lucifer's automotive counterpart and namesake, the Diablo, uses its thundering growl to keep its driver alert and respectful, and all bystanders bedazzled and bewitched. Wait now and allow the fluids to begin to circulate around the beast. Trundle out of the garage slowly, taking care not to rev the engine while the lubricating oils are still cold.

The steering on early Diablos is heavy at walking pace, but lightens up considerably once at jogging speed. Thereafter steering weight is not a problem, and the steering response is direct, immediate and linear. The later variants feature power-assisted steering, which is brilliant – not too light at parking speed, and weighting up perfectly in the higher speed ranges. Depress the clutch and brake pedals when it is safe to do so, just to get a feel for their weight and consistency: they are significantly heavier than in a normal car, but by no means unmanageable. You should already know where each of the control stalks and buttons are, but you might not yet fully appreciate the extreme width of the Diablo, so drive slowly and carefully, especially as outward visibility is one of the Diablo's greatest weaknesses.

Later when you are familiar with the Diablo (which will actually take years if not decades) push the beast and hear its incomparable V12 symphony – the deep bass still dominates and grows in volume with the revs, but it is now accompanied by several sopranos singing out different high-pitched metallic shrieks – and savour its vibrations and thrust and drama, the likes of which you will never have experienced before. As the Diablo's engine speed increases, each new gear change engages with ever more fluidity and ever greater tactility, which is hugely satisfying. The clutch pedal is heavy but manageable. The large-capacity, naturally aspirated Bizzarrini engine responds in a very linear fashion to each micropascal of accelerator pedal pressure, and to every millimetre of accelerator pedal travel. The resultant push in the back is definite, forceful, refined and feels inexhaustible. The Diablo never startles its driver or passenger with the abrupt and coarse thump you get when the turbo suddenly starts spooling in a forced induction engine. Sant'Agata is far too polished and sophisticated to indulge in such inelegant and uncultured shenanigans. The brake pedal is firm at the very top of its travel, and then remains proportionately responsive throughout the rest of its range. It does not exhibit any fade even in hard road use, but it is heavy and demands that the driver works for any retardation that he wants.

It is only at speed that the Diablo reveals its true inner soul. Then it hunkers down and shows that it is truly a genuine supercar. When most sports cars are slowing down and

It is only at speed that the Diablo reveals its true inner soul. Then it hunkers down and shows that it is a genuine supercar – truly the real thing.

losing the battle against the forces of wind resistance and tarmac-tyre friction, the Diablo is just getting into its stride. It simply accelerates on relentlessly, and surprisingly, becomes more poised and feels more planted as the speedometer gauge needle sweeps ever further to the right. It effortlessly reaches speeds that are quite frankly, irrelevant. But the Diablo is so much more than mere acceleration and speed. It is also about heritage, glamour, advanced technology, engineering prowess, avant-garde design and styling, environmental awareness despite a V12 engine, comfort and safety. The Diablo immediately established itself as an important chapter in the great Italian supercar story. It is indisputably one of the most notable of Ferruccio Lamborghini's 'perfect' grand touring cars and a worthy successor to the Miura and the Countach. Hail to the marvellous, glorious Lamborghini Diablo.

APPENDIX: LAMBORGHINI DIABLO SPECIFICATIONS

	Diablo	Diablo VT	Diablo SE30	Diablo SV	Diablo Roadster
Introduction date	1990	1993	1993	1995	1995
Kerb weight	1,576kg (3,475lb)	1,623kg (3,579lb)	1,449kg (3,194lb)	1,530kg (3,373lb)	1,625kg (3,583lb)
Engine capacity	5707cc	5707cc	5707cc	5707cc	5707cc
Bore	87mm	87mm	87mm	87mm	87mm
Stroke	80mm	80mm	80mm	80mm	80mm
Compression ratio	10:1	10:1	10:1	10:1	10:1
Peak power	492bhp @ 6,800rpm	492bhp @ 6,800rpm	520bhp @ 7,100rpm	510bhp @ 7,100rpm	492bhp @ 7,000rpm
Peak torque	580Nm @ 5,200rpm	580Nm @ 5,200rpm	580Nm @ 5,900rpm	580Nm @ 5,900rpm	580Nm @ 5,200rpm
Top speed	328km/h (204mph)	325km/h (203mph)	333km/h (207mph)	328km/h (204mph)	328km/h (204mph)
0–100km/h	4.09s	4.09s	3.90s	3.90s	4.00s
Length	4,460mm	4,460mm	4,550mm	4,470mm	4,470mm
Width	2,040mm	2,040mm	2,040mm	2,040mm	2,040mm
Height	1,105mm	1,105mm	1,105mm	1,105mm	1,105mm
Wheelbase	2,650mm	2,650mm	2,650mm	2,650mm	2,650mm
Ground clearance	140mm	140mm	140mm	140mm	140mm
Front disc diameter	330mm	330mm	330mm	330mm	330mm
Rear disc diameter	284mm	284mm	284mm	310mm	310mm
Steering	Manual rack + pinion	Power-assisted rack + pinion	Manual rack + pinion	Power-assisted rack + pinion	Power-assisted rack + pinion
Drive	Rear-wheel-drive	Four-wheel-drive	Rear-wheel-drive	Rear-wheel-drive	Four-wheel-drive
Wheels front	8.5 x 17	8.5 x 17	8.5 x 17	8.5 x 17	8.5 x 17
Wheels rear	13 x 17	13 x 17	13 x 18	13 x 18	13 x 17
Tyres front	245/40ZR17	245/40ZR17	235/40ZR17	235/40ZR17	235/40ZR17
Tyres rear	335/35ZR17	335/35ZR17	335/30ZR18	335/35ZR18	335/35ZR17
Gearbox	Manual 5-speed + reverse	Manual 5-speed + reverse	Manual 5-speed + reverse	Manual 5-speed + reverse	Manual 5-speed + reverse
Suspension	Independent with double wishbones; coil springs; conventional dampers	Independent with double wishbones; coil springs; electronic damper control	Independent with double wishbones; conventional dampers	Independent with double wishbones; coil springs; conventional dampers	Independent with double wishbones; coil springs; electronic damper control

Various figures are available from a variety of reputable sources and it would be presumptuous for the authors to claim to know which if any is absolutely correct. We have selected plausible representations and clear trends are immediately visible. The variants have been arranged according to year of introduction.

2nd generation MY 1999

	Diablo VT	Diablo Roadster	Diablo SV	Diablo GT	Diablo 6.0 VT
Introduction date	1998	1998	1998	1999	2000
Kerb weight	1,625kg (3,583lb)	1,625kg (3,583lb)	1,530kg (3,374lb)	1,490kg (3,284lb)	1,625kg (3,582lb)
Engine capacity	5707cc	5707cc	5707cc	5992cc	5992cc
Bore	87mm	87mm	87mm	87mm	87mm
Stroke	80mm	80mm	80mm	84mm	84mm
Compression ratio	10:1	10:1	10:1	10.7:1	10.7:1
Peak power	530bhp @ 7,100rpm	530bhp @ 7,100rpm	530bhp @ 7,100rpm	575bhp @ 7,300rpm	550bhp @ 7,100rpm
Peak torque	605Nm @ 5,500rpm	605Nm @ 5,500rpm	605Nm @ 5,500rpm	630Nm @ 5,500rpm	620Nm @ 5,500rpm
Top speed	335km/h (208mph)	335km/h (208mph)	320km/h (201mph)	338km/h (211mph)	335km/h (208mph)
0–100km/h	3.95s	3.95s	3.85s	3.70s	3.95s
Length	4,470mm	4,470mm	4,470mm	4,430mm	4,470mm
Width	2,040mm	2,040mm	2,040mm	2,040mm	2,040mm
Height	1,115mm	1,105mm	1,115mm	1,115mm	1,105mm
Wheelbase	2,650mm	2,650mm	2,650mm	2,650mm	2,650mm
Ground clearance	140mm	140mm	140mm	140mm	140mm
Front disc diameter	355mm	355mm	355mm	355mm	355mm
Rear disc diameter	335mm	335mm	335mm	335mm	335mm
Steering	Power-assisted rack + pinion	Power-assisted rack + pinion	Power-assisted rack + pinion	Power-assisted rack + pinion	Power-assisted rack + pinion
Drive	Four-wheel-drive	Four-wheel-drive	Rear-wheel-drive	Rear-wheel-drive	Four-wheel-drive
Wheels front	8.5 x 18	8.5 x 18	8.5 x 18	8.5 x 18	8.5 x 18
Wheels rear	13 x 18	13 x 18	13 x 18	13 x 18	13 x 18
Tyres front	235/35ZR18	235/35ZR18	235/35ZR18	245/35ZR18	235/35ZR18
Tyres rear	335/30ZR18	335/30ZR18	335/30ZR18	335/30ZR18	335/30ZR18
Gearbox	Manual 5-speed + reverse	Manual 5-speed + reverse	Manual 5-speed + reverse	Manual 5-speed + reverse	Manual 5-speed + reverse
Suspension	Independent with double wishbones; coil springs; electronic damper control	Independent with double wishbones; coil springs; electronic damper control	Independent with double wishbones; coil springs; electronic damper control	Independent with double wishbones; coil springs; electronic damper control	Independent with double wishbones; coil springs; electronic damper control

ACKNOWLEDGEMENTS

This book has been a collaborative effort with contributors from four continents, without whose generosity the authors would not have been able to even start on this project.

Foremost amongst these has been Automobili Lamborghini SpA and the Audi Group. Maurizio Reggiani, Gerald Kahlke, Francesco Stevanin, Elena Ruosi, Chiara Sandoni and Dario Lucchese of Lamborghini SpA and Polo Storico were very generous with their time, in giving us precious information, and in letting us use various pictures, drawings and images from the owner's and workshop manuals, brochures and news bulletins. We are hugely grateful. Similarly, Archivio Automobili Lamborghini and its consultant Barbara Grillini were very generous in providing us with invaluable photographs and information – thank you.

Cav. Comm. Ing. Tonino Lamborghini, Ferruccio Lamborghini Junior and the Ferruccio Lamborghini Museo, Funo di Argelato, Historical Archive, have been very generous in providing precious text, photographs and inside knowledge of the Lamborghini family. We cannot thank Tonino enough.

Valentino Balboni cannot be separated from Sant'Agata, and we are very grateful to him for his signature kindness through the years.

Paolo Stanzani, Giampaolo Dallara, Umberto Marchesi, Horacio Pagani and Loris Bicocchi were all kind enough to engage with us, and provided deep and invaluable insight into Lamborghini's inner workings.

Ian Hunt has mentored us through four books, and his advice, cheerful support and photographs have all been priceless.

We have been very lucky to have had on board acknowledged world-class Lamborghini experts like Robert Forstner and Vanessa Forstner of Bob Forstner, and Mike Pullen and Roberto Grimaldi.

We are immensely grateful to Rod Grainger of Veloce Publishing for having had the courage to give us our first writing break a few years ago. Taking on two enthusiastic but virginal authors was always a risk. He and Jeff 'Jai' Danton, Kevin Quinn and Kevin Atkins gently mentored us, and we cannot thank them enough. Similarly we are immeasurably indebted to Mark Hughes, Evro's Publishing Director, whose truly humbling depth of knowledge and breadth of overview genuinely educated us in how to write a motoring book.

Jim Holder of *Autocar*, Colin Overland of *CAR* and Stuart Gallagher, Ryan Chambers and Nick Trott of *EVO* have been hugely kind and encouraging to two amateurs throughout this enterprise, and we would like to thank them for allowing us to use excerpts from their magazines.

The National Motor Museum at Beaulieu, Hampshire, is the second home for many of our cars and we are deeply grateful to Jonathan Day, Tim David Wood, Russell Bowman and Stephen Munn for the use of the wonderful images taken in the Beaulieu photographic studio.

Special thanks to Mark Bogard, Benjamin Somner-Bogard, Simon Furlonger, Matthew Honeysett and Hassan Harake of Furlonger Specialist Cars; Dion Speak of the Elms Collection; Bill Sherlock of PPM Milton Keynes; Bryan Moullet of Lamborghini Porrentruy; Franco Granell and Joe Macari of Joe Macari Performance Cars; Filippo Balzano and his effeNovanta YouTube channel; Achim Joos of Lamborghini Singen; Allan Fiedler; Lucas Hutchings of the Octane Collection; Charles Myers and Paul Whinney of Redline Specialist Cars; Wikimedia Commons and its contributing author Arnaud 25 (Creative Commons Attribution-Share Alike 3.0 license; no changes made; Musee Lamborghini 0110;0111;0113); Jeron Holy; John Gordon; Mark and Stephanie Jansen of Oldtimer Australia; Tony Mullen; Frank Jacob of Springbok Sportwagen; Mink Hwee of Sunning, Hong Kong; Brian Owen; Dylan Miles; Russell Gilbert of Hexagon Classics; Dominique Franssens and Vincent Breukers of Legendary Classics Ethen; and Gary Tolson and Ian Kershaw of Kaaimans International, all of whose help was invaluable.

Peter Dron, Mel Nichols, Ian and Antony Fraser, Gautam Sen, Kaare Byberg, Branko Radovinivic, Raymond Stofer, Marcel Wallenburg, Robert Hennessy, Nigel Ratledge, Paolo Grasso, David Lillywhite, Robert Westall, Maurice Rizzuto, Peter Griffiths, Ryan Upward, Nick Elkan, Kirsty Pullen, Mark Sheldon-Lloyd, Sourein Jabourian and Alan Robb all helped enormously with information, contacts and photographs. Thank you.

Almost lastly we must thank Crowood for their expertise and dedication in bringing this book to fruition.

Finally, we must acknowledge and thank those invaluable contributors who have asked to remain nameless. Some of your offerings were beyond priceless – your request for anonymity will always be respected.

INDEX

RELATED TITLES AVAILABLE FROM CROWOOD

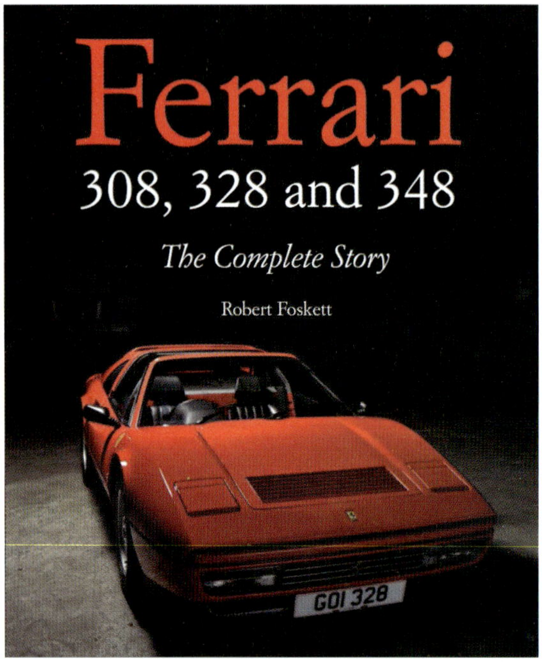

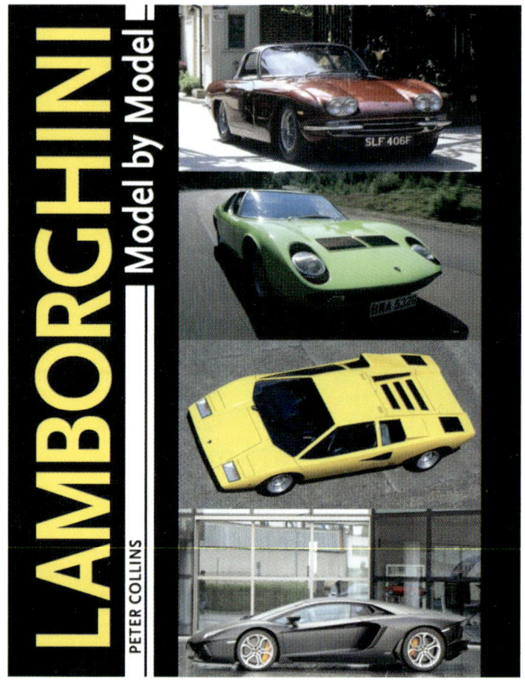

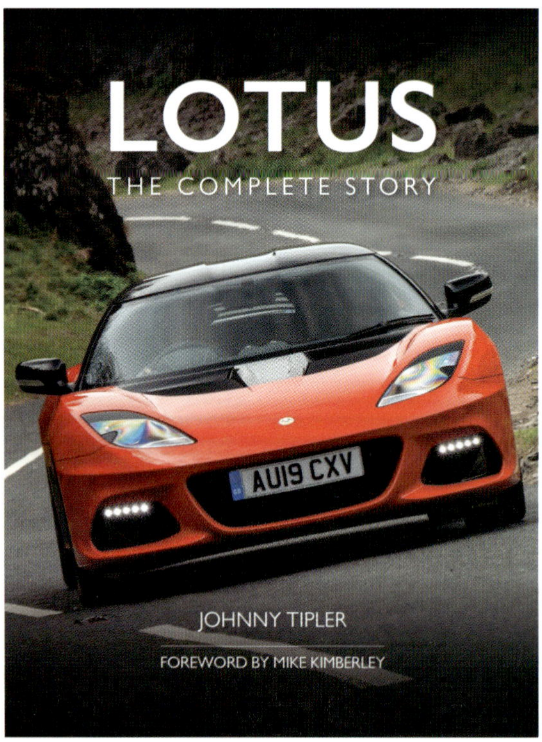